THE
EVERYTHING
GUIDE TO CAREERS IN
HEALTH CARE

Dear Reader,

As you explore the possibilities of a career in health care, you will find that it can be one of the most rewarding and yet most challenging choices you will make in your lifetime.

In the post-9/11 era, many people have come to the realization that they want to do something with their lives that will make a difference in the lives of others. In their quest, many have found that health care careers offer a means to achieve that goal.

Today, hundreds of jobs exist in the health care industry. Just a few years ago, the only real jobs for health care providers were doctors, nurses, and dentists, along with a few ancillary support positions. Technological advances and an aging population have brought about vast changes.

As the population continues to age and the baby-boom generation moves into retirement, the health care industry will continue to face and meet the demands of the public. In contrast to fields that have seen sharp declines with the downturn of the economy in the early years of this new millennium, health care has grown and will continue to grow for many years to come. In fact, some health care fields such as nursing have experienced shortages that are approaching crisis levels. This is due in part to the many choices now available to those who wish to enter a caring profession.

Tomorrow promises more health care career choices, some of which are completely unknown today.

Kathy Quan RN BSN

CENTER FOR CAREER SERVICES
JOHN CARROLL UNIVERSITY
20700 NORTH PARK BLVD.
UNIVERSITY HEIGHTS, OH 44118

THE

EVERYTHING®

GUIDE TO CAREERS IN
HEALTH CARE

Find the job that's right for you

Kathy Quan, R.N., B.S.N., P.H.N.

Adams Media
Avon, Massachusetts

Dedication
To the loves of my life, who are always here for me:
my husband, Tim, and my children, Amy, Rob, and Becky!

• • •

Publishing Director: Gary M. Krebs
Associate Managing Editor: Laura M. Daly
Associate Copy Chief: Brett Palana-Shanahan
Acquisitions Editor: Lisa Laing
Development Editor: Jessica LaPointe
Associate Production Editor: Casey Ebert

Director of Manufacturing: Susan Beale
Associate Director of Production: Michelle Roy Kelly
Cover Design: Paul Beatrice, Erick DaCosta,
    Matt LeBlanc
Layout and Graphics: Heather Barrett,
    Brewster Brownville, Colleen Cunningham,
    Jennifer Oliveira

An Everything® Series Book.
Everything® and everything.com® are registered trademarks of F+W Publications, Inc.

Published by Adams Media, an F+W Publications Company
57 Littlefield Street, Avon, MA 02322 U.S.A.
www.adamsmedia.com

ISBN 10: 1-59337-725-8
ISBN 13: 978-1-59337-725-0

Printed in the United States of America.

J I H G F E D C B A

Library of Congress Cataloging-in-Publication Data
available from publisher

This publication is designed to provide accurate and authoritative information with regard to the subject matter covered. It is sold with the understanding that the publisher is not engaged in rendering legal, accounting, or other professional advice. If legal advice or other expert assistance is required, the services of a competent professional person should be sought.
—From a *Declaration of Principles* jointly adopted by a Committee of the American Bar Association and a Committee of Publishers and Associations

Many of the designations used by manufacturers and sellers to distinguish their products are claimed as trademarks. Where those designations appear in this book and Adams Media was aware of a trademark claim, the designations have been printed with initial capital letters.

This book is available at quantity discounts for bulk purchases.
For information, please call 1-800-289-0963

Visit the entire Everything® series at *www.everything.com*

Contents

Acknowledgments

I would like to express my deepest gratitude and appreciation to all of the health care professionals with whom I have worked over the past thirty years, and those whom I have observed and interviewed for this book.

Next I want to thank my family for their love, devotion, and help throughout the writing of this book: my husband, Tim; my children, Amy, Rob, and Becky; and our extended family of children, Chase, Heather, and Dana. Many thanks to my mother, who has always been my biggest fan and most honest critic. She has been a tremendous help and influence in writing this book. And to "the girls," who have always encouraged me to reach beyond my comfort zone and follow my dreams. Thanks for your love and inspiration. Many thanks also to the rest of my family and friends for their encouragement and support throughout this effort. I love you!

To Barb Doyen, my agent, who has been a great source of support and encouragement through all the bumps along the way, thank you.

Thanks so very much to all of you!

Top Ten Things You Need to Know about Careers in Health Care

1. If you want to pursue a career in health care you should have a solid foundation of math, sciences, and a foreign language.

2. Some of the most important characteristics you need for any health care career include attention to detail, good communication skills (both written and oral), and a strong desire to help others.

3. Opportunities in health care will continue to grow and expand well into the next decade and beyond, despite any economic downturn.

4. Many health care careers have similar basic-education requirements and can open doors to other opportunities in the field.

5. Many of tomorrow's jobs don't even exist today. Technological advances and scientific discoveries will bring about many more changes in the future.

6. Health care requires a commitment to lifelong learning based on the advances and discoveries that come to light every day.

7. Health care careers are some of the most physically and emotionally demanding careers, and yet they offer some of the most rewarding opportunities.

8. Health careers are professions, not gender roles; a nurse isn't necessarily a woman, and a doctor isn't necessarily a man.

9. Many Americans are turning to health care for second and even third careers.

10. It is essential that those who enter health care careers do so with a clear understanding of the responsibilities and challenges of the profession, and not with false hopes and expectations.

Introduction

How many times in recent years have you picked up a newspaper or a business magazine and read a headline about college graduates unable to find jobs? Or read about the vast numbers of unemployed workers? Or perhaps lived through a downturn in the economy in which your position was eliminated and you were laid off?

The health care industry is booming and expanding its needs almost daily. There are many, many choices and vast shortages of workers in numerous areas. You don't have to be a doctor, dentist, or nurse. You don't even have to like the sight of blood or have a strong desire to work with the sick to join the health care team.

Health care today is comprised of a huge team of diverse industries. Technology has brought about, and continues to provide for, tremendous advancements in areas such as diagnostics, treatments and procedures, documentation, billing, insurance reimbursement, and general health care delivery. With these advancements comes the need for many more workers to perform the associated jobs.

Health care is a team effort, and each member is vital to the success of the whole. This includes those workers with direct patient contact as well as those who may never have any contact at all with patients, such as medical librarians and information technologists. The patient is the central character, and everything that happens revolves around the needs of the patient.

The needs of the patient drive the demand for better diagnostics, better treatments, and better health care delivery systems—which, in turn, provides the impetus for technological advancements.

As the population ages, the demand for health care will increase. The baby-boom generation (those born between 1946 and 1964) is rapidly approaching retirement age. The firstborn of this generation turned 60 in 2006. By 2012, baby boomers will be 48 to 66 years old.

According to statistics from the U.S. Department of Labor's Bureau of Labor Statistics, in the decade spanning 2002 to 2012, the number of people age 55 to 64 will increase by greater than 43 percent (by over 11 million persons). During that same time period, those in the age bracket from 35 to 44 will decrease, but those aged 16 to 24 will increase by 7 percent.

The demand for health care is going to increase for at least the next several decades, while the workforce is going to diminish. That equates to a very strong job market in the health care industry for years to come.

The U.S. Department of Labor issues a report on job opportunities and prospects for each decade. The report issued for 2000 to 2010 had to be modified by 2002 due in large part to the events of September 11, 2001, and the economic downturn that the country experienced in 2001 and 2002. Suddenly, Americans felt a strong urge to have careers that made a difference in the lives of others. The demands of an aging population and the economic factors have forced a long-term shift from goods-producing jobs to service jobs.

Of the ten fastest-growing jobs in the United States, nine are in the health care or computer information technology industry. For those who are seeking a challenging, rewarding career with long-range job security and growth opportunities, health care is the industry to choose.

The background and basic education requirements will translate to many different avenues within the industry. In health care, learning and education is a lifelong process. Therefore, the opportunities for career growth and changes as technological advancements continue are ever-present, and afford many more choices than any other industry.

Enjoy your search, and keep your eyes and mind open for many different opportunities throughout your working years. Remember that many of tomorrow's jobs don't even exist today.

Chapter 1

Why Choose a Career in Health Care?

The health care field is now growing at an exponential rate, and it is predicted to continue to do so well into the next decade and beyond. The U.S. Bureau of Labor Statistics records that there were 146 million jobs in 2004; of that number, the health care industry provided 13.5 million jobs. Wage and salary jobs accounted for 13.1 million of these jobs, while 411,000 were self-employed workers.

The Health Care Explosion

The general population is expected to increase by 23.9 million from 2004 to 2014. A large portion of the current population is composed of members of the baby-boom generation. These are the 76 million children born after World War II, from 1946 to 1964. By 2014 this group of adults will be 50 to 68 years of age. As such, this large group will be close to retirement or retired by 2014.

The generation following the baby boomers is known as the baby-bust generation. After 1964, births declined dramatically, accounting for current and predicted future shortages in the prime-age workforce.

 Fact

The U.S. Department of Labor's Bureau of Labor Statistics studies the relationships between the demands for goods and services, the labor force, and the demographics of the population to understand the past and present trends as well as to predict future opportunities. Their findings indicate an explosion in health care jobs, now and in the near future.

From 1965 to 1976 births slowed to 3.4 million per year. This equates to 37.4 million births, or roughly half of the total births in the baby-boom generation. As baby boomers retire, there are only half as many people available to move into their vacant positions, and the younger workforce—even considering the Echo Boom (the children of baby boomers) generation—leaves huge gaps in the numbers of workers entering professions.

In some fields, retirement for the baby boomers will not come until they reach their seventies or eighties, if then. But in the health care industry, this isn't expected to hold true. The physical and emotional demands of the health care profession will take their toll, and as we have already begun to see in several fields, such as nursing and therapies, retirement will come early to these workers.

The physical demands such as prolonged standing, walking, lifting, assisting, and transferring patients become more difficult for the older health care worker. Strength and stamina are as important to safety as proper body mechanics, and age is not kind when it comes to either.

Alert

Many fields are exploring options to assist older health care workers transition into other positions such as desk jobs, management, teaching, and mentoring in order to keep them working in the field to lessen the critical effects of shortages. Their knowledge base and level of experience are invaluable, and finding creative solutions to keeping them as active members of the profession is an important challenge.

As the baby-boom generation ages, they will begin to need more and more health care services. There is already a shift to preventative care and promoting wellness that has increased the demand for health care services. This combined with the demands that will be exacerbated by aging, such as arthritis, hypertension, diabetes, Alzheimer's disease, heart disease, and stroke, will also increase the demand for health care services.

This demand will cause an increase in the demand for health care workers. For some providers the demand will be greater than for others. Predictions are based on data gathered by the U.S. Department of Labor's Bureau of Labor Statistics.

Shift from Goods to Services

Services industries will continue to benefit from the ongoing shift away from goods-producing industries. Approximately 18.7 million of the 18.9 million projected new wage and salary jobs from 2004 to 2014 will be service-providing positions. Since the 1980s the production of goods in the United States has steadily declined, and with this decline jobs in these industries have been lost. Construction is the only goods-producing industry expected to experience growth.

E ssential

In order to offset rising materials and labor costs, manufacturing and technology companies in the United States have moved much of their operations to foreign countries. This practice is called *outsourcing*. Today when you need assistance with your computer or cell phone, the technician on the other end of the phone is most likely in another country, such as India.

Over the next decade the service-providing fields that are expected to experience the greatest growth include health care, social assistance, and educational services. The U.S Department of Labor estimates that three out of every ten jobs created in the coming decade will be in this sector. An aging population and longer life expectancies drive this demand. As a result, approximately 4.3 million new jobs are expected to be created in health care and social assistance areas such as hospitals, nursing and residential care facilities, and family and individual services. Other areas such as sales, financial planning, defense, and security jobs are expected to grow as well; however, the long-range job security projections are not as strong for these industries as they are for health care and education.

Unlike other industries, health care cannot be outsourced to another part of the world. Hands-on care must be provided in person. Some technological developments have already begun, and will likely continue, to provide long-distance diagnostics, such as the periodic checkups for pacemakers and implanted defibrillators, but for the most part health care will continue to require the personal touch.

Demographics of the Health Care Industry

The health care workforce is made up of a wide array of professionals, including administrators, hands-on caregivers and practitioners, scientists, illustrators, and photographers, and those who provide support, such as counselors and social workers. The industry provides twenty-four-hour care to humans and animals from newborns to the chronically and critically ill. Their job is to combine the art of caring with scientific technology to provide patients with the best possible level of care.

 Fact

About three-quarters of health care establishments are offices of practitioners such as doctors, dentists, veterinarians, and chiropractors. Hospitals only account for about 2 percent of health care establishments, although they employ approximately 40 percent of the health care workers.

Health care workers in general tend to be older and remain employed in their field longer than workers in other industries. This is due in part to the length of time required to obtain the high level of education necessary for many health care professions.

The vast majority of the health care professionals work in approximately 545,000 establishments that have various degrees of staffing patterns and organizational structures. They can range from very small private practices to very large organizations and facilities.

In 2004, health care was the largest industry in the United States. The 13.1 million wage and salary jobs were primarily divided between offices of physicians (16 percent), nursing or residential care facilities (22 percent), and hospitals (41 percent). The majority of the 411,000 self-employed and unpaid family workers worked in offices of practitioners such as doctors, dentists, chiropractors, and veterinarians. Geographically the jobs were concentrated in the largest states such as California, Pennsylvania, New York, Texas, and Florida, although health care jobs can be found all over the country.

Twenty percent of health care workers were part-timers who were parents with young children, students, older workers, and those holding dual jobs. Many health care workers hold more than one job. This is especially true of those who work shifts, such as nurses. Part-time workers comprised 39 percent of those employed in dentists' offices and 33 percent of the workforce in offices of other practitioners.

Health Care Outside the Box

The world of health care extends beyond the realm of hospitals, clinics, and practitioners' offices. It includes all of the educational institutions, medical libraries, pharmaceutical companies, bioengineering firms, and medical publishers.

The Rest of the Health Care Industry

Health insurance companies employ nurses, therapists, and physicians to assist in reviewing as well as authorizing care. Financial services and management companies, whether in-house or outsourced, support such things as human resources, medical billing, medical coding, and accounts receivable functions for both small practices and large corporations throughout the medical field.

Nurses, doctors, dentists, and others become educators to teach new students how to become health care professionals. Scientists develop new technology to improve diagnostics and treatment modalities.

Not all of these workers are included in the statistics of health care workers. Facilities also hire food service workers, security personnel, janitorial services, and numerous administrative support personnel to run the day-to-day operations of their facilities and ensure clean and safe environments for patients as well as health care professionals. Many of these workers further their education and eventually become full-fledged members of the health care team as doctors, nurses, and other practitioners.

Have Degree, Will Travel?

There is a romantic notion that the exciting and dramatic hospital setting portrayed on shows such as *ER*, *House*, *Scrubs*, or *Grey's Anatomy* is the norm. On the other hand, not all rural sites and their country doctors are as quaint and inviting as the settings for *Everwood* and *Doc Hollywood*. There are over 5 million people employed in the health care industry in the United States today, and they don't all work in such places.

E ssential

Not every health care issue requires highly specialized modalities, and not every health care worker desires to work in a high-stress environment. Health care offers opportunities to meet the diverse needs of the public as well as the workforce. Sometimes the less-desirable locations will offer you interesting and creative incentives.

Another notion is that if the patient requires specialized care he'll only get good care—and possibly be cured—if he travels to a large medical facility such as the Mayo Clinic or Johns Hopkins. While these are, of course, top-notch facilities, they are not the only places where patients can receive superior medical diagnosis and treatment. They do create situations for the less-desirable areas to compete for health care professionals. Geographically, wherever people live there will always be a need for health care, but because of this strong competition, the care is not always adequate.

The Health Care Shortage: Causes and Solutions

As the baby-boom generation ages and retires or moves into other positions, replacements will be needed. As technology creates new diagnostics and treatments, new positions may be created as well. As the demand for more services grows, so will the need for larger staffs.

There is a shortage of health care professionals in many fields today. Physicians are still scarce in rural areas and lower socioeconomic sections of the country despite efforts to recruit them with tuition forgiveness and other package deals of benefits and incentives. Nurses are in short supply all across the country. Not long ago when women sought to join the health care team they were limited to becoming nurses. Now women are members of all health care professions. Low salaries and poor benefits in the field of nursing have long been ignored, resulting in a lack of incentive for anyone to pursue a career as a nurse. Creative solutions are way behind in filling the growing need for nurses.

Critical shortages of nurses have encouraged creative recruiting efforts and financial incentives that are enticing many into the field. However, the shortage of nurse educators will be a major factor in keeping this shortage at critical levels for years to come.

Tighter immigration laws will affect the health care profession as a whole. As fewer immigrants are available to step in and fill the openings, the need for new health care professionals will also grow.

Cost containment issues have forced a shift in the health care industry as well, which has led to a shortage of home health care workers. There has been a major shift from inpatient to outpatient care. Patients no longer spend a week to ten days in the hospital recovering from surgery. They go home in two to three days and are expected to care for themselves, or have family members or hired help assist them. When necessary, home health care agencies address these needs. But even then, the ultimate responsibility for the care rests upon the patient and family or caregivers, as the home health care is not unlimited. Medicare and insurance companies restrict the number of visits allowed, and in most instances expect the patient or caregiver to learn to perform the care needed.

Many times diagnostics and treatment are provided as outpatient services rather than as inpatient services. The series of tests a patient may have been hospitalized for in the past is now performed over several days in outpatient diagnostic centers.

Managed-care systems imposed by insurance companies dictate inpatient versus outpatient care and have resulted in waiting periods for authorization for procedures and treatment as well.

All of these scenarios have influenced staffing issues and roles within the field of health care. For instance, where nurses and therapists once treated patients in the hospital until they no longer required care and went home, now they are expected to do much more teaching so that patients can go home and care for themselves.

 Fact

Registered nurses top the list of most-needed workers in the United States, and indeed there is a critical shortage of nurses that is only expected to worsen. Nursing is one of the most physically and emotionally demanding jobs, and the workforce of nurses is aging. One of the challenges that nurses have faced in this crisis is that there are so many other health care career choices available now.

Those who work in outpatient and home care environments now deal with patients who are much sicker and weaker and require more care and instruction than ever before. This shift has created tremendous growth in the need for home health aides as well as personal and home care aides. Home health aides visit patients on an intermittent short-term basis to assist with bathing and personal care under the supervision of skilled nurses or therapists. Personal and home care aides are hired privately to assist patients with personal as well as custodial care in their homes.

Roles change, but staffing levels, pay, and benefits don't always keep pace. This can cause severe retention and recruitment issues for employers and lead to shortages.

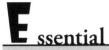

Essential

Efficiency and cost-effectiveness have forced role changes. Nurses, physicians' assistants, pharmacy techs, and veterinary technologists now handle a larger portion of the examination and patient teaching process. The practitioner's time is too costly for them to spend it taking temperatures, asking questions, and instructing in care and prescriptions.

Solutions will come from thinking outside the box as well as examining the usual issues such as salaries, benefits, and work conditions. Flexibility is going to be a key issue.

Salaries and Job Security

Health care practitioners are some of the most educated and skilled workers in the country, and as such are also some of the best compensated as well. Others in health care are highly skilled experts in technological fields such as sonography. Still others are highly skilled caregivers such as nurses. The education, skills, and caring required in these careers makes these workers not only in high demand, but also extremely valuable in a field that is destined to grow faster than others well into the next decade and beyond.

In some health care fields salaries are still lagging, but shortages and demands are forcing them upward. Sign-on bonuses and other benefit packages and perks are also increasing. It isn't uncommon to find employers offering child care services, house-cleaning services, company cars, and other personal services to attract the finest in various professions.

Negotiating power may not be as strong for entry-level personnel as it can be for more seasoned professionals and managers, but the potential for job growth and advancement is enticing many to enter the field.

Alert

With the high demand for health care professionals in most areas, there is frequently a shortage of teachers. Consequently, competition is fierce in many fields for spots in education programs, and students must put forth their best efforts at grades, test scores, essays, personal presentation, and interviews.

Education standards and expectations are high and courses are tough. Almost all fields require a strong command of English (both spoken and written language)—at least a tenth-grade reading comprehension level—as well as strong backgrounds in math and science.

The payoff is that salaries are often attractive because of the education and skills required as well as the growing demands for qualified candidates to fill the positions. Additionally, in an economy that is not very stable, the job security is a strong incentive to enter the field of health care. Even as roles change and paradigms shift, health care professionals are secure in knowing that they can find suitable employment somewhere in the country. It may not necessarily be in their small rural hospital, but they can find a job perhaps in a nearby community or in a larger metropolis a further distance away. This security is expected to hold well into the next decade and beyond.

One of the best perks of any job in the health care field is that it can be one of the most rewarding jobs you can find. Making a difference in someone's life every day is the major reward for all health care workers.

Chapter 2

The Growing Opportunities in Health Care

While opportunities in other fields are diminishing and even disappearing, the broad field of health care is booming. Because so much of health care is a team effort, there are no nonessential jobs. They span from entry-level positions to top-level scientists with Ph.D.s. The demands of the population and the advances in technology ensure that health care has a solid foundation and that it will continue to be a growing field for decades to come.

The Occupations Most in Demand

Changes and improvements in technology, combined with strict efforts to contain the skyrocketing costs of health care, will have tremendous influence and impact on which health care occupations grow the fastest. Out of the top twenty occupations expected to grow the fastest between 2004 and 2014, fourteen of them are in the health care industry.

Home health aides are expected to have the largest percentage of change over the next decade. Medical assistants ranked third, and physicians' assistants ranked fourth. Ranking sixth and seventh, respectively, are physical therapy assistants and dental hygienists. Dental assistants and personal care and home care aides ranked ninth and tenth. (Note: home health aides have more specific training than home care aides.)

Physical therapists ranked in thirteenth place. Veterinary technicians and technologists ranked fifteenth. Diagnostic medical sonographers ranked sixteenth. Ranking seventeenth through twentieth, respectively, are physical therapy aides, occupational therapy assistants, medical scientists (except epidemiologists), and occupational therapists. (Again, there is a difference in training between physical therapy assistants and aides.)

 Fact

In the top twenty occupations expected to have the largest numerical increases, registered nurses rank second, home health aides rank eighth, nurses' aides (including the titles of C.N.A., orderly, and attendant) rank ninth. Personal and home care aides rank eleventh.

All of these positions require some degree of postsecondary formal education or training. This can include on-the-job training opportunities for medical assistants, dental assistants, and personal and home care aides, but in most instances employers will expect some training from a vocational school or adult education program. Physical therapy aides and home health aides require additional training as well.

For twelve of the occupations in this group, an associate's or bachelor's degree is minimal, and for three of these—physician assistants, and physical and occupational therapists—a master's degree is required.

Health Care Roles Defined

There are several categories of health care careers. The most commonly recognized roles are:

- Primary care practitioners: diagnose and prescribe treatment; includes M.D.s, dentists, chiropractors, and veterinarians
- Partners and associates: work side by side with the primary care practitioners to provide primary treatment; includes nurses and physician assistants
- The rehab team: provides rehabilitative treatment; includes physical, occupational, and speech therapists

- Assistants and aides: help the team to provide bedside care, personal care, and other assistive services; includes physical therapy aides, certified occupational aides, and certified nurses' aides
- Administrative team members: manage facilities and personnel

Other roles for health care workers include such fields as medical writers and illustrators, biomedical engineers, athletic trainers, medical records technicians and information technologists, medical librarians, phlebotomists and laboratory technicians, radiology technologists and x-ray technicians, sonographers, health insurance reps, and genetic counselors, among others.

The Nine Major Segments of Health Care

When people think of health care, they often conjure up images from their own experiences in doctors' offices, clinics, and hospitals. Then there are the images of intense drama and hustling and bustling in hospitals and emergency rooms such as those presented on television and in the movies. These are all part of the health care arena, but it extends far beyond the emergency room.

While the majority of the health care industry operates from inpatient and outpatient facilities, there are other sites as well. Health care establishments include nine major segments. These are:

- **Hospitals:** They can be general or specific and provide complete medical care primarily on an inpatient basis.
- **Nursing and residential care facilities:** These include rehab, convalescent, and long-term care facilities as well as independent and assisted-living facilities.
- **Physicians' offices:** These are the offices of physicians and surgeons.
- **Dentists' offices:** These include the offices of general or specialized dentists and dental surgeons.
- **Home health care agencies:** They provide skilled-nursing care as well as physical, occupational, and speech therapy; social

work; and home health aide services for patients at home (on an intermittent basis).

- **Offices of other health care practitioners:** These Include chiropractors, optometrists, podiatrists, outpatient therapists (physical, occupational, and speech), dietitians, psychologists, audiologists, alternative medicine practitioners, and veterinarians.
- **Outpatient care centers:** These include urgent-care centers, kidney dialysis centers, outpatient mental health centers, and clinics.
- **Other ambulatory care centers:** These include patient transport services (ambulance, helicopter), blood banks, organ donation banks, and smoking cessation centers.
- **Medical and diagnostic laboratories:** These include x-rays, MRI, CAT scans, mammography, and clinical laboratory studies.

Many of these sectors operate around the clock and require workers on all shifts. Some offer only on-call assistance after hours, on weekends, and holidays, in which case workers may share or rotate the on-call duties.

Inpatient Facilities

Inpatient health care facilities include hospitals, skilled nursing and long-term care facilities, and residential care facilities. Each of these has many different specialties ranging from generic to highly specialized levels of care.

Hospitals

The majority of health care workers are employed by hospitals. Hospitals fit into two categories: They are dedicated to either acute care or long-term rehabilitative care. Acute care facilities treat sudden and acute illness or injuries, and patients typically stay less than ten days unless their care involves more intense treatment (such as that which requires being admitted to an intensive care unit).

Long-term hospitals treat illnesses such as psychiatric issues; chronic illness, like respiratory issues; and rehabilitative issues. The rehab can be for substance abuse. Other rehabilitation is for post-acute illness or severe injury such as massive strokes, spinal cord injuries, and major or multiple orthopedic injuries. The long-term stays in these facilities can range from a few weeks to several months. The key element is progress and the potential to continue progressing.

Hospitals are generally owned and operated by three different groups:

- **For-Profit:** These are proprietary facilities usually owned by individuals or companies. Sometimes groups of physicians own the hospital.
- **Nonprofit:** These are usually local, private hospitals most often run by religious organizations. Other nonprofit organizations, such as the Shriners, operate specialty hospitals in some areas of the country.
- **Government owned and operated:** These are run by the local, state, or federal government. The Veterans Administration is an example. State hospitals are usually psychiatric hospitals, and local governments have community or county hospitals.

Specialty hospitals, such as children's hospitals, are usually run by local city and county governments. There are also hospitals designed to treat specific illnesses, such as respiratory disease, orthopedic and neuromuscular conditions, and cancer. These are usually either run by local governments or are privately owned, and often are nonprofit.

On the other hand, for-profit organizations are in the business of making money and paying large dividends to the owners and shareholders. The philosophical approach to *how* they provide care can be very different. The types of salaries they pay may or may not reflect their profit status, except perhaps at the CEO level.

Some nonprofit hospitals provide free care to all who seek it and cannot afford to pay. They depend heavily on donations and endowments to provide this level of care. For-profit institutions are less likely to offer free care, but may allow for sliding-scale payments based on the ability to pay.

Question

What are nonprofit organizations?
They are organizations that have been granted tax-exempt status. They usually depend on donations from the private sector or from government agencies. Nonprofit organizations can engage in moneymaking operations; however, they cannot distribute the profits to owners and shareholders as a for-profit company would. How they earn and spend money is restricted by their tax-exempt status.

Skilled-Nursing and Long-Term Care Facilities

A skilled-nursing facility, also known as a *SNF* (pronounced "sniff"), provides continuing care to patients who still require skilled care from either a nurse or a therapist (or both), have a potential to improve, and no longer require as acute a level of care as they did in the hospital.

Patients at a SNF are usually recovering from an acute illness and are not yet able to return home. They may have had a stroke, major illness, or surgery, or may be recovering from an orthopedic injury such as a fractured hip or a joint replacement, and require continued nursing care and/or physical, occupational, or speech therapy. The rehabilitative nature of a SNF is far less intense than that of a long-term rehab hospital.

A long-term care facility is one in which the residents require twenty-four-hour care or supervision, but it is custodial in nature rather than skilled. That is, they require supervision and varying levels of assistance with activities of daily living (ADLs), like bathing, grooming, feeding, mobility, and toileting. This can also include those patients who are in vegetative states and require total care, as long as they don't require any *skilled* care.

These two types of facilities are often lumped together and referred to as *nursing homes*. The distinction becomes necessary when it comes to billing and reimbursement issues. Staffing is generally less skilled in the long-term care facilities due to the non-skilled, custodial nature of the job. For those seeking careers in these facilities, the difference will affect the hiring potential. If your small community has only one such facility and you have your heart set on becoming a P.T. and working there, you need to explore whether employment is a possibility.

 Fact

Most insurance will reimburse for either a finite period of time, or as long as there is a need for skilled care and the potential to improve. However, once there is no further requirement for skilled care or there is no potential to improve, the reimbursement will usually end. The patient's only option may be to move to a long-term care facility, where his out-of-pocket expense will be lower.

Residential Care

The most common residential care facilities are senior residences, whether they are small board-and-care homes or large assisted-living facilities. There are a variety of senior residences offering several levels of care, from independent living to moderate levels of assistance. (Those who require maximum assistance should be placed in a long-term care facility.)

In independent living, seniors require little to no assistance, but have the advantage that someone will check to be sure they are okay each day, and an option of community dining. In assisted-living facilities, residents can require minimal assistance (such as help with medications), more moderate assistance with activities of daily living (such as bathing and dressing), or may even require twenty-four-hour supervision. The higher the level of care, the higher the cost for the care. Residents do, however, have to be able to ambulate (walk). They can require the use of a cane or walker, but if they are wheelchair bound, even though they transfer independently, they should be living in a facility with a higher level of care.

In board-and-care homes, residents can be wheelchair bound, depending on the home's licensing and staffing ratios. A board-and-care home is a private home that is licensed by the state to house one or more residents who can require varying levels of care, from only supervision to a moderate level of assistance with activities of daily living (ADLs), depending on the skill and number of staff available twenty-four hours a day to care for the residents.

Other residential care facilities serve special needs. These include, but are not limited to, homes for those with autism or severe birth defects; the mentally challenged and retarded; and emotionally disturbed individuals. There are also facilities such as halfway houses for substance abuse and alcohol rehabilitation.

Outpatient Facilities

Some of the most common facilities include physicians' and other health care practitioners' offices, dentists' offices, veterinary clinics, public health clinics, and clinical laboratories. These are primarily facilities where patients go to receive care and where more than 500,000 people are employed nationwide.

Other outpatient facilities include same-day surgery centers, emergency care centers, blood banks, family-planning facilities, mental health clinics, imaging centers, and outpatient rehab centers for physical, occupational, or speech therapy. Vision care centers, wellness facilities, E.M.T./ambulance services, pharmacies, and home health care are also examples of outpatient care.

Other facilities that fit into a broader definition of outpatient facilities include insurance companies, health education agencies, professional health organizations, research facilities, and manufacturers and distributors of durable medical equipment and pharmaceuticals.

Skills of Health Care Workers

As you can imagine, all inpatient and outpatient facilities require health care workers at all levels, from administrative, office, and support personnel to the highly skilled scientists and practitioners. Currently well over 5 million people are employed at the scientific and highly skilled levels, and another 1 million support personnel work in the health care industry. As the population ages and the demand for health care increases over the next few years, many more openings will exist for workers of all levels of skill, ability, and education.

Technology advances have also brought about new opportunities for health care workers and will continue to do so far into the future. Imagine, for example, how the advent of MRI and CAT scan technology expanded the opportunities for specialized technologists beyond the realm of simple x-rays. Many new diagnostic and treatment modalities will continue to emerge and with them a wide variety of career opportunities.

E ssential

The ever-increasing costs of health care will most likely bring about many changes and reforms in the health care industry that will have an impact on job prospects. Some positions may be eliminated, but many more may be created that cannot be anticipated at this point. The fact is, however, that there will continue to be a high demand for health care workers for many decades to come.

An important advantage to the health care industry is that almost anywhere in the country, you can find a job in health care. Many of the non-skilled positions translate or are easily adaptable to other positions in health care. Many of the skilled professions build upon or represent building blocks to other skilled positions. This is not true for most other career paths.

Many of the skills developed by health care workers also transfer to positions outside of health care. For example, there are eight basic skills employers desire in the ideal employee. Nurses usually possess all eight of these skills and are highly sought after for that reason, especially for positions outside the nursing field. These eight skills are:

- Leadership/persuasiveness
- Problem solving
- Physical stamina
- Networking skills
- Teamwork
- Manual dexterity
- Initiative
- Ability to teach others

Physical, occupational, and recreation therapists as well as E.M.T.s and paramedics usually possess most, if not all, of these transferable skills. This makes these health care workers highly desirable in other positions as well as in their own realms of health care.

As community volunteers, health care workers set the bar high, demanding a level of excellence that usually equates to very successful community programs.

Alert

The economy, the stability of the local population, changes in health care trends, and government support will all affect the reliability of the data and information you collect. In some instances, we can't even predict all of the types of jobs that will be available and in demand in ten years, but we do know that health care careers will continue to be in high demand because we have a population that is aging and will present a growing need for health care in the future.

Health care workers and professionals are generally in high demand in rural areas as well as in large metropolises. The exact needs may vary from one area to another, but simple research will give you an idea of the opportunities available where you want to live and work. Classified ads, Internet job search engines, and networking are just three of the easiest ways to determine the current needs in your area.

There is a wide range of career opportunities in health care. There is a need for administrative support personnel, personal care assistants, practitioners, and diagnosticians, as well as highly skilled scientists who are needed to develop new drugs, treatments, and diagnostics. Some positions will grow at a faster pace than others, but there are really no health care fields that are saturated at this point, and none that are predicted to be in the near future.

The opportunities for women and minorities in the health care field are wide open, and many more women and minorities are filling openings and attending schools. Medical schools have made concerted efforts to recruit women, and today almost 50 percent of the freshmen entering medical school are women, and over 15 percent are minorities.

Women especially find themselves turning to health care as a second career. Many pursue nursing or medicine after raising families. Men who are searching for a more meaningful career have begun to turn to nursing and other health care careers as second careers as well, particularly in the aftermath of September 11.

Economic changes combined with the high cost of medical care have forced changes in the industry. For instance, a physician's time is very costly and valuable. For a physician to spend his time instructing a patient in how to take a medication or in the specifics of a new diagnosis is not cost-effective. The physician's time is better spent assessing and diagnosing. Nurses, and sometimes physician assistants, have assumed the role of instructing patients in medications, diseases, and necessary lifestyle changes.

Nurse practitioners and physician assistants may be your primary health care practitioners unless your needs extend beyond a wellness or simple-illness exam and treatment. Dental hygienists today have an expanded role in your dental care, and if there is nothing significant to be found at routine teeth-cleaning sessions, you might not even see the dentist.

Alert

Many of the lower-paid positions such as nursing and therapy aides are seen as stepping stones to becoming R.N.s, P.T.s, O.T.s, and S.T.s, leaving these positions open to be filled by a new generation of young workers who also aspire to one day become nurses and therapists. This turnover will continue to fuel the need for more workers.

Responsibilities of Health Care Workers

All health care workers carry a tremendous responsibility to assist and provide for the best possible outcomes for the patient. Sometimes that responsibility reaches to life or death circumstances, but most frequently relates to everyday health and wellness.

There is not room for mediocrity in health care, and health care professionals must demand excellence from themselves and their peers. The general public expects perfection, as evidenced by the high volume of malpractice cases each year.

Unlike trading in a car that doesn't live up to your expectations, you cannot exchange your body for a new one if it malfunctions or wears out. You depend on health care professionals to assist you in keeping your body fine-tuned and functioning at its best, and to repair it when necessary. You expect nothing short of excellence.

Take Care of Yourself

Because of the high degree of responsibility involved, health care professions are some of the most physically and emotionally demanding of all. This is especially true for nurses and doctors, which helps to explain the high level of burnout for nurses. This is an important fact to understand as you explore your options in the health care field. One of the biggest reasons that heath care workers leave the field after only one to three years is that they did not understand the impact it could have on their private lives. They became disenchanted with their jobs and quickly burned out.

Most health care professionals work long and varied hours. Sick people don't conveniently develop illnesses during banker's hours. Nor do they suddenly become well for holidays and vacations. Health care jobs in many instances span twenty-four hours per day, seven days a week. Depending on your chosen career, you may work any of several different shifts and possibly be on call for a significant portion of time as well. Health care doesn't take a break because you are sick, either.

There are no nonessential jobs in health care, and it takes a team effort to provide patients with the very best in care. The ability to be a team player and not have to be a star player is essential to the success of the effort. Not everyone can adapt to the fact that there is "no *I* in *team.*"

Take Care of Others

Health care workers are usually selfless and always put others first. In order to replenish themselves, however, they need to be able to take care of themselves. They need to understand that they have a responsibility to both themselves and their patients to do so. They are usually the worst patients, and they need to learn to become better at doing what they preach.

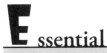

E ssential

A positive outcome does not always indicate a cure or an improvement. Sometimes a positive outcome can involve a person dying in a dignified, pain-free manner. Health care careers often require the ability to think outside the box and see things from a different perspective.

Honesty and integrity are two primary and essential characteristics that health care professionals must possess. The ability to think on their feet, even under duress, and to make decisions goes without saying. The ability to accept responsibility and to be accountable for their decisions and actions is an absolutely necessity. Human beings make mistakes. Health care professionals have to do their very best to avoid mistakes, but sometimes they are unavoidable. In those instances, a health care worker cannot try to hide or cover up the mistake. They must report it, and be accountable.

They must also be honest and forthcoming about their skills and abilities. Health care presents a lifelong learning opportunity to all who work in the industry, but you must never exceed the scope of practice nor what you have been trained to do. In the learning process there will always be a first time, but not without proper preparation, education, and supervision.

Chapter 3

Making the Choice for You

Choosing a career is one of the most important choices you will make in your life. It will involve a large portion of your future life, including the time you spend obtaining the necessary education. You will need to consider carefully the things you like to do and those you don't enjoy at all. The job you train for today may not be the exact job you perform throughout even the majority of your career, but it's a place to begin the process.

Self-Assessment and Evaluation

As technology continues to make advances in the field of health care possible, new jobs will be created and existing jobs will be expanded and changed to meet the needs and demands of the public. Consequently you will have many opportunities to grow and change throughout your career.

Some people seem to be born knowing exactly what they want to do "when they grow up," and others struggle to find even a clue. One of the best aspects of health care is that there is such a broad variety of skills, talents, and abilities that can adapt well to a career and afford you an opportunity to combine your personal interests and talents with the skills and abilities needed to help people strive to improve their lives. This can provide you with one of the most rewarding and meaningful careers possible.

Not all health care careers will require an intense study of science and math, but most do require an understanding of human anatomy and basic bodily functions. For example, if you enjoy art, photography, music, dance, or even gardening, you may find that these talents and skills apply to health care careers and may not require such an extensive study of math or science.

Begin with a self-evaluation. How many of the following items can you identify as having a priority in your future career?

- Teaching others
- Working with a team or group
- Working with your hands or using instruments
- Precision and accuracy; detail oriented
- Working with and/or helping people
- Completing complex tasks with detailed steps
- A need to see tangible results
- Problem solving
- Job security with ample employment opportunities well into the future

If five or more of these appeal to you, you should further explore opportunities in health care. There are more issues to be explored later that will serve to support this and to help you choose more specifically which aspect of health care you might want to explore.

Question

But how do I know if I am suited for, or should even consider, a career in health care?
One of the primary issues you should evaluate is whether or not you like people and want to help them. Another important issue you should consider is whether or not you enjoy science and math. Most health care professions combine the art of caring with the skills of science and technology.

Think about the qualities and characteristics you would need for certain aspects of health care professions. These are not exclusive and, of course, they overlap, but they do tend to describe the individuals who migrate to these health care careers. Think about your skills and attributes as well as your interests. Where do they tend to fall?

Some of the characteristics of health care practitioners and administrators include being personable, objective, logical, resourceful, forceful, creative, organized, practical, and having excellent problem-solving skills.

Therapists, social workers, and counselors need to be persuasive, outspoken, motivating, innovative, personable, and determined, and they need to enjoy challenges.

Nurses, health educators, athletic trainers, medical writers, and photographers need to be creative, imaginative, emotional, sensitive, and reflective. They also need to be conceptual and abstract thinkers.

Biomedical engineers, health librarians, medical coders, and health scientists need to be organized, methodical, systematic, detail oriented, and controlling, and they must enjoy working with numbers and systems.

The Art of Caring Is Essential

Caring is an important aspect of life and it is essential to health care. Some feel it is a lost art, and some will tell you that nurses are the only health care professionals who understand the art of caring. Nurses do the caring, doctors do the curing, and the rest just participate along the way: that may have been the way in the past, but it certainly isn't true today. As members of each health care profession have come to learn that caring, compassion, and empathy have made them better professionals, and helped to improve patient outcomes as a result, this perhaps lost art is returning to the health care profession as a whole. Learning the art of caring is essential to success in the field today and for the future.

The stigma that caring shows weakness, and that needing to be cared for means dependence and demonstrates an even greater weakness, is losing in the battle to create a dignified means of promoting wellness and an emphasis on improving one's health status.

Fact

Events such as September 11, the tsunami in Asia, and the devastating hurricanes of 2005 have been vivid reminders that life is short and not always fair. Many people have turned to health care to find careers, even second or third careers, which bring meaning and substance to their own lives as they search for a way to help others.

As these positive moves intensify, health care professionals become more integrated and have improved teamwork. This has been especially evident in the improved relationships between doctors and nurses over the last few years. As roles and responsibilities shift in this new paradigm, respect for each other as professionals as well as team members grows, as does the understanding that each member has a different but essential role in the care of and outcome for the patient. Doctors and nurses have come to form true partnerships in their quest to provide the very best of care to their patients.

What Appeals to You?

Consider your own interests and hobbies. What kinds of things do you like to do and do well? Are you good at working with your hands? Are you a born leader, or would you rather be a follower? Do you like teaching others? Do you have a talent for art or music? Do you love math and science? All of these things can play a big part in determining your career focus and decisions.

You should begin to make an inventory of the things you like to do and are good at so that you can compare them to the skills and talents needed for the various health care positions discussed later in this book. Get a pad of paper and write them down.

Some of the following questions will assist you in assessing your likes and dislikes, as well as the skills and talents that would be assets in your future employment. Make a list of these points as well.

- What are your strong points? Are you dependable? Are you a leader? Can you work independently? Do you learn new things quickly? Are you organized? Are you ambitious? Can you think on your feet? Can you make good decisions quickly?
- What are your weaknesses? *Be honest with yourself or ask others to help you out with this.* Are you abrasive or aggressive? Do you have annoying habits? Are you lazy or hard to motivate? Does it take you a long time to learn new things? Are you confrontational? Do you have a temper and do you have difficulty controlling it? Do you take criticism well?
- What kinds of hobbies do you have? This could even include sports or other extra-curricular activities you participate in. Do you like to read? Do you build or create things with your hands? Do you like photography? Are you artistic? Do you play a musical instrument or dance or sing? Do you like to write or create stories?
- What useful skills do you have? This will include computer literacy as well as other computer skills and proficiency at computer programs. Can you program your thermostat? Automatic sprinklers? Can you set your VCR or TiVo to record a program? Do you speak a foreign language? Do you know American Sign Language? Can you speed-read, do you have an excellent or "photographic" memory, and do you have legible handwriting? All are among items to consider when determining the skills you possess.

Prior Work Experience or Volunteer Work

Certain courses of study such as nursing and physical or occupational therapy require some experience or volunteer work in the field before you can be accepted into the program major. For nurses, often a C.N.A. (certified nursing assistant) is required. For therapy, volunteer hours in a therapy department are often required. Sometimes working in a medical office can count for some credit toward this requirement.

For other health care fields as well as these, other work experience and responsibilities will always be counted, so think about all of the responsibilities of your prior jobs. Are there skills or talents that you learned or perfected that can be an asset? Any lessons learned in customer service, for example, apply here as well. Experiences with problem solving, teaching, giving detailed instructions, patience, motivating others, leadership, supervision of others, and team building are all valuable experiences you should highlight.

Personal Likes and Dislikes

In this category you need to consider and list personal preferences that could influence your career choices. This could include a multitude of considerations: Do you want to work inside or outside? Can you stay awake for long periods of time, or do you require ten or more hours of sleep? Do you have allergies? Do you have racial or ethnic biases that would prevent you from working with people of all nationalities and colors? Do you have an attitude about diseases such as AIDS or mental illness? Do you prefer small companies or large organizations? Are you willing to relocate? Do you like fast-paced environments, or do you prefer a slow-paced, quiet environment?

These are very important things to consider. Be honest with yourself. Perhaps you have a real aversion to children or older people. If you tend to make judgments about people of color, people with disabilities, or those with certain ailments such as HIV or AIDS, then you need to understand why and whether or not you can learn to be nonjudgmental or tolerant. List these items and explore them along with your career options.

Educational Commitment

How long are you willing and or able to commit to the education or training you will need for your professional choice? For instance, some health care professions require several months of training, while becoming a physician could take upwards of eight to ten years of college and medical school/residency. Do you like school? Are you interested in learning? Do you have the patience to spend another ten years in school? Do you have the time to spend?

Or perhaps you need to take it in steps, such as becoming a nurse first so that you can support yourself and your family while you pursue your dream of becoming a doctor. Or maybe you could become a therapy aide so that you can support yourself through physical therapy school. The educational building blocks are a huge perk for students at all levels in the health care field.

Tackling Math and Science

Perhaps you have a burning desire to work in a profession where you can help others, but you cannot pass math. What can you do? Most of the health care professions will deal with math and science because you are working with the human body and its functions. However, there are choices to be made that will not require such an extensive background of math and science.

Working in study groups can be most beneficial as well. Perhaps a fellow student can help explain concepts in a way that you can better understand. Also consider options such as talking with other students and counselors who can offer advice about a professor who is particularly good or helpful for students who have difficulty with the subject.

For most health care professions that involve hands-on patient contact, you will need a significant amount of math and science. This usually means basic algebra, at least.

Essential

If you struggle with math, don't be completely discouraged. You can get some additional help with any of the courses you may need to take. Hire a private tutor or seek out additional help or tutoring from your teacher. Sometimes you might need to consider taking only one class for a particular term so that you can concentrate solely on it.

Sciences will include biology, anatomy and physiology, and microbiology. Some programs may require physics and organic chemistry. Basic chemistry will be required for many. Courses in sociology and basic psychology may also be required. To be able to comprehend the reading required for these courses, you will have to have at least a tenth-grade reading/comprehension level. This will require a thorough understanding of the English language, both written and oral.

These courses could be abbreviated for some professions, such as for massage therapists, nurses' aides, and therapy aides, or much more advanced for fields like biomedical engineering. If you really cannot pass math or science, consider some of the ancillary positions in the medical field.

Narrowing Down the Choices

Once you have made your lists of attributes and considered all of your possible skills and talents as well as your personal preferences, you will need to begin to research the various health care careers and compare the requirements and expectations with your lists. You may want to make new lists of side-by-side comparisons of the requirements and attributes of the profession in one column and your personal characteristics and attributes in another column. You might even find that you have more in common with a career than you thought, or that you have nothing in common with one you have long considered to be your primary choice.

Once you have narrowed down some of your choices, you need to begin to investigate the profession further. Here are a few suggestions:

- Find opportunities to observe these professionals at work. Contact a facility where these professionals work, and inquire about a tour of the facility and the possibility of shadowing the professional for a day. Make an appointment and call to confirm. Be on time.
- Contact the professional organization and request information about the profession. Ask if they offer any mentoring programs or shadowing opportunities for potential students.

- A number of health sciences camps are becoming popular all over the country. They are offered primarily by colleges, universities, and professional organizations to provide high school students with a week-long, in-depth view of the profession. (See Appendix A, search the Internet for "health sciences camps," or search by vocation such as "nursing camps.") The camps offer experiences such as shadowing opportunities, CPR certification, and peanut-gallery views of such sites as the ER and of diagnostic and treatment procedures, such as CAT scans and hyperbaric chambers.
- Be sure to research the prospective job opportunities in your area. You can do this through classified ads in your local paper. You can also search the Internet at sites such as Monster.com, CareerBuilders.com, HealthcareJobs.org, or Medzilla.com.

Many health care education programs limit the number of spaces available for students. This is due in large part to the shortage of qualified teachers in the particular area, and may also be due to the shortage of available facilities willing to allow for clinical rotations. Therefore, it is essential that students entering the programs have an understanding of what they're getting into so that they have a better chance of graduating from the program as well as entering the profession.

Making a Decision

Once you have narrowed down your choices and explored these options more carefully, you should be able to make a decision about which field you want to pursue. This may or may not be the career you end up in, but it will provide you with a starting point and a focus for your education.

Very few health care fields require only on-the-job training. Almost all will call for some form of classroom time as well as clinical or practical experience. Depending on the field you choose, this could be a few months to several years of education.

Alert

It's important to research the opportunities for your chosen profession in the geographic location where you hope to reside. For example, if you live in a small community, how many sonographers does your one rural hospital need? Would your time and education be better spent becoming a nurse or therapist?

Health care professions are not just learned from reading a book. It requires hands-on experience to learn and perfect techniques while under the direct supervision of qualified teachers.

By the same token, many health care options build upon each other. In other words, if you begin your career as a physical therapy aide, you could eventually choose to go on and become a physical therapist. Your experience and education will serve as valuable assets and will fulfill many of the prerequisites necessary to achieve your new career goal.

Or if you plan to become a physician, and halfway through decide that you cannot devote that much time and effort at this point, you could shift gears and pursue a role as a physician's assistant, or you might find yourself looking into becoming a nurse practitioner. Again, the knowledge acquired and most of the courses taken will easily transfer to the new program.

Chapter 4

The Education Process

Once you've chosen the area of health care you want to pursue, you must investigate how to obtain the necessary education. Most health care careers will require ongoing continuing education until retirement, but you first have to find out how to get into the field you've chosen. There are two important factors to keep in mind: find the most rigorous program that you can get into and afford; and make sure that the program or school you choose is accredited.

Prepare in High School

If you're still in high school, make the most of the opportunity to prepare for further education in health care. In most instances, you will need a strong background in math and sciences. Almost all health care jobs require a college degree. This can be from vocational or technical schools, professional schools, community colleges, or universities, depending on the program or degree required. The career path you have chosen will determine the type of school you need to attend.

Basic algebra is probably the minimal math requirement for most health care positions. In some you will need even higher math. Very few positions won't have a math requirement, and in order to pass most college-level entrance exams, you will need to have a grasp of basic algebra. Most schools have some sort of entrance exam and/or placement tests.

Science Courses

Life sciences such as biology, anatomy, or physiology are recommended, as are physical sciences such as chemistry and physics. Computer skills such as keyboarding and word processing are a must, and Internet search skills are highly recommended.

E ssential

Social sciences such as psychology or sociology are suggested as well to help you gain an understanding of cultural differences, coping mechanisms, and emotional issues you may face in the course of interacting with patients.

Communication Skills Are Essential

Of course, excellent written and verbal communication skills are extremely important. You must be able to clearly convey information and to document or even just interpret what care has been given. In order to complete college-level course work, you need to have at least a tenth-grade reading and comprehension level.

If you have chosen to do something that will involve another skill, such as art or photography, basic courses of study in these areas should be taken. Medical writers would be well advised to take a class in journalism.

Entrance Exams

Many schools will require an entrance exam of some sort. Preparation courses and practice tests may be available in your school library or online. These will usually test at least your basic reading-comprehension level as well as basic math skills. Other college entrance exams such as the SAT or ACT will test your knowledge of other areas as well, including social studies, science, foreign language, and literature. Prep courses and practice tests are readily available for these two popular exams.

Choosing the Program for You

If you have a specific career objective in mind, this will dictate the type of school or program you need to attend. If you are unsure, it may be more difficult, but a well-rounded basic college degree with an emphasis on math and life science courses can provide you with a basic foundation for many health care careers. If you didn't begin to prepare for this type of study in high school, you may have a few more math and science classes to take to bring you up to speed.

Always make sure that any school you attend is accredited. Not all schools are, and some have accreditation for some programs and not for others. Be sure to ask—never assume. Accreditation is achieved when an independent agency evaluates the school's program for quality of the faculty; content or curriculum; and the facilities available for the education, such as libraries, classrooms, and laboratories. This independent agency submits its findings in a report to the accrediting agency, and the agency decides whether or not to offer accreditation.

One of the best ways to begin your search for a program is to talk to people who work in the field that interests you. Find out where they got their education and what they recommend. Did the program work well for them? Would they do it the same way again or do something different, and why?

Technical or Vocational Schools

These schools offer health care education programs such as medical transcription, medical and dental assisting, EKG technology, and phlebotomy. Most C.N.A. (certified nurse's aide) and licensed practical or vocation nurse (L.V.N./L.P.N.) programs are now run by vocational schools. These programs combine classroom study with practical experience. Upon completion of the program you receive a certificate. If the position requires a license, then you will be duly qualified to sit for a licensure exam.

Community College

Community colleges, or junior colleges as they may be referred to in some areas, offer some of the same programs that vocational schools do, as well as other certificated programs such as certified nurse's aide training. They also offer associate's (two-year) degree programs in such areas as nursing, dental hygiene, and x-ray and other radiology technology areas. Community colleges also offer an excellent opportunity to fulfill general-education requirements before transfering to a bachelor's degree program at a four-year college or university. It is important that all professional programs be accredited so that graduates are eligible to sit for licensing or certification exams. It is also important to make sure your course work is transferable to a four-year college or university whether or not that is your goal at the present time. For example, not all anatomy and physiology courses taken at the community college level will transfer. Make sure you take the one that does, or be prepared to take it again at the higher-level institution.

E Alert

Accreditation can be rescinded if standards are not maintained, so make sure to ask the school about its current status. Stay informed. Employers seek employees with appropriate credentials, and if you cannot prove that you have received your education from an accredited institution, you may not be allowed to sit for licensing examinations or become certified.

Four-Year Colleges and Universities

Complex health care careers such as practitioner, therapist, dietitian, physician assistant, pharmacist, and psychologist all require a bachelor's degree. Many also require several years of postgraduate study and internship or training. A bachelor's degree includes basic education studies such as English, history, and humanities in addition to the math and science required by the specific career path.

Postgraduate study can include studies to obtain a master's degree or beyond, or specialized education such as medical school, which includes internship and residency responsibilities.

Finding the Right School

Once you've decided on the career path and the type of schooling you'll need, it's time to make a few more decisions and find the right school. You should apply to several in order to better ensure that you'll get in, particularly if your program is one that has a limited number of openings for students.

What Are You Looking For?

Some things you should consider when investigating possibilities include:

- Do you want to go away to school?
- Do you want to live on or off campus?
- Are you looking for a large school or a small one?
- Do you want to attend a religious school, a private school, or a state school?
- Should it be a conservative or a liberal environment?
- Does the ethnic makeup of the school matter to you?

You can find information about potential schools on the Internet, by talking with friends and family, or through your local or school library. One of the most helpful resources is *Peterson's College Guides*. You can access them online at *www.petersons.com*. These and other guides like them provide information about the school, the demographics, the degree options, and what majors and minors they offer. They tell you how many students apply each year and how many are accepted. And they break out the ethnic and socio-economic information about the students. They also include contact information, instructions on how to apply, and a list of the prerequisites.

Comparing Schools

When you have a few schools in mind, you should begin to fill out a comparison sheet for yourself. This can include a space to record which steps you have completed in the application process.

The information you might write down includes:

- The name of the school
- The cost of tuition, books and supplies, and room and board
- Application deadline (and another place to indicate when you sent in your application)
- Other cost considerations, such as transportation to and from the school (will you need a car?)
- Length of the program
- Additional prerequisites
- Entrance exams and fees
- Contact information and Web address

Leave additional room for any other comments or pertinent information you might want to access quickly or frequently.

When you have completed these comparisons, you should prioritize your choices and then begin to further your investigation. Write or e-mail the admissions department and request information and an application. If you can, you should visit each of your choices. This is not always feasible, so you should try to get to a campus or two near your home. They may not even be among your chosen few, but there are many things you can learn from visiting a campus.

Your Campus Tour

Take care not to disrupt classes, but do try to see what you can. Check out the layout of the campus. Peak in classrooms and check out the types of lab facilities available. Visit the library, computer labs, and health care clinic, and check out the food services. What kinds of extracurricular activities are available? What is the general atmosphere like? Do the students seem happy and friendly? If you're going to live on campus, where are the dorms? Try to visit one or two. What is the community like? Can you easily get to off-campus places such as shopping centers?

Make note of the things that are important to you and that you like. Also make note of the things you don't like or that are inconvenient. Even if this is not a campus you are considering, you will have something by which to measure those you do choose.

E ssential

Write or e-mail the department chair for your major and ask if there is a student or two who would be willing to share their experiences with you via phone or e-mail. If you make a visit to the campus, see if they'll be available to meet with you and possibly show you around a little bit. The more that you can do to ensure this will be a good fit, the more successful your experience will be. Talk with these students about what they like and dislike about the campus and the program.

Your Application

When you have narrowed down your choices, make your applications. Be aware of deadlines, as they will vary from one school to another. These are usually absolute deadlines, and if you miss them, you'll have to wait for the open application period for the next available term. Each application will require a fee, so you likely won't be applying to more than a few, but don't put all of your eggs in one basket.

If you need written recommendations from others, be sure to ask early enough and clearly identify deadlines. You should pad your dates so that if they are late, you still have time. Remind them at least ten days before the deadline. Be sure to thank them appropriately.

Never assume that because you have a 4.0 you're a shoe-in. Someone with a lower GPA and tons of community service and extracurricular activities may just beat you out. Read about the student population. Know what they look for in a student, and work to highlight your qualifications that fit that mold; or find a better match for yourself. Schools are usually well aware of the academics of the schools from which they usually accept students, so don't try to embellish your qualifications beyond what you can actually live up to. But don't forget to think outside the box and give yourself credit for your accomplishments.

 **Alert**

Be sure that you provide all of the information requested. Be neat and organized. Your application represents you to the school, so be sure to put your best foot forward. A messy paper with coffee stains, or ink that's too light because your pen just ran out, will not make a good first impression. If you have to write an essay, give it plenty of thought and polish it.

The competition may be very fierce depending on the type of program you are entering. This is especially true for nursing students. There is a tremendous shortage of nurses, but there is also a shortage of nurse educators, so the programs have a limited number of openings. There are waiting lists, and schools use many tactics to weed out those who are not serious or likely to complete the program.

It will be several weeks or even a few months before you hear back from schools. Usually they will include information in your application packet as to how long the process takes. Relax, and hopefully you'll get into the school or program you most desire.

Financial Aid

Now it's time to figure out how you're going to pay for all of this and not kill yourself working three jobs and going to school full-time. Hopefully you will have some funds saved up, but not everyone does. You will need to figure out a realistic budget of school and living expenses. If you're going away to school, be sure to include transportation costs. Don't forget to include coming home for holidays.

Some dorms close down for the summer, and if you decide to stay at school, you'll have to arrange other housing.

The first step you need to take in the process is to complete what is called a FAFSA. This is your Free Application for Federal Student Aid. You can get the forms from your career center or you can fill out the entire form online, at *www.fafsa.ed.gov*. They have placed a great deal of helpful information on this site, and a special section to help you identify and avoid financial aid scams.

All schools, including most vocational/technical schools, will require the information from your FAFSA. It determines your financial need as well as your EFC (expected family commitment). Once you complete the FAFSA, if you are eligible for federal grants, you will receive information about how to apply. As you fill out your financial aid applications, pay special attention to deadlines and carefully read the background materials so that you portray yourself as an ideal candidate.

 Fact

There are many forms of financial aid available. They include grants, scholarships, low-interest student loans for students and parents, and work-study programs. If you're still in high school, your guidance counselor has probably steered you toward scholarship and grant information. Be sure to apply for as many as you can.

If you are a dependent and being claimed as such by your parents for income tax purposes, you will have an EFC. This commitment can be met by PLUS loans, which your parents can apply for. If you are single and independent, then you will not have an EFC and will be eligible for larger student loan amounts.

Once your school has received your FAFSA, the financial aid officer will send you an award letter. This will tell you about any grants or scholarships that have been given, and will direct you to an appropriate lender should you need student loans. Your financial aid department should become your best friend for this process. They will help you, and there is no fee for their service.

There are other helpful Web sites to explore to get an understanding of the financial aid process and for links to other resources for possible scholarship and grant considerations. These include:

- *www.collegeboard.com/pay*
- *http://fastweb.com*
- *www.srnexpress.com* (Scholarship Resource Network Express)

Alert

There are many reputable firms and financial aid counselors, but there are also many scams that appear to be just as reputable. You can do everything for yourself that a reputable firm can do for you. If you seriously do need help, investigate the firm's credentials before you choose. If their promise seems too good to be true, it probably is.

Other sources of financial aid include private loans and tuition reimbursement plans from employers. Many employers offer tuition assistance of some sort to their employees and even to their employees' children. These can be valuable sources, but be sure to explore any associated obligations. The money could be offered in exchange for a guarantee of employment for a set period of time, and you may have to repay it in a lump sum if that obligation is not met. Just be sure you can commit to their requirements.

The government from time to time offers programs for loans that are forgiven either in full or a large part for workers in areas of critical shortage. Currently there are some of these available for nurses. They require a commitment to work in disadvantaged areas for a designated time frame. Be sure to investigate opportunities such as these. Your financial aid officer should be able to assist you. Or you can search the Internet for "loan forgiveness programs for [your particular field]."

E Fact

Don't overlook even the smallest scholarships if you are eligible. Any amount of money—$100, $500—will help defray the cost of books or supplies. Several of these small amounts could cover your books for a semester, and that's money that doesn't ever need to be repaid.

Surviving School

The education process for health care careers will be an intense one. You will be dealing with the human body, and you will have to understand anatomy and physiology on some level for almost every aspect of health care. That will be true even for those who don't have direct patient contact. To code a diagnosis, to illustrate a body part, to coordinate insurance benefits, you will have to have some understanding of the body, its functions, and its dysfunctions.

You will have some fun courses, but you will have plenty of math and science to contend with. You will probably have laboratory and clinical classes that will provide you with practical experience. Most of your classes will be essential; that is, you cannot skip classes and expect to learn what you need to know in order to work in the health care field. Mrs. Jones will not understand when her physical therapist can't help her with her back pain because he was up all night partying and missed those classes, or when her doctor ignores her issues with her ear because she chose to sleep through classes and still doesn't understand much about the ears.

This can be a stressful time, and if you have multiple commitments such as family and a job as well as school, it can quickly become overwhelming. Many people are turning to health care for second and third careers, and find themselves in this position. The high school graduate may be no better prepared to cope with an intense schedule.

It is vital to your success in school to learn two basic skills that will help you in your career as well. They are stress management and time management.

E ssential

This is serious business, and you need to attend classes and learn all that you can. Health care is a lifelong learning experience, as new techniques, technologies, and medications are constantly becoming available. You will never stop learning, but the foundation you receive in your basic education is very important to your success and to the health of your patients.

Stress Management

If you are able to manage your time wisely, you will be better able to manage your stress. That goes without saying; however, you will not always be able to control the time issue, and you need to be able to learn to cope and to de-stress.

In fact, at times such as midterms and finals, you may find that taking time to relax and clear your mind is far more effective than forcing yourself to study and fighting the fatigue and pain.

There are many techniques that work well, but they are very individual. The most important point is that you value yourself and take care of yourself. Schedule time for yourself. Go to the gym, join a yoga class, or practice self-hypnosis or meditation. Relax on your bed and let some guided imagery take you to a special place for a few moments, a mini-vacation. Have a massage or spend an hour window-shopping. Think about whatever works for you to take you away from it all for an hour.

You can also steal a few minutes between classes to close your eyes and take a few deep breaths. Tune out the world and just simply relax. This works well just before you take a test. Clear your mind of all the clutter so that you can concentrate and access the information you've crammed in.

Fact

Stress is one of the leading causes of burnout among health care professionals. Health care is a highly demanding field, both physically and emotionally. Learning to manage your stress as a student will be a great asset to you when you become a professional.

Time Management

Organization is an essential factor for effective time management. If you are not an organized person, find someone who is and ask her or him for advice and help. Clutter is a terrible time waster, whether it is all in your mind or is physical; you need to clear out the clutter.

If you have a family that is feeling neglected because of your intense schedule, it's important to create opportunities to spend quality time with them. You may even need to schedule time for them.

There are several online resources to assist you with time management issues. Yahoo! Groups is one such resource and is useful if you have a study group. You can send bulletins and share information without having to meet in person. Or you can plan your study group activities and remind each other of deadlines.

Study Groups

Working with a study group is one of the most effective means of learning, especially in the health care sciences. There are lots of theories and abstract examples that may make perfect sense to someone else and not you or vice versa. Perhaps your study group can find a better way to understand and explain certain concepts to you and the others. It also gives you an opportunity to reinforce what you know, and to remember facts and figures when you discuss them aloud.

E ssential

Buy a day planner or a PDA and learn to use it. Write down your entire schedule of test dates, deadlines for papers and presentations, etc., as well as your personal schedule of work and appointments. Keep it up to date and check it every morning. On Monday, check the whole week so that you have a clear picture of what you need to accomplish.

A study group also helps to keep you on your toes, makes you keep up with time frames, and offers you an opportunity to vent and share frustrations and fears. Not everyone looks forward to dissecting a fetal pig, and sharing your concerns can be very helpful.

Health care is a team experience. Forming study groups helps you learn the value of team experiences and how to work with a diverse group of people. This will be a valuable tool throughout your professional life.

Take Advantage of Spare Moments

Another useful tip for using time wisely is to take full advantage of every spare moment you have. Do homework between classes when the subject is fresh in your mind and so it's out of the way. If you take a bus to and from school, read or review your notes from the day's classes. Write notes with important information and hang them on your mirror or on the refrigerator so you can review them often. If you take advantage of the time you have to spend waiting for something, you'll have more free time later to relax and de-stress. Study as you go along; don't wait and cram just at test time. This is information you need to retain and use in your career.

Chapter 5

Understanding the Patients

The patients are the core of the health care industry. They are your customers and consumers, and at times they will be you or your loved ones. As the population ages, there will be many more patients requiring various stages of health care. How much involvement you wish to have with patients will be a driving force behind your career decisions. Some aspects of health care require a lot of hands-on care, and others involve virtually no patient contact.

Patients Are Your Customers

The most effective health care delivery systems place the patient at the center, making him the central player. The patient should be the most important member of any health care provider's organizational chart. Without patients, there would be no need for any health care services. There will always be patients, and the fact that the population is aging ensures that there will be a growing number of patients in need of many levels of care. The high cost of health care ensures that there will also be many new positions created as time goes by in an attempt to control costs.

Because health care is service oriented, customer service is a vital to success in this field. The "customer is always right" attitude is undergoing some changes of late, but the basis of this statement is that good manners and good customer service are skills that are essential skills in any business.

The responsibility of the health care team is to assist the patient in understanding and learning how to take control of his own health care, as well as how to maintain a healthy lifestyle. As a member of the health care team, your job may entail some aspect of assisting or teaching the patient how to achieve this goal. At times you may have to be very firm and pushy, at other times you will have to be an enthusiastic, bubbly, and encouraging cheerleader. Sometimes you'll have to be emotionally strong and a good listener. At other times you'll have to bite your tongue and silently seethe while you smile and politely remind your obnoxious patient or their family member that you're just trying to help her or him get better.

Patients Cope in Various Ways

One thing that is fairly certain is that people are uncomfortable with and often fearful of the unknown, particularly when the unknown involves their health status and could involve pain, suffering, and even death. How that fear manifests itself in their behavior can vary greatly from stoicism, to anger and emotional outbursts, to tears, withdrawal, and isolation.

E Alert

The primary responsibility for a patient's health status is shifting to the shoulders of the patient and/or caregivers, and is not solely on the health care practitioner. The patient has a responsibility to understand and to participate actively in developing, implementing, and evaluating a health care plan. This plan should be re-evaluated and modified on an ongoing basis as needed.

Sick people are not at their best, and caring for them is an art. How they react to a situation may, and often will, be entirely different from how they would act if they were not sick. The ability to accept this and go forward involves a special form of patience and understanding inherent in a caregiver. This is an essential characteristic for health care professionals of all levels who will have direct and even indirect patient contact.

Society values independence and youth and casts a stigma on age and those who become dependent on others. This affects a person's ability to cope with an illness or injury and his ability to heal.

Some people cannot cope at all with just a simple cold or flu or a paper cut, and others aren't fazed unless the situation becomes truly life threatening. A lot of this depends on their own self-image and how comfortable they are with themselves. If a person was teased mercilessly all of his life for any little sign of frailty, then that individual is less likely to cope well with being even the slightest bit ill and being seen as momentarily weak.

On the other hand, those who are more comfortable with themselves may take things in stride and allow their bodies to react and then to heal and recover without a lot of angst and drama.

Others thrive on the attention and may even do things to intentionally delay the healing process in order to continue to reap the attention. They may also seek to find other illnesses and conditions that warrant or prolong the attention.

Consider the Whole Person

Health care professionals have to remember to look at the whole person, not just the illness or the injury. Patients are not numbers or diseases. Patients are mothers and fathers, sisters and brothers, sons and daughters. They are coworkers, bosses, and friends, and even perhaps enemies. They have families to care for, jobs to hold down, bills to pay, and lives to live.

 Fact

Patients come in all shapes and sizes, races and genders. A patient may be an infant who has been born several months premature, or an elderly gentleman who has seen the better part of ten decades. Some are sweet, adorable, and cooperative, and some are just plain mean and obnoxious. Illness affects people in very many ways. Some cope with it better than others.

The sum of all of these factors can influence a patient's health status in a helpful manner or hinder the situation. Health care is most effective when the team has an understanding of who the patient is and why she reacts or behaves in certain ways. Beliefs, customs, and cultural diversity all play a role in how a person reacts to an illness, copes with changes, and adapts to the healing process.

The patients (customers) may not always be right, but they have to come first and are your priority for the moment. Always treat your patients as you would expect to be treated, and more importantly, as you would expect your most precious loved ones to be treated.

Communication and Health Care Literacy Issues

The ability to translate scientific facts into layman's terms will be one of your biggest assets. Convincing a patient who is in denial to learn to do something will become one of your most admired qualities. But how do you do this? The simple answer is communication. However, the more complex answer is also communication.

Speaking and Listening

Communication is a two-way process. In simple terms, it implies both speaking and listening. Some people think communication is just the process of getting their ideas across. But how do they know they got the idea across? Because the listener understood what they said and reacted to it in a meaningful way.

Communication is also nonverbal. Hand gestures, facial expressions, body language, attitude, and eye contact all play a role in communication. In dealing with someone who is deaf or speaks another language, communication may have to be all nonverbal.

Listening is vital to successful communication. You cannot listen effectively if you are talking or paying attention to something else, or if you're not willing to listen or hear what is being said.

Effective verbal communication in the health care arena is essential. Literacy (the ability to read and write) is a major issue in this country. Health care professionals often take it for granted that people can read and write, and yet, for more than 40 million Americans this is not true. According to the U.S. Department of Education, another 10 million Americans can barely read and write their names and simple information.

Health care literacy experts report that almost 90 million Americans (half of the population) will have at least some degree of difficulty understanding information and forms regarding their own health care. They will also have some degree of difficulty in accessing their health care system because of literacy issues.

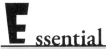

E ssential

Sometimes listening is the most important form of communication for the health care professional. You must always listen carefully to what your patients and their friends and family are telling you. Whether they are telling you something new or telling you what they think you said to them, the information is vital to a successful outcome.

Here's Something to Read . . .

One of the first inclinations in explaining something new to someone is to hand the person something to read on the subject. This happens most often when time is limited, and the literature is meant as a reference source to reinforce the teaching and answer questions. In health care, time is always limited, because time is money, and health care costs are skyrocketing. So you give the patient the simple explanation, hand them a pamphlet to read, and tell them to come back next time with questions!

Illiteracy carries a stigma of shame. It is highly doubtful that the patient will tell you he can't read that pamphlet. You may not even have a clue about his literacy issues because he seems too bright and knowledgeable to not be able to read. If you ask him to read it to you, or just to sit and read it for a few minutes and then you'll discuss it, you might at least glean that he doesn't "understand" what he "read" and you'll have a clue that you need to change your teaching approach with this patient.

In fact, as health care professionals began to grasp the concept and the vast extent of health care illiteracy, patient education roles for nurses and physician's assistants and pharmacists, for example, expanded tremendously, and they continue to do so. Today when you get a new prescription filled at a retail pharmacy, the pharmacist comes over to explain the drug to you and answer your questions in addition to providing you with a few precautionary labels on the bottle and a drug pamphlet from the manufacturer.

Communication not only involves delivering a message and listening to that message, but it also includes validating that the message was received and understood. In order for health care to be effective and the outcomes to be optimal, effective communication is essential. Communication is an art, and it needs to be polished regularly.

Dealing with Difficult Patients and Family Members

Draw from your own experiences. If you aren't feeling well, you're probably short with people, cranky, unsocial, and just wanting to be coddled or totally left alone, depending on the moment. Combine this with being poked and prodded and asked a million questions, all while sitting on a cold table in a paper gown.

Fear of the unknown, fear of pain, fear of suffering, and fear of death are all racing through your body and your mind. The medical terminology seems completely Greek to you, and, along with losing your dignity, you feel like you just might freeze to death in that paper gown. Coping skills, if you had any, fly out the window.

Fear of loss of control is a huge problem for many people, and it is most often the root of the behavior issues you will encounter with demanding and difficult patients and families. They will grasp at anything to try to control some aspect of the situation. Because of this, they might threaten to have your head on a platter if you don't do things their way.

Just Listen

One of the simplest ways to diffuse a situation is to validate feelings. You can do this by listening. Be calm and don't react. Let the patient or the family member vent. Don't try to say things such as, "I know how you feel." That always infuriates people. You can say something like, "I would certainly be angry if this happened to me," or "I understand how something like this could make someone very angry." Or even better, "You certainly have a right to be upset about this. What I can do to help the situation?"

Don't make excuses, and at the same time, don't accept responsibility for something you did not do. Offer to assist in finding out what happened or why it happened, or why it hasn't happened, and tell the patient that you'll get back to her or him. Let your patient know that you will take care of the situation. Then do it, and get back to your patient as soon as possible. Keep them updated and informed. Just show that you care, that you are trying to help, and that the person is important to you.

Learn what the patient or family members perceive to be the problem. Perhaps it's a misunderstanding. Perhaps there are huge gaps in communication, or in the patient education process. Perhaps they just perceive something to be more serious than it is or are more fearful of something than they need to be, and a little explanation can go a long way in resolving an issue.

E ssential

If possible, give patients and their families a time frame of when you hope to have some answers for them. Check back with them in an hour or two to let them know of any progress and to reassure them that you are working on a solution.

Anticipate Needs

Many times you can avoid an unpleasant situation altogether if you anticipate the needs of the patient or family member. Keep them informed and updated. Always explain procedures before you start and again as you go along.

If you know that the doctor is running at least forty-five minutes behind and has two important phone calls to return before she'll get to the patient, let the patient know. Then update him periodically as to the progress.

If the waiting room in the ER was empty when Mr. Gable arrived after trying to slice off his thumb with a carving knife, he's going to assume he will be seen soon. However, there might be several more critical patients being attended to, and the doctor won't get to him right away. Let him know that the doctor is tied up with someone who's in cardiac arrest and it'll be awhile before he gets seen. Meanwhile, explain that he is stable and won't bleed to death, and that you are going to keep an eye on him and make him comfortable.

Wherever you may work in the health care industry, if you keep your patients informed about how things work in your area, how the schedule is flowing or backed up, what they can expect to happen and when, you'll alleviate a lot of fears, stress, and concern about the unknown. You'll also be letting them know that things are under control and not just run-amok chaos. Perhaps schedules aren't as precisely controlled as many would like, but if you let people know that you individualize your care to meet the needs of the patients, and that when someone needs extra time or care you stop and provide it, then perhaps you can infuse a little humility and humanity into the mix. Command respect by showing that you value quality, not quantity. Patients need to respect the rights of other patients, but they also need to know that they will receive the same quality care and consideration.

The Patient's Role and Responsibilities

Health care is a team effort, and it is not a passive activity. The patient is the primary team member and is expected to be an active participant. For the most part, the patient should be the captain of the team. But patients come in all ages, and some are not old enough to make decisions for their care, while others are too old, ill, or otherwise impaired to make decisions for themselves.

Many institutions have adopted patient rules and responsibilities that are given to the patients at their first visit or upon admission to a facility. Usually a signed copy must be entered into the medical record acknowledging the patient's awareness of and promise to adhere to the rules. These rules are designed to help reduce the possibility of errors due to misunderstandings, miscommunications, and improper identification. They also help to protect providers from being expected to shoulder the entire responsibility for the health status of a patient, and/or from being considered to be infallible. They also help to reduce the high costs of health care by encouraging and enacting preventative measures. The patient's responsibilities include:

- Providing health care workers with accurate and complete information about current symptoms and complaints; current medications and treatments; allergies; and past medical history, including illness, injury, and treatments
- Keeping all appointments and notifying providers in advance if this is not possible
- Notifying providers of any significant change in condition or reaction to treatment or diagnostics
- Actively participating in all decisions about treatments and asking questions if there is any confusion—and continuing to ask questions if they still don't understand
- Complying with prescribed treatments and lifestyle changes or discussing options or alternatives with the providers, and asking questions or asking for help if they don't understand how to perform or comply
- Never assuming that the health care provider is infallible, and correcting or reminding the health care provider of issues such as allergies or previously successful or failed treatments; to question anything that doesn't seem right

With the trend moving more toward preventative medicine and promoting wellness, there has been a shift of responsibility for health status and treatment outcomes to the patients and their caregivers.

Patients cannot expect the physician or other health care practitioner to heal them or to fix the problem alone. Health care is a team experience, and all members have essential roles to fill and responsibilities to honor.

Chapter 6

Your Role as a Health Care Provider

As a health care professional you will have many responsibilities, not only to yourself and perhaps to your own practice, but to your patients/clients and to your coworkers and fellow professionals as well. There are many rules about confidentiality and patient/provider privilege to live by. There are also expectations to live up to and a reputation to build and maintain.

The Skills You Will Need

Health care careers are not just jobs, they are professions. As such they require you to conduct yourself in a professional manner and to live by a code of ethics at all times, not just while on duty. This responsibility is not something that everyone is willing to take on, and it needs to be considered carefully by all who enter this field.

In the course of your education you will develop a wide variety of professional skills, including technical skills, communication skills, leadership skills, and problem-solving skills. Throughout your career you will continue to learn new aspects of these skills, and you'll never stop striving to perfect them.

Technical Skills

These are the hands-on skills for those who have direct patient contact. They are the skills to diagnose or assess and treat as well as to evaluate the accuracy and effectiveness of your assessment and treatment. For those in positions without direct patient care, these will be the skills involved in the performance of your job, such as the operation of the machinery, the coding of the diagnosis, the transcription of records, photography skills, illustration skills, etc.

The process for learning new technical skills involves clinical hands-on practice. First you will learn about the process and the reason for a skill. Then you will observe the skill being performed by a professional. Next you should try to assist the professional with this skill. Then you might perform it on a classmate or yourself under supervision. The next time you'll be given an opportunity to perform the skill on a patient under direct supervision. When it is determined you are safe to perform it alone, you will be notified. You should then seek every possible opportunity to perfect your skill.

Communication Skills

Effective communication is vital to the health care professions. It is an integral part of the job. Documentation is a major element of the medical field. Verbal communication sometimes has to be instantaneous and accurate. Remember that communication is a two-way process. Listening is as important as speaking. Health care professionals have to be excellent communicators, in both written and spoken communications. Communication is an art and needs constant practice to perfect.

Leadership Skills

Health care is a profession that depends on teamwork. The more efficient and effective the teamwork, the better the care will be. You may never be a manager supervising many others, but as a team member, it is important to remember that each member is vital to the success of the whole. In such situations, there will be occasions when you will need to become the leader and direct others in order to complete a task or to meet the needs of a situation.

E ssential

Leadership does not come easily to everyone. It requires taking personal risks and exposing your weaknesses as well as your strengths. With time you will learn to build on your strengths as you strive to improve your weak areas.

Problem-Solving Skills

Meeting the health care needs and demands of the public is challenging. They are constantly changing and will only continue to do so as technology continues to advance. Health care professionals need to be innovative and flexible. Problem solving is a part of almost every level of health care. Practitioners, nurses, and therapists must perfect and utilize these skills perhaps more than others.

Problem solving involves analyzing a situation, determining what needs to be done or what is wrong, and making a plan and implementing it. It then requires periodically re-evaluating the situation to determine what works and what does not, and making changes as needed.

Your Attitude and Bedside Manner

You need to develop a positive attitude and a pleasant bedside manner. The patients/clients you deal with will come from every walk of life, every ethnic group, socioeconomic level, gender, etc. Remember that sick people are not always at their best, so they could be tired, cranky, impatient, anxious, whiny, and any combination of characteristics you hate the most, but you will be expected to deal with them in the same manner as you would the most pleasant people. There is not room for discrimination in health care. You can, of course, be firm and set boundaries and expectations, but there will be times when you have to deal with the worst of behaviors in a calm, sensible, nonreactive manner.

Health care also presents a lifelong learning process. You need to be open to new ideas and to continuing your formal as well as informal education. You need to have an inquisitive nature and a desire to find answers, as this will help you to develop an expertise. You must also be committed to excellence and always strive to put forth your best effort.

In developing a bedside manner you need to keep in mind that you are there to *help* others. You and your patients will work together as partners to address their health care needs. You will develop a therapeutic relationship with clients and patients.

To accomplish this you will:

- Utilize your skills and talents to work toward improving the outcome for the patient.
- Encourage the patient to strive for independence and not become dependent on you (the professional).
- Refer the patient to another professional if the services and skills needed exceed your expertise, or if personality conflicts impede progress toward the goals.

Alert

Improved patient outcomes are always primary goals for health care. That does not necessarily mean that the patient improves and recovers. If a patient's pain and suffering are minimized and his dignity is preserved, even if he dies, the outcome is still a positive one. This is a difficult concept to learn, but death does not always represent failure.

You may also need to refer the patient to another professional if an assistant such as a nurse practitioner or physician assistant can offer a lower-cost care option that provides the same quality of care and will not compromise the outcome. This is not always an option that makes everyone happy, but health care costs have skyrocketed, and all health care professionals are expected to do what they can to help contain the costs without compromising patient outcomes.

Confidentiality Issues

One of the hardest things for many health care students and novice professionals to learn is how to maintain patient confidentiality. New laws have made this even more of an issue. It's only natural to want to rush home and tell your spouse about the celebrity you got to meet today and will be treating, but you can't do it. You can't discuss any client's care with your spouse, family, or friends. In reality, it does happen, but it is illegal unless it is done with great discretion to protect the identity of the patient.

Under new laws such as HIPAA, you must have express permission from the patient to discuss his condition or treatment even with any next of kin and family members. There are other privacy issues that have caused health care facilities to rearrange offices, designate new lines and waiting areas, and re-create forms and sign-in sheets to protect the privacy and identity of patients.

One of the easiest ways to deal with these issues is to neither deny nor confirm information, but to refer the person inquiring to the patient for an answer. Of course, you also need to inform the patient that this has transpired.

If you are discussing a patient with a colleague, you need to be discreet and make sure that others can't overhear your conversation. Never reveal anything specific that could identify a patient if you aren't sure that you won't be overheard.

Records and charts must be kept confidential as well. Never leave documentation where it can be seen or read by others. If you have electronic access, be sure it's secure before leaving the workstation. Protect passwords.

E ssential

Trust is an essential element in establishing a professional-patient relationship. Patients need to know that they can safely discuss sensitive information with their health care providers and that the information will remain privileged. Exceptions to this privilege are rare but include public health issues such as sexually transmitted diseases, TB, or hepatitis, which require reporting.

Confidentiality also encompasses privacy. Always be sure that you close doors or curtains to protect a patient's modesty, dignity, and privacy. Use towels, sheets, gowns, and paper drapes to ensure the patient is not exposed.

Teamwork

Teamwork seems to come naturally for some and not for others. It is defined simply as a collaborative effort toward a common goal. Health care naturally lends itself to teamwork, as there is not usually a time when one single person is solely responsible for a patient's outcomes.

One person could cause a downfall or occasionally the untimely death of a patient, but that happens most often when the teamwork effort fails. When the team works together toward a common goal to improve the outcome for a patient, usually the effort is successful. Again, this can be true even when the patient dies, such as if the goal was to reduce pain and suffering and provide for a peaceful death. Reducing or minimizing pain and suffering is always a goal in responsible health care.

Alert

The health care team members will have supplementary and/or complementary roles. The team needs to have a clear understanding of the roles and responsibilities of each member and to accommodate professional differences. It is important to understand your role and to stay within your scope of practice. Each member has to uphold her responsibilities to the team.

One of the best examples of a health care team in action is that depicted in ER (emergency room) scenes on television or in the movies, where groups of physicians, nurses, paramedics, technicians, and ancillary staff all work together to save a life. Each member has a separate role, but they all have one common goal.

It is vital to understand the hierarchy of the team. The patient is the ultimate decision maker if he is capable of fulfilling this role. If, for example, he is unconscious, then consent is implied and the highest-ranking health care team member makes the decisions. This person will then direct the team in the course of action to be taken.

Each team member will perform her duties as assigned and within her scope of practice. Your scope of practice will be defined by your license and education and training.

One of the advantages of teamwork is that as members put forth their best efforts, team members learn from one another. Over time they perfect and improve their own professional skills and abilities, including those vital communication, leadership, problem-solving, and technical skills.

Combining Caring with Science

When the health care team works together toward a common goal of reducing pain and suffering and improving the quality of life and outcomes for the patient, caring becomes a natural element of this process.

However, there are some team members who will be more wrapped up in the process of caring than others. They will be more intimately involved in the day-to-day care of the patient and will perhaps express more emotion and empathy than others. Nurses often spend far more time with patients, especially in a hospital setting, so they are said to be the ones who are best at caring.

Caring is an art, and it will take time to find a balance point. With time and experience, it will come. Science and technology will continue to evolve and it's important to continue the learning process. As better treatments and cures are discovered, it becomes easier to improve outcomes and reduce pain and suffering.

There will always be times when something will go wrong when you least expect it, no matter how hard you try to keep it from happening. Learn to expect the unexpected, and you will be better equipped to deal with it and to continue to care and to maintain objectivity.

Always treat your patients and clients in a manner that you would expect for your most cherished loved ones. Walk a mile in your patient's shoes before you condemn him for his actions. Before you decide your patient is noncompliant, remember that literacy is an issue affecting almost half of all Americans. Perhaps he just doesn't understand.

Caring is not a sign of weakness. It brings a human side to a scientific situation. It helps to reduce fears and anxiety, to build trust, and to ease pain and suffering. It is essential to achieving positive outcomes for your patients.

E ssential

Medicine is not an exact science, because no two people will respond exactly the same way to a disease or treatment. However, there are strong similarities among patient responses, and that's how diagnoses and treatments evolve. It's important not to lose objectivity by becoming emotionally involved with your patients; such an attachment makes it easier to lose sight of a diagnosis or a response.

For those aspects of health care that are not hands-on, the art of caring is also essential. If you understand that your job carries a high degree of importance in your patients' lives, you will always strive to put forth your best effort. Your job will have meaning and bring satisfaction to your life. For instance, if you are a medical illustrator and you take extra care to be exact in your drawings, you may at some point make a difference between another health care worker making or missing a diagnosis. You may never know it, but if there's a chance it can happen, you will always try to do a better job.

Finding Your Own Rewards

Health care is not a job in which you will always see tangible results. Knowing that you have given your best effort and that in some small way you have made a difference in someone's life is a reward that cannot compare to most tangible ones. However, health care is not always a positive experience. Disease and death cause pain and suffering. Not all of it can be eliminated, and that takes a toll sooner or later. You will at times find that the guilt, the anger, and the horror that you feel in some situations will get to you. Sometimes you won't understand why something affected you so much. Sometimes it's just because of an accumulative effect of which you aren't even aware.

You may only spend small snippets of time with a patient and never see that your efforts did have a positive impact or make a difference, no matter how small. You need to be confident that because you gave your best effort, the long-range goals will be met. Remember, you are part of a team effort, and as long as you uphold your responsibilities, you can take pride in your work and know that you have done your best to help someone.

Alert

The physical and emotional demands of health care careers can be overwhelming at times. You will need to find ways to replenish and recharge yourself so that you can always be at your best.

A smile, a thank you, a handshake will take on greater meaning for you, as they may be all the acknowledgment you receive. And sometimes you may not even get that, even at a time when you may have gone way above and beyond. The knowledge that you gave it the very best you could will suffice.

Capture the moments and take mental photographs. Start a journal of "How I Made a Difference in Someone's Life Today." Fill a shoebox with notes about your experiences. When you need a boost, read them and remember why you made this choice to work in health care, and remind yourself that you do make a difference every day.

Reward yourself with things that make you happy and help you to relax and replenish yourself. It could be a massage, a day at a spa, or tickets to a ballgame or the theater or a concert. It could be buying yourself a new piece of equipment, such as a stethoscope, or that PDA you've always wanted. Or maybe you need a change, like a new hairstyle or new clothes.

Do something for you, and do it regularly. You work hard and give so very much of yourself to your work. Give something back to yourself. This is essential and cannot be overemphasized.

Coping with the Facts of Life and Death

Death is part of life and everyone will have to deal with it sometime. Dead bodies are actually the easy part. Telling someone they're going to die or holding their loved ones while they cry can be much more difficult. After a lengthy, painful illness, death is usually a relief, but the loss is still difficult. Sudden and unexpected death adds a whole new dimension to the situation.

Question

Are health care workers born knowing how to deal with these issues? There are those who have such a strong sense of curiosity about blood, guts, and gore that they have no problem with them, but for others the ability to deal with these things must be learned. The passion to help others and to ease their pain and suffering drives you to learn to find ways to handle all of this.

Helping someone to come to grips with his own impending death or the loss of a loved one is not easy, but it can be very rewarding when peaceful acceptance is achieved. It can also be very rewarding to watch someone slip away quietly and peacefully when you know that his pain and suffering were minimized and that he was surrounded by loved ones.

You will not enter the health care field fully prepared for all of the possible unknown factors. You will not enter fully prepared for each and every situation. You are a warm, caring, passionate individual, and that is why you will make a terrific health care professional. You will learn the skills and develop the talents necessary to help you deal with the situations that you will face. You will learn how to cope. Health care is a lifelong learning experience.

Chapter 7

Primary Care Practitioners

The health care team is divided into many categories. Primary care practitioners are those who diagnose and treat illnesses. Only those who are specifically trained and licensed in the art and science of diagnosis may do so. Once a diagnosis is made, the primary care practitioners will order and direct treatment, which will come from other health care team members such as pharmacists, nurses, and therapists. They may also solicit assistance and consultation from other primary practitioners in diagnosis and treatment aspects.

Physicians

There are approximately 125 areas of general practice, specialties, and subspecialties for physicians. Physicians are trained to diagnose and treat diseases. Medicine and surgery are the two main categories from which the other specialties branch. Most physicians practice *allopathic medicine*, in which the remedies they prescribe produce effects that are different from those that cause the disease. Others practice *homeopathy*, wherein the physician treats a patient's disease by administering small doses of drugs that, if given in large doses to a healthy person, would cause symptoms of the disease.

Duties/Activities/Scope of Practice

Physicians are the diagnosticians and the coordinators of care. They are the detectives who seek out answers to the mysteries of illness and injury. They collect data from physical examinations, lab tests, and other diagnostics to determine the nature and extent of the illness or injury. Once they have determined a diagnosis, they direct the treatment or refer the patient to another physician for more specialized diagnosis and treatment.

In medicine, there are generalists, also known as the GP (general practitioner). Family practice and internal medicine are also fairly general. There are also specialists who concentrate on certain aspects of health care, such as pediatricians, cardiologists, urologists, and obstetricians and gynecologists.

Surgeons are classified as generalists or specialists as well. There are general surgeons and there are specialists, such as vascular surgeons, orthopedic surgeons, and oncology surgeons. Some cross over from medicine to surgery in specialized areas such as orthopedics, gynecology, and urology.

Education and Training

A bachelor's degree is the primary prerequisite for attending medical school. Most students intending to become physicians major in biology or chemistry. In addition, medical schools require that the BS degree include one year of English, math (algebra or higher), physics, and biology, and two years of chemistry, including both inorganic and organic. Candidates for medical school must also pass the MCAT (Medical College Admissions Test.) See Appendix B for more information on admissions exams. Medical school consists of another four years of study.

Alert

Getting into medical school is a highly competitive process. Grades from the pre-med program (BS degree), MCAT scores, letters of recommendation, and participation in extracurricular activities are all taken into consideration. In-person interviews are usually conducted with the admissions committee. There are 126 allopathic medical schools in the United States.

The first two years of medical school are spent studying anatomy and physiology, pharmacology, pathology, microbiology, medical ethics and laws governing medicine, psychology, and biochemistry. These are classroom and laboratory courses.

After that, students begin rotations through each of the major clinical areas, including internal medicine, obstetrics and gynecology, pediatrics, surgery, and psychiatry. They will also be exposed to specialty areas, and during their fourth year will be encouraged to take electives in these areas. These are clinical, hands-on courses taught in hospitals and clinics associated with the medical school under the direct supervision of physicians. After graduation, medical students become interns. Internship lasts one year. After that, another one to seven years of residency training in the specialty of choice is required. This is paid, on-the-job experience.

Licensure/Certification

Physicians have to pass a minimum of three board examinations in order to practice medicine. The first one is given at the end of the first two years of classroom and lab study. The second is given after the third year of medical school, and the third is given at the end of the first year of postgraduate study (internship). After successfully passing all three, they are given the title M.D., and they begin their residency training.

To be board certified as a specialist, physicians have to satisfy residency training requirements and pass another examination given by the specialty board. Board certification in subspecialties requires even longer residency and more examinations.

Each state and the District of Columbia license physicians separately. Each state administers its own licensing exam. Some states allow for reciprocity without another exam, but there may be some limitations.

Graduates of foreign medical schools can be licensed in the United States after completing a residency requirement and passing an examination. Some Americans attend medical schools outside of the United States because of the stiff competition for admission to U.S. schools.

Work Settings and Salaries

The nature of the specialty will define where the physician will work. In general, physicians work in offices or clinics, in hospitals, or in both. Surgeons, for example will spend more of their time in hospitals either performing surgery or visiting patients, and less time in an office examining patients pre- and post-op. Family practice M.D.s and pediatricians will spend more time in offices or clinics. In some instances, physicians will form practices with several physicians, and one will cover all hospital visits, while the others see patients in the office only.

Physicians and surgeons work long and irregular hours. According to the U.S. Department of Labor's Bureau of Labor Statistics, in 2004, almost one-third of physicians worked sixty or more hours each week. In addition to scheduled appointments and procedures, there is always the unexpected in almost every practice. After hours, physicians are on call for patients, other physicians needing consultations, and hospitals in need of orders for patients or patient consultations.

The high costs of health care continue to affect the structure of private practices. Where doctors once hung a shingle on their own front porch and saw patients in their own homes, today most combine their practice with several doctors to share costs of capital and medical equipment, staff, and office space. They also share their practice and cover each other's time off so that they can spend quality time with their own families, and relax and replenish themselves as needed.

 **Question**

What are the most important qualities that a physician should have? Physicians need to be self-motivated, and they need to be able to withstand the pressures of working long hours. They have to have stamina, and physical and emotional stability. Precision, an eye for detail, and accuracy are all vital characteristics as well.

One in seven physicians in 2004 was self-employed and not incorporated, according to the U.S. Department of Labor. Of the 567,000 physicians working in 2004, about half worked for office-based practices, a quarter were employed by hospitals, and the rest worked for federal, state, and local governments in clinics and educational services.

Physicians make some of the highest salaries of any occupation. Their education costs and the costs of maintaining a practice with state-of-the-art equipment are also very high. Salaries typically range from $150,000 to $320,000 per year depending upon the area of practice. Family practice and pediatricians typically earn less than more specialized M.D.s.

Career Potential and Additional Information

The U.S. Department of Labor predicts that employment for physicians and surgeons will continue to grow at an average pace through 2014. As with all health care fields, the aging population will increase demands for continued and improved health care.

Some of the factors that will heavily influence physicians, however, include the increasing costs for health care and health care coverage. In order to contain costs, insurance companies and consumers have pushed for lower-cost options for many services in health care, such as employing the services of physician assistants, nurse practitioners, and nurse anesthetists.

Technology and advancements in areas such as telemedicine and the use of electronic medical records will also impact physician practices. In many ways these advances will improve productivity and reduce costs as well as improve patients' access to care.

Shortages of physicians in rural and low-income areas continue and will give rise to even more creative recruitment and retention methods. These areas will provide opportunities for many years to come, especially to new physicians.

Technology advancements along with pharmacologic changes, which happen at a frantic pace, will continue to give rise to the need to continue education. Health care is a lifelong learning experience. Those who keep up and are flexible will adapt well to changes in the field and find new opportunities.

For a list of medical schools and residency programs, as well as information about financial aid and careers in medicine, contact the Association of American Medical Colleges. Their Web site is *www.aamc.org*. Their address is 2450 N Street NW, Washington, DC 20037-1126, Attn. Student Services.

For information on physicians, contact the American Medical Association. The Web site is *www.ama-assn.org*. Their address is 515 N. State Street, Chicago, IL 60610.

For licensing information, contact your State Board of Medical Examiners. You should be able to link to this from your state's official Web site.

Dentists

The majority of dentists are general practitioners who handle all varieties of dental emergencies and dental diseases as well as preventative care. There are several specialties including the largest, orthodontics, which involves the straightening of teeth. Oral and maxillofacial surgeons operate on the mouth and jaw for such issues as impacted wisdom teeth or diseases of the jawbones. Others include pediatric dentists, periodontists (gum and jawbone diseases), prosthodontists (who deal with bridges, crowns, dentures, etc.), and endodontists (who specialize in root canals).

Duties, Activities, and Scope of Practice

Dentists diagnose and treat diseases of the teeth, gums, jawbones, and mouth tissue. Their primary goal is to provide preventative care and to encourage good oral hygiene. They correct defects such as decay, and cavities, and misalignment of teeth. They replace missing teeth and repair or remove broken or fractured teeth.

Dentists instruct in oral hygiene measures including brushing, flossing, diet, and using fluorides. They examine for diseases and infection of the gums, mouth tissue, tongue, and supporting bones. They prescribe treatments and refer to specialists for follow-up care as needed.

Education and Training

In the United States there are fifty-six dental schools that are currently accredited by the American Dental Association. Each of the fifty states requires that a dentist be licensed. In order to become licensed, the candidate has to have graduated from one of the accredited schools and then must pass a written and a practical exam.

Dental schools require applicants to have completed at least two years of undergraduate studies at a college or university. Most applicants will have their bachelor's degree, and many major in biology or chemistry. One year of biology and physics is required, along with two years of chemistry, including organic and inorganic chemistry. They must also take the DAT (Dental Admissions Test). See Appendix B for more information.

Essential

Competition for entrance to dental school is stiff. Admissions departments consider grades, DAT score, personal recommendations, extracurricular activities, and personal interviews. Specialization in such areas as orthodontics requires postgraduate education, usually two to four years of study. Dentists who wish to teach dentistry spend an additional two to five years training in programs run by dental schools.

The dental program consists of four academic years of study. The first year is primarily classroom and laboratory experience of basic sciences such as anatomy, physiology, microbiology, and biochemistry. The second year typically includes such things as endodontics, dental surgery, and making dentures. Second-year students also begin treating patients under the supervision of dentists. The third year includes the study of building crowns and bridges, periodontics, and how to diagnose oral issues. In the fourth year specialty areas are explored. Upon successful graduation, students are awarded a D.D.S. (Doctor of Dental Surgery) or D.M.D. (Doctor of Dental Medicine), depending on the school.

Licensure/Certification

Dentists are licensed by the state in which they intend to practice. (All fifty states plus the District of Columbia require this.) They must graduate from an accredited school of dentistry and then pass a written exam (the National Board Dental Examinations) and a practical exam. Some states require written and practical examinations in any specialty areas as well if the dentist intends to practice specialized care.

Work Settings and Salaries

According to the U.S. Department of Labor, most dental school graduates will buy an established dental practice or open their own after graduation. Some will work as associates with other dentists to gain experience and earn enough to move into their own practice. About 12 percent will enter specialty training.

Most dentists work in private offices, some in hospitals or clinics. They usually work thirty-five to forty hours per week, and many offer flexible hours, working some evenings or weekend hours to meet the needs of their patients. Some work part-time, and, in fact, there are a considerable number of dentists working part-time today who are well beyond retirement age.

The U.S. Department of Labor's Bureau of Statistics reports that there were 150,000 dentists working in 2004, and their median salary was $129,920. One third of the dentists were self-employed. According to the American Dental Association, approximately 80 percent of dentists are sole proprietors, 13 percent belong to partnerships, and others are salaried and work for hospitals or physicians.

Career Potential and Additional Information

Employment for dentists is expected to grow more slowly than average through 2014, but there will continue to be an increasing demand for dentists. As the population ages, there will be more demand for such technologies as dental implants as well as maintenance on bridges and crowns. Also as the population ages, so will the baby-boomer dentists, leaving many openings for replacements as this group retires from practice.

To obtain more information about careers in dentistry and a list of accredited dental schools, contact the American Dental Association. Their Web site is *www.ada.org*. Or contact them by mail at 211 E. Chicago Avenue, Chicago, IL 60611.

Contact the American Dental Education Association for information on admission to dental schools. The Web site is *www.adea*
.org. Their address is 1400 K Street, NW, Suite 1100 Washington, DC 20005.

Chiropractors

Chiropractors are holistic practitioners who provide nonsurgical, drugless treatments to promote wellness. They believe that interference with the spine, the muscles, and the nervous system impairs the body's natural functions and results in illness and disease. Many people believe that chiropractors treat only pain issues, but in fact chiropractors deal with all health issues, and refer to other practitioners as appropriate.

Duties, Activities, and Scope of Practice

Chiropractors take a full medical and lifestyle history; complete a physical examination, including neurological and orthopedic systems; and order x-rays and laboratory tests as needed to complete a diagnostic study. They will then employ manual adjustments of the spine or other joints to correct alignment issues. If needed, they will direct other treatments such as ultrasound, heat and ice therapy, massage, water and light therapy, and electrical stimulation.

Chiropractors are holistic practitioners, and as such, they will counsel in wellness as well as nutrition, exercise, stress management, and any lifestyle changes needed to improve the health status of patients. They may recommend dietary supplements, but they do not prescribe medications or perform surgery. They may utilize traction and apply braces, tapes, or straps.

Education/Training

A minimum of two years of undergraduate study is required, but an increasing number of states now require a bachelor's degree as well as graduation from an accredited four-year chiropractic college with a Doctor of Chiropractic degree. The undergraduate education must include at least ninety units in courses in general chemistry, biology, and physics as well as general-education courses in English, social sciences, and psychology.

There are currently sixteen chiropractic programs and two chiropractic institutions in the United States that are accredited by the Council on Chiropractic Education.

The chiropractic program consists of eight semesters of study. The first two years are spent in classroom and laboratory courses in the basic sciences of biology, biochemistry, anatomy and physiology, microbiology, and pathology. The last two years concentrate on manipulation and spinal adjustment procedures, including theory and practical experience, and diagnostic studies, which includes physical examination and examination of clinical and laboratory findings. During this time, students also study nutrition, orthopedics, geriatrics, physiotherapy, neurology, obstetrics and gynecology, pediatrics, and emergency procedures.

Licensure/Certification

The National Board of Chiropractic Examiners administers a four-part written and practical exam to graduates of accredited programs, which most states accept. Some states administer supplemental testing as well. To maintain licensure, most states require continuing-education courses each year. The number of units varies from state to state. Some states allow reciprocity provided the education, licensing, and examinations meet their specific standards. Otherwise, becoming licensed in another state may require additional training or examinations.

Some chiropractic associations offer specialty training and offer a "diplomate" certification in those areas. Specialty areas include sports injuries, occupational and industrial health, nutrition, neurology, and orthopedics.

Work Settings and Salaries

Chiropractors who are newly licensed have the option to open their own practice, purchase an established one, or work as a salaried associate or partner with other chiropractors. Typically chiropractors work forty hours per week in private offices, alternative health care centers or spas, or even at chiropractic colleges. They may offer evening or weekend hours to accommodate the needs of their patients.

 Fact

According to the American Chiropractic Association, the average income for salaried as well as self-employed chiropractors in 2005 was $105,363 after all expenses. According to the U.S. Department of Labor's Bureau of Statistics, the median income for salaried chiropractors in 2004 was $69,110.

Career Potential and Additional Information

The job outlook for chiropractors over the next decade is a positive one. Growth is expected to be faster than the average for all occupations due to the increasing need posed by an aging population seeking alternative means of improving and maintaining their health status.

The majority of chiropractors stay in this field until retirement, and therefore the opportunities are based on replacing retiring practitioners. Geographically there is an iniquity, and more opportunities for a successful practice exist in those areas not overpopulated with chiropractors. Specialization opportunities through chiropractic associations may increase the chances of finding a niche even in areas where many chiropractors are located. Educating the community about the benefits of chiropractic care is an important part of establishing and maintaining a successful practice.

General information about chiropractic careers is available from the American Chiropractic Association. Their Web site is *www.amerchiro.org.* Their address is 1701 Clarendon Blvd., Arlington, VA 22209.

For information about chiropractic programs contact the Council on Chiropractic Education. Their Web site is *www.cce-usa.org.* Their address is 8049 North 85th Way, Scottsdale, AZ 85258-4321.

Licensing information is available from the Federation of Chiropractic Licensing Boards. Their Web site is *www.fclb.org.* Their address is 5401 W. 10th Street, Suite 101, Greeley, CO 80634-4400.

Veterinarians

These health care practitioners have a broad role in the field, not only in the care of animals, but in helping humans as well. Most care for pets or livestock, but others care for zoo animals or research animals, and some participate in research on diseases and problems that affect humans as well as animals. In fact, veterinarians participated in research that helped to find clues to malaria and yellow fever, as well as botulism. Those who work with livestock deal with issues such as transmittable diseases as well as slaughtering and processing techniques to improve food purity for human consumption. Joint, limb, and organ transplants were first perfected for animals, and that knowledge was passed along for human use. Medications such as anticoagulants were first developed to treat heart problems in animals.

Duties, Activities, and Scope of Practice

Veterinarians diagnose and treat animals. They educate owners on the care, behavior, feeding, and breeding of pets, sporting animals, and livestock. They vaccinate animals, treat injuries and illnesses, set fractures, and perform surgeries as indicated.

Usually veterinarians choose to practice the care of small animals such as dogs, cat, birds, and other pets, or large animals such as racehorses, horses, cows, and other ranch or farm animals. Some may choose to work for zoos and care for either small or large animals or a combination of both. And some work in the food inspection and packing industry to ensure the proper breeding, care, and slaughtering of animals.

Education/Training

The veterinary program is a four-year postgraduate course that bestows the Doctor of Veterinary Medicine (D.V.M. or V.D.M.) degree. Twenty-eight schools are accredited by the American Veterinary Medical Association. Prerequisites vary by school, but all require at least some undergraduate work of forty-five to ninety units.

Entrance exams are required and vary from school to school. They may include the GRE (Graduate Record Exam), the VCAT (Veterinary College Admission Test), or the MCAT (Medical College Admission Test). See Appendix B for more information on these exams. Experience working with animals either in a veterinary setting or on a farm or ranch is also helpful, as many schools place a heavy consideration on this.

Alert

Admission to veterinary programs is highly competitive and almost all applicants do have a bachelor's degree. The number of applicants has risen significantly in recent years, and in 2004 only one in three applicants was accepted. Most veterinary schools are public, state-supported institutions. That means they reserve the majority of the openings for in-state residents. Consequently, the competition for out-of-state applicants is very keen.

Veterinary programs include the study of sciences such as organic and inorganic chemistry, physics, biochemistry, microbiology, zoology, animal biology and nutrition, genetics, vertebrate embryology, and cellular biology. Math requirements may include calculus, and most require algebra or statistics. Courses in practice management and career development are also becoming part of the core program.

The first two years are spent on sciences and core courses. Students spend the final two years in clinical practice learning diagnostics, clinical procedures, and surgery.

For those who wish to specialize in areas such as pathology, veterinary dentistry, ophthalmology, internal medicine, radiology, or laboratory animal medicine, an additional two years of internship and study is required. Board certification in areas such as oncology, exotica, small-animal medicine, radiology, dermatology, anesthesiology, and neurology require a three to four year residency for additional education and training.

Licensure/Certification

Upon completion of an accredited program, candidates take the North American Veterinary Licensing Exam (NAVLE), which is administered by computer and consists of 360 questions (multiple-choice) covering all aspects of veterinary medicine. Ten percent of the exam is visual and tests diagnostic skills.

All states require veterinarians to be licensed. Most administer an additional licensing exam that covers laws and regulations relating to animals, and some require a practical exam as well. Most states require continuing education for re-licensure.

Work Settings and Salaries

Salaries for veterinarians as reported by the U.S. Department of Labor for 2004 ranged from $38,000 to slightly over $120,000. The median income was $66,590. Most begin their careers working for other veterinarians, but usually set up or purchase their own practice as soon as they can. Some work for zoos, horseracing farms, aquariums, or research laboratories. In 2004, there were 61,000 veterinarians. About 28 percent were in solo private practice. Most of the rest were working for a veterinary practice.

Veterinarians usually work long hours. They may take night and weekend calls on a rotating basis, and work weekends to accommodate their clients. And some rotate through after-hours emergency clinics. Those who work with large animals usually make house calls to ranches and farms, and may have to perform surgery or treatments onsite and often under unsanitary conditions. They will spend many hours each week traveling to see patients.

Career Potential and Additional Information

The outlook for employment for veterinarians through 2014 looks very good. The numbers will grow faster than average for all occupations during this time period. Most veterinarians practice small-animal care in animal hospitals and clinics. Companion animals are increasingly viewed as part of the family, so the amount of time and money devoted to their care is increasing, creating a growing demand for small-animal care. The need for large-animal care is not expected to grow as fast.

Federal agencies dealing with public health and food safety as well as the biomedical research industry will continue to have a demand for new veterinarians.

Additional information on veterinary careers and a list of accredited schools is available from the American Veterinary Medical Association. Their Web site is *www.avma.org*. Their address is 1931 N. Meacham Rd. Suite 100, Schaumberg, IL 60173-4360.

For more information about veterinary education contact the Association of American Veterinary Medical Colleges. Their Web site is *www.aavmc.org*. Their address is 1101 Vermont Ave NW, Suite 301, Washington, DC 20005.

For information about employment as a veterinarian with the federal government, contact the U.S. Office of Personnel Management (OPM) through their Web site: *www.usajobs.opm.gov*. Or call (703) 724-1850.

Optometrists

Optometrists are Doctors of Optometry, also known as O.D.s. They provide primary vision care and prescribe eyeglasses and contact lenses. Over half of the population in the United States today requires glasses or contact lenses. Optometrists should not be confused with ophthalmologists, who are medical doctors who treat eye diseases and perform eye surgery, or with opticians, who dispense eyeglasses and contact lenses from prescriptions written by optometrists and ophthalmologists.

Duties, Activities, and Scope of Practice

Optometrists perform comprehensive exams on the external and internal structures of the eye and prescribe eyeglasses or contact lenses to correct vision problems. If they suspect disease or other medically related problems with the eye, they refer the patient to an ophthalmologist for follow-up care, or to other physicians as indicated.

They may prescribe topical or oral medications for certain eye conditions. They can also care for patients before and after cataract and laser vision-correction surgery. Optometrists also work with low-vision patients in a rehabilitative manner. Emergency treatment and first aid for eye injuries also come under their scope of practice.

Education and Training

Doctors of Optometry are graduates of an accredited four-year program. The first two years are spent primarily on classroom and laboratory courses, and the last two include clinical hands-on practice under the supervision of optometrists. This is also a postgraduate program and requires a minimum of three years of undergraduate college work. In most cases, applicants will have completed a bachelor's degree with an emphasis on sciences. Applicants must also take the Optometry Admissions Test (see Appendix B for more information). Admission is competitive.

 Fact

As with other primary practitioners, optometry school includes many sciences, such as biology and chemistry, in addition to pharmacology, vision science, optics, biochemistry, and the study of systemic diseases.

Most optometrists are generalists, but some specialize in pediatrics, geriatrics, or low-vision care.

Licensure/Certification

All states and the District of Columbia require optometrists to be licensed. They must graduate from an accredited school of optometry and pass a written and practical state board exam. They take the National Board of Examiners in Optometry Exam during their academic study, and some states accept all or part of this for the written exam.

Licenses must be renewed periodically, usually every one to three years, and many states require continuing education in order to renew.

Work Settings and Salaries

Most optometrists work forty hours per week with flexible evening and weekend hours to accommodate the needs of patients. Now that optometrists have medication-prescribing privileges, they have obligations to be on call for emergencies. The number of jobs outnumbers the number of practicing optometrists, and therefore many work two or more jobs. They may work in private practice or for vision centers, or both.

According to the American Optometric Association, approximately two-thirds of practicing optometrists are in private practice. Some are in solo practice, but a growing number are in partnerships or work in group practices. Some work in ophthalmologists' offices.

The median income in 2004 was $88,410 for salaried optometrists, and for salaried combined with self-employed, the median was $114,000, according to the U.S. Department of Labor.

Career Potential and Additional Information

The vast majority of optometrists retire from the profession, and therefore new optometrists are needed to replace them. Growth potential between now and 2014 is expected to be as fast as the average occupation. As the population ages, vision changes are inevitable for most. Technology advances that will allow optometrists to see more patients in a day, and the use of optometric assistants, will keep the need for more optometrists in check somewhat.

Advances in laser surgery will reduce the need for glasses and contact lenses for more of the population, at least for several years at a stretch. Pre- and post-op care of these patients will still be needed, and optometrists are well qualified for this.

Contact the Association of Schools and Colleges of Optometry for more information about optometry as a career, as well as for information about accredited schools of optometry. Their Web site is *www.opted.org*. Their address is 6110 Executive Blvd., Suite 510, Rockville, MD 20852.

For more information about optometry careers, contact the American Optometric Association. The Web site is *www.aoanet. org*. Their address is 243 N. Lindbergh Blvd., 1st Floor, St. Louis, MO 63141-7881.

Podiatrists

The foot is a very complex piece of human anatomy designed for balance and mobility. Doctors of Podiatric Medicine (DPMs) diagnose and treat diseases, injuries, and disorders of the foot and ankle. They also specialize in treatment to prevent disorders and diseases. The fifty-two bones in human feet (twenty-six in each foot) make up one-fourth of all the bones in the body.

Duties, Activities, and Scope of Practice

Podiatrists utilize medical, surgical, mechanical, and physical treatment modalities. They prescribe corrective footwear and orthotics. They treat corns, bunions, heel spurs, calluses, ingrown toenails, and other disorders of the feet and ankles. Diseases such as diabetes, arthritis, and heart disease often manifest in foot problems. Diabetics, for example, are prone to foot ulcers and infections. In these cases, podiatrists consult with or refer to other practitioners to provide appropriate care.

Education and Training

There are seven accredited schools of podiatric medicine in the United States. The Doctor of Podiatric Medicine is bestowed on graduates of a four-year postgraduate course of study at an accredited school of podiatric medicine. Applicants must have completed at least ninety units of undergraduate study, including the same basic sciences of chemistry, physics, and biology required for premed students. Most applicants will have completed a bachelor's degree. They also have to take the MCAT. Some schools accept the GRE or DAT. (See Appendix B for more information.) Extracurricular activities as well as letters of recommendation are scrutinized, and applicants are also evaluated on personal interviews in this highly competitive arena.

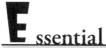

Essential

Podiatrists can prescribe medications, perform surgery, set fractures, and direct physical therapy treatments. They apply casts and splints, and can design custom-made shoes, splints, and braces to help correct problems and prevent complications. Specialty areas for podiatrists include surgery, dermatology, orthopedics, sports medicine, pediatrics, and diabetic foot care.

Podiatric students spend four years in formal education similar to that of other medical schools. The first two years concentrate on classroom instruction in sciences, and the last two years are spent in a clinical environment working under the supervision of licensed podiatrists. After graduation, a residency program is required, which can range from one to three years. Specialization requires a longer residency.

Licensure/Certification

Each state and the District of Columbia requires a podiatrist to be licensed in the state in which she practices. Many offer reciprocity. The National Board of Podiatric Examiners administers a board exam in two parts. The first part is taken at the end of the second year of podiatric school, and the second part is taken during the second semester of the fourth year. Most states accept the scores from these tests and do not require another written exam. Some states also require an oral or practical exam. A one-year minimum residency program is also required for licensure. Board certification is also available in several specialty areas and requires additional practical and written exams.

Work Settings and Salaries

Podiatrists generally have their own practices and offices. Some visit patients in their homes or in senior housing and nursing homes. Some work in clinics or hospitals. Today, group practices are becoming more popular. These practitioners have far fewer after-hours calls than other practitioners.

The median income for podiatrists in 2004 was $94,400 according to the U.S. Department of Labor. *Podiatric Magazine* reported that the median income for 2004 was $113,000.

Career Potential and Additional Information

The field of podiatric medicine is expected to grow as fast as the average occupations through 2014. An aging population will need more services for all health issues, including foot and ankle problems. Be aware, however, that routine preventative foot care and such things as the removal of corns and calluses are not generally covered under insurance or Medicare, so this portion of the business would be more popular in affluent communities where more disposable income is available.

Contact the American Podiatric Medical Association for further information about careers in podiatry. Their Web site is *www.apma. org*. Or write to them at 9312 Old Georgetown Rd., Bethesda, MD 20814-1621.

For information about podiatric colleges of medicine, contact the American Association of Colleges of Podiatric Medicine. Their Web site is *www.aacpm.org*. Their address is 15850 Crabbs Branch Way, Suite 320, Rockville, MD 20855-2622.

Chapter 8

Partners and Associates

In today's heath care arena, the practitioners (physicians and dentists in particular) often delegate care because their time is limited and costly. They continue to oversee and direct all aspects of care, as does any level of health care professional who delegates care. The partners and associates to whom care is delegated are well-educated, highly skilled professionals who participate in the health care team and perform the duties for which they have been educated and trained.

Nurses and Nurse Practitioners

Nurses are highly skilled professionals who care for the sick, help to educate the population on health care issues, and promote wellness. Licensed practical nurses (L.P.N.s) or licensed vocational nurses (L.V.N.s), depending on the state, perform most of the bedside care. In hospitals they may have more opportunities for expanded care, which they learn on the job. However, L.P.N.s are being phased out in most areas of the country. Those who were grandfathered in still work in hospitals, but new L.P.N.s find work primarily in skilled-nursing facilities (nursing homes) or doctors' offices. Registered nurses (R.N.s) perform many expanded roles and have multiple avenues for specialization and advanced education.

Duties, Activities, and Scope of Practice

Nurses were once thought to be handmaidens of physicians, but today that couldn't be further from the truth. Nursing is a profession, and the nurse's role complements the physician's role on the health care team.

R.N.s assess patients, educate and counsel patients, and carry out treatments and procedures as directed by physicians. They apprise physicians of significant changes. There are many roles for nurses, from positions in hospitals and clinics to working in schools and business organizations.

Nurse practitioners are advanced-practice nurses with a master's degree and specialized training in diagnosing and prescribing. (In forty-eight states they can prescribe medications.) They specialize in an area, such as family practice, pediatrics, women's health, mental health, or geriatrics, and they work under a physician. They conduct physical exams, order tests, diagnose and treat minor illnesses and injuries, and refer to the physician as needed.

There are many advanced-practice roles for nurses, such as in clinical settings, midwifery, anesthesia, and education. These require additional training and education such as master's and doctoral degrees.

Education and Training

All nursing programs require a high school diploma. Math and sciences are included in all nursing curriculums to varying degrees. Algebra is required. Chemistry, biology, anatomy and physiology, and microbiology are also required.

Most nursing programs require applicants to have a C.N.A. (certified nursing assistant) and some level of experience in the health care field. Many schools also require the NET (Nursing Entrance Test). See Appendix B for more information.

R.N. programs begin at three levels. There are still a few diploma nursing schools in existence, but most R.N.s attend either a community college and earn an associate's degree, or a four-year college or university and obtain a B.S.N. (Bachelor of Science in Nursing). Advanced degrees of Masters of Science in Nursing or a doctoral in nursing are also available, as well as several other master's and doctoral degrees in health care, health care administration, nursing education, etc.

All nursing programs consist of classroom education as well as supervised practical/clinical rotations in hospitals and other facilities. These clinical rotations include medical, surgical, orthopedics, pediatrics, labor and delivery, and mental health. Some include other areas such as public health and home health.

Associate's and bachelor's degree programs have general-education requirements, as well as math, sciences, and nursing courses. General-education courses are typically taken in the first year for the A.D.N. program and the first two years in the B.S.N. program. Nursing courses, both classroom and clinical, usually make up the latter year(s) of the program.

 Fact

L.P.N./L.V.N. programs are offered through technical or vocation schools and adult education programs, as well as some community colleges. The course of study is about fifteen to eighteen months. Upon graduation the L.P.N. (or L.V.N. in California and Texas) can take the NCLEX-L.P.N. exam for licensure.

Licensure/Certification

Upon graduation from an accredited school of nursing, L.P.N.s and R.N.s are required by all states to pass the NCLEX (National Council Licensure Examination) for licensure. This test is administered by the National Council of State Boards of Nursing. It is given via computers at testing centers across the country at various times. It tests both scientific and math knowledge, as well as nursing situations. Reciprocity is available in most states. Renewal is done on a periodic basis of every one to three years. Most states require continuing education in order to renew. If a license lapses, the nurse must retake the NCLEX in order to practice again.

Work Settings and Salaries

Nursing is one of the most physically and emotionally demanding careers. Nurses cover shifts and patient needs in hospitals and home health care 24 hours per day, 365 days per year. Many situations require nurses to be on call and available on short notice. Nurses spend a considerable amount of time standing and walking.

Nursing constitutes the largest health care occupation. According to the U.S. Department of Labor, nurses accounted for 2.4 million jobs in 2004. One out of every four nurses worked part-time in 2004, and nearly 7 percent held more than one job. Almost 60 percent of the jobs were in hospitals, in inpatient and outpatient departments. The other 40 percent of jobs were primarily in nursing homes, home health, physicians' offices, clinics and outpatient facilities, schools, insurance and managed care companies, pharmaceutical companies, industry, and government agencies.

Salaries for nurses can vary greatly, especially for those working more than one job. However, the U.S. Department of Labor reports that for 2004, the median salary for an R.N. was $45,330, and for an L.P.N. it was $33,970. Advanced-practice R.N.s typically earn between $50,000 and $85,000 annually.

Career Potential and Additional Information

In recent history there have been cycles of nursing shortages followed by a surplus and another shortage and another surplus. Changes in health care management have greatly reduced the number of R.N. jobs available, as hospitals have needed to cut down on nursing staff in order to deal with reduced reimbursement issues. Nonetheless, the nursing shortage has increased over the past few years, as women have taken advantage of other health care opportunities. Critical shortages of nurses over the past two decades have led to increased salaries and improved working conditions.

The average age of nurses today is forty-five and older, and nurses entering the field are older as well. As the population ages and the baby boomers retire, the number of nurses will continue to fall.

Nursing will be the fastest-growing occupation from now until 2014. This will be due to advances in technology and the need for health education. The need for nurses in hospitals may shrink, but the need for nurses in outpatient settings, day surgeries, home health, and ambulatory care settings will rapidly increase. Advanced training and education will be needed for nurses in many of these areas. There is a significant shortage at the present time of nurse educators, which is severely limiting the number of new nurses who can be trained. Most nursing schools have waiting lists.

For more information about nursing as a career contact the American Nurses Association. Their Web site is *www.nursingworld.org*. Their address is 8515 Georgian Avenue, Suite 400, Silver Spring, MD 20910.

For information about accredited nursing programs contact the National League for Nursing. Their Web site is *www.nln.org*. Their address is 61 Broadway, 33rd Floor, New York, NY 10006.

Physician Assistants

Physician assistants, also known as P.A.s, are formally trained to diagnose and treat patients as directed by and under the supervision of a physician. P.A.s assume many of the duties physicians used to, allowing physicians to concentrate on more complex tasks with their patients. P.A.s usually practice in primary care, such as family practice, pediatrics, mental health, internal medicine, or geriatrics. They can work in surgical specialties where they perform pre- and post-op care, or may serve as first or second assistants in the OR.

Duties, Activities, and Scope of Practice

P.A.s perform physical examinations, take medical histories, and diagnose and treat illnesses and injuries. They can apply casts and splints, suture wounds, order diagnostic tests, and educate and counsel patients in treatments and preventative care as delegated by the physician. They can make house calls and check up on patients in hospitals and skilled-nursing facilities and report back to the physician.

Education and Training

The P.A. program is about two years. Applicants are required to have completed a minimum of two years of college and have some health care experience. Most applicants have a bachelor's degree, and many a master's degree. Many have backgrounds as an R.N.. Undergraduate requirements include biology, chemistry, English, math, psychology, and social sciences.

E ssential

The P.A. program includes biochemistry, pharmacology, microbiology, anatomy and physiology, clinical medicine, geriatrics, home health care, medical ethics, and disease prevention. Clinical training is supervised and includes rotations through geriatrics, obstetrics, emergency medicine, primary care, mental health, surgery, and pediatrics.

Additional training and residency programs are available for those who seek added responsibilities and advancement.

Licensure/Certification

Upon completion of an accredited P.A. program, all states and the District of Columbia require P.A.s to pass the Physicians' Assistants National Certifying Examination, which is administered by the National Commission on Certification of Physician Assistants (NCCPA). In order to remain certified, P.A.s must complete 100 hours of continuing education every two years. Additionally, every six years they must pass a recertification exam or an alternative program, which consists of additional training and a take-home exam.

Work Settings and Salaries

Today, about one-third of P.A.s work in rural settings and towns with populations under 50,000. Almost half work in cities with populations over 500,000. Most work in clinics and M.D. offices with physicians in primary or family practice. However, P.A.s can work in any specialty alongside physicians who supervise and delegate their work. P.A.s also work in such settings as hospitals, prisons, nursing homes, and student health care services. Many help to meet the needs of underserved areas.

The normal workweek is forty to forty-five hours and often includes working evening and weekend on-call hours to meet the needs of patients.

The U.S. Department of Labor reports that the median salary for 2004 was $69,410. The Academy of Physician Assistants reports a median income of $74,264 for 2004 for P.A.s in full-time clinical practice.

Career Potential and Additional Information

The first P.A. program was started in 1965 at Duke University. Many medics returning from Vietnam seeking employment in the medical field influenced the formation of this profession. Only recently did Medicare begin to allow reimbursement for P.A. visits and care. This, along with the acceptance of P.A.s by the general public, and recognition of the cost-effectiveness of P.A.s by insurance companies and HMOs, has caused the profession to grow rapidly. An expected 50 percent increase in positions for P.A.s over the next decade is possibly a conservative estimate.

An aging population will present many new and increased demands for health care, and recognition of the cost-effectiveness of P.A.s will represent one solution to the rising costs and help to meet the demands.

For further information about physician assistant careers and programs, contact the American Academy of Physician Assistants. Their Web site is *www.aapa.org*. Their address is 950 North Washington Street, Alexandria, VA 22314-1552.

Dental Hygienists

The primary function of dental hygienists could be said to be teeth cleaning, which involves the removal of hard and soft deposits on the teeth. However, their role in the health care team extends to assessment and patient education as well.

Duties, Activities, and Scope of Practice

Duties can vary by state as defined by each state's "practice act" for dental hygienists. A practice act is the set of laws as determined by each state to protect the public by regulating who can be a dental hygienist. The practice act also sets requirements for education and licensure, and can include disciplinary procedures for those who violate the practice act. Beyond cleaning teeth, in some states hygienists are allowed to take impressions for making appliances and teeth. Some hygienists can also place temporary fillings and polish existing fillings and other restorations.

 Question

Do dental hygienists always work with dentists?
In most instances, dental hygienists work under the supervision of the dentist. However, they can also work independently, as they often do in facilities such as skilled-nursing homes and hospitals.

Hygienists apply fluorides and sealants for preventative care; they assess for mouth and gum problems, such as gingivitis and oral cancers, and notify the dentist. They educate patients about appropriate oral care, including brushing and flossing, and about a proper diet to help maintain a healthy mouth. They counsel patients about the hazards of smoking and dipping tobacco as well as other harmful habits. Hygienists take x-rays and perform chair-side assistance to dentists during procedures.

Education and Training

Many dental hygiene schools require at least one year of college for admission. Accredited schools bestow an associate's degree on graduates, and this is adequate to work in private practice. A bachelor's degree from an accredited school is required to work in public health or a public school program. To teach or to work in research, a master's degree is required.

Dental hygiene programs include classroom and laboratory study of chemistry, microbiology, anatomy and physiology, oral anatomy and pathology, radiography, histology, pharmacology, dental materials, periodontology, and nutrition. The second portion of the program includes supervised clinical practice.

Licensure/Certification

All states and the District of Columbia require dental hygienists to be licensed. This requires completion of an accredited program and successfully passing written and clinical exams. The written exam is administered by the American Dental Association Joint Commission on National Dental Examinations and is accepted by all states. The clinical portion is administered by state or regional testing agencies. Most states also require an exam on the legal practices of dental hygiene.

Work Settings and Salaries

More than half of all dental hygienists work part-time (less than thirty-five hours per week). The U.S. Department of Labor reports that there were 158,000 jobs for dental hygienists in 2004. Since dentists usually hire hygienists to work only two to three days per week, many hygienists hold more than one job. They may work flexible hours, including evenings and weekends, to meet the needs of the patients. Almost all hygienists work in dentists' offices. There is a growing need for hygienists who will work in nursing care facilities, senior housing, and hospitals.

The U.S. Department of Labor reports that the mean hourly salary for dental hygienists in 2004 was $28.05. Salaries were reported to vary from $18.05 to $40.70 per hour. Benefits varied from one employer to another, because most hygienists work part-time. (The ADA reports that 9 out of 10 have dental coverage.)

Career Potential and Additional Information

The potential for careers in this area is expected to grow faster than for the average occupation due to the aging population who will require more dental care. The effectiveness of fluorides and other sealants, as well as improved preventative dental education, has resulted in the retention of natural teeth, which will require more care.

If you would like more information on a career in dental hygiene, contact the American Dental Hygienists' Association (ADHA). Their Web site is *www.adha.org.* Their address is 444 North Michigan Avenue, Suite 3400, Chicago, IL 60611. For information about accredited schools, contact the Commission on Dental Education of the American Dental Hygienists' Association at the same Web site and address.

Dietitians and Nutritionists

The trend in health care today is to involve the patient in the responsibility and accountability for his own health care status. A healthy and nutritious diet is an important aspect of a healthy lifestyle. Dietitians and nutritionists are trained in food selection and preparation, nutrition, and how to adjust for specific needs due to allergies and diseases.

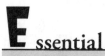

E ssential

Dietitians have been members of the health care team for over 100 years, but in recent decades, more interest in healthy eating has brought them to the foreground. Dietitians are experts in nutrition, and they understand the correlation of disease to nutritional deficiencies.

Duties, Activities, and Scope of Practice

Dietitians plan and select meals based on the needs of the patients. They also supervise the preparation and serving of meals. They suggest modifications as appropriate to promote wellness and prevent disease. There are four main specialties and several subspecialties. The primary specialties are clinical, community, management, and consulting.

Clinical Dietitians

Clinical dietitians work in hospitals and nursing homes. They evaluate patients' needs and formulate and supervise plans for improved nutrition for the patients. They confer with the members of the health care team to determine the needs of the patient, with the patient to determine habits and likes/dislikes, and with the family to educate them regarding the maintenance of proper diet and nutrition upon discharge.

Community Dietitians

This group of professionals is more commonly known as *nutritionists*. They work with individuals and groups to advise about proper nutrition and dietary habits to promote wellness. They usually work in clinics or for home health agencies, nursing homes, HMOs, and hospitals, and they teach patients and families about proper nutrition and habits to promote wellness. They help patients develop nutritional care plans.

Management Dietitians

In this specialty, dietitians work for long-term care facilities, senior residences, restaurants, hotels, schools, and prisons to supervise large-scale food preparation and meal planning to meet the general needs of the population they serve. They help to plan and implement budgets, meet and maintain sanitary food and safety standards, and train food-preparation workers.

Consultant Dietitians

These professionals work in private practice to consult with individuals and institutions. They provide nutrition screenings, and they design plans for patients with issues such as weight control or disease control. Consultants may work for health care facilities, individuals, sports teams, or wellness programs.

Education and Training

Nutritionists and dietitians must obtain at least a bachelor's degree in dietetics, food service management, foods and nutrition, or other areas approved and accredited by the American Dietetic Association.

The areas of study include biology, biochemistry, microbiology, organic and inorganic chemistry, anatomy and physiology, diet therapy, nutrition, food service management, and food preparation in quantity. The program includes both classroom and laboratory studies and practical experience.

Licensure/Certification

Forty-six states have laws governing dietitians and nutritionists. Thirty of these states require a license, and fifteen require certification. Although only one state requires registration (the minimum professional status), most dietitians are registered. At one time registration was the only professional distinction, and most states still honor this. To become registered, candidates must meet the requirements set by the Commission on Dietetic Registration for classroom and clinical experience, and pass an examination. This can be accomplished in one of two ways. The first involves the completion of an accredited bachelor's degree in dietetics and an internship or ADA-approved prepractice program of 900 hours of supervised practice. The other route is to enroll in an ADA-approved coordinated program that combines academic studies with practical experience. When this program is completed, the student earns either a bachelor's or master's degree and has also completed the necessary hours of practical experience. When either of these programs is completed, the dietitian sits for a written exam given by the Commission on Dietetic Registration. This exam is given in October and April and is a half-day test of knowledge of normal nutrition, clinical nutrition, community nutrition, food service systems and management, and food science.

To maintain registration the dietitian must accumulate seventy-five hours of approved continuing education every five years.

Work Settings and Salaries

In 2004, dietitians and nutritionists held about 50,000 jobs, according to the U.S. Department of Labor. More than half of the dietitians worked in hospitals, nursing homes, outpatient settings, and doctors' offices. Others worked in a variety of settings such as private practice or for agencies that provide food service to schools, corporations, airlines, colleges and universities, prisons, home health care, and care facilities for seniors.

The median income reported by the U.S. Department of Labor for 2004 was $43,630. According to the ADA, dietitian salaries in 2005 ranged from approximately $45,000 to $60,000.

Career Potential and Additional Information

Increasing emphasis on improved dietary habits, promotion of wellness, and prevention of diseases will help to ensure that the outlook for employment for dietitians and nutritionists will continue to grow about as fast as the average for all occupations through 2014. There will be some areas where the needs for dietitians will most likely decline, such as in nursing homes and state agencies, because of the use of contract food services.

Growth will be increased if reimbursement issues are resolved and Medicare recognizes the need for these professional services.

For more information about careers in dietetics and nutrition, contact the American Dietetic Association. Their Web site is *www. eatright.org*. Their address is 120 South Riverside Plaza, Suite 2000, Chicago, IL 60606-6995.

Pharmacists

Dispensing medications as prescribed by practitioners is the primary function of pharmacists today. Long ago, pharmacists compounded ingredients and chemicals into capsules or solutions or ointments to fill prescriptions for the treatment and cure of diseases and illnesses. Today, large pharmaceutical manufacturers compound the medications, and pharmacists fill the amounts prescribed, educate patients on the use of the medications, and keep records of health history to ensure the safe use of the prescriptions. In some instances, pharmacists still do some compounding.

Duties, Activities, and Scope of Practice

Doctors, dentists, and others with prescribing privileges write prescriptions for medications to treat or cure illness and disease. The pharmacist interprets and reviews those prescriptions—considering the patient's medical history, any allergies, and any other medications that patient may be taking—to ensure the safe use of the prescribed medications. Pharmacists dispense medications as prescribed.

Pharmacists also educate patients in the dose, use, action, and possible side effects of the medications. And they assist patients in the choice of over-the-counter medications for such things as colds, digestive disorders, flu, headaches, and pain relief.

Education and Training

Pharmacists receive a Doctor of Pharmacy degree (PharmD), which requires a minimum of six years of college. The program includes the study of sciences, math, and general-education courses, as well as practical experience under the supervision of licensed pharmacists in the dispensing of medication and the counseling of patients. The PharmD program is a four-year (or longer) program following a minimum of two years of college studies. Most applicants to pharmacy programs have at least three years of college and some have completed bachelor's degrees with majors in biology, chemistry, or other science courses. Half of the pharmacy schools require applicants to take the Pharmacy College Admissions Test (see Appendix B for more information). Pharmacy schools are accredited by the American Council on Pharmaceutical Education (ACPE).

For those who wish to do research for drug companies or to teach, master's degrees and Ph.D.s are available from most schools of pharmacy. Pharmacists who wish to run their own pharmacy may also consider an M.B.A. (master's degree in business administration).

Fact

The American Association of Colleges of Pharmacy recently launched a Web-based application process that allows applicants to use one set of transcripts and one application to apply to multiple PharmD programs.

Postgraduate internship under the supervision of a licensed pharmacist or an externship during pharmacy school may be required by some states.

Licensure/Certification

All states and the District of Columbia require pharmacists to have a license in order to practice. To become licensed, pharmacists must graduate from an accredited school of pharmacy and pass an examination. Not all states require the same written examination, and some require more than one. Many states offer reciprocity. Check with the state board of pharmacy for the state in which you intend to practice for details.

Work Settings and Salaries

Most pharmacies today are located in hospitals, drug store chains, discount stores, and grocery stores. Some small pharmacies can be found in medical office buildings or clinics. A few free-standing pharmacies can be found, usually in smaller communities.

Community and hospital pharmacies often offer extended hours, and even some drug store chains are beginning to offer twenty-four-hour availability. This means pharmacists work various shifts, which may include nights and weekends. Some small independent pharmacies offer on-call availability for such services as home health care and hospice. Some pharmacies specialize in IV (intravenous) medications and supplies.

According to the U.S. Department of Labor, there were 230,000 jobs for pharmacists in 2004. Approximately 61 percent of the pharmacists worked in community pharmacies, which are part of drug store chains, grocery stores, and discount stores. These pharmacists were mostly salaried employees, although some were independent, self-employed owners. About 24 percent of the pharmacists were salaried employees in hospital pharmacies. Other pharmacists worked in mail-order pharmacies, clinics, home health care agencies, and for pharmaceutical wholesalers or the federal government.

Salaries reported for 2004 ranged from $61,200 to $109,850, with a median salary of $84,900.

Career Potential and Additional Information

As health insurance companies recognize that the high cost of medications does not even come close to the exorbitant cost of treating patients with diseases that have not been controlled with medications, the role of pharmacists in the health care team is increasing. Pharmacists are vital members of health care teams, and their part in educating the public in preventative care and promoting wellness is essential. Preventing injury and illness from allergies and incompatible medications also plays a big role in reducing costs as well as promoting wellness.

The outlook for employment for pharmacists thorough 2014 is very good. Enrollment in pharmacy schools is increasing, but the need for pharmacists is expected to continue to exceed the number of pharmacists seeking employment.

For more information about careers in pharmacy, contact the American Society of Health-System Pharmacists. Their Web site is *www.ashp.org*. Their address is 7272 Wisconsin Avenue, Bethesda, MD 20814.

For information on pharmacy schools, contact the American Association of Colleges of Pharmacy. Their Web site is *www.aacp .org*. Their address is 1426 Prince Street, Alexandria, VA 22314.

Psychologists

Psychologists are employed in many fields, including health care. They study human behavior and the human mind. Rising costs of health care cause those who reimburse for care to examine the factors that contribute to an unhealthy lifestyle. Some of those factors include smoking, overeating, job stress, and addiction. Psychologists who specialize in health care issues are trained to help people deal with these and other issues affecting their health status.

Duties, Activities, and Scope of Practice

Clinical and counseling psychologists work with patients to help improve their lifestyle, promote wellness, and achieve an improved health status. Clinical psychologists in the three areas of health care include health psychologists, neuropsychologists, and geropsychologists.

Health psychologists help patients achieve goals such as losing weight and quitting smoking. Neuropsychologists work with patients with brain injuries and strokes to help them to adjust to the limitations imposed by the injury to the brain. They study the relationship between the brain and behavior and help patients to improve their behavior. Geropsychologists help patients to cope with the problems and lifestyle changes presented by aging.

Education and Training

To become an independent licensed clinical or counseling psychologist, a doctoral degree in psychology (a Psy.D.) is required. A bachelor's degree is the first step, followed by graduate study, which usually takes five to seven years to accomplish. The degree is usually based on examinations and practical work instead of a dissertation. For clinical and counseling work, an internship of one or two years is also required. Those with a bachelor's degree in psychology can assist psychologists in mental health centers.

Licensure/Certification

Psychologists involved in patient care must meet certification or licensing requirements set by each state and the District of Columbia. These requirements vary by state and are specific to the type of position in which the psychologist has been educated and trained. The American Board of Professional Psychology (ABPP) recognizes clinical and counseling psychologists. They require a doctoral degree, postdoctoral training in the specialty area, and one to two years of professional experience. In addition, a candidate must pass a state licensing examination.

Work Settings and Salaries

Clinical and counseling psychologists practice most often from private offices and in clinics. They usually set their own hours and often offer evening and weekend hours in order to accommodate the needs of their patients.

Hospitals, nursing homes, and other health care facilities may hire psychologists to work as members of the staff. In these cases, the psychologists may work varying shifts, which can include evenings and weekends as well.

According to the U.S. Department of Labor, in 2004 clinical, counseling, and school psychologists made a median income of $54,950. Salaries ranged from about $32,000 to $93,000. The median income for industrial organization psychologists was $71,400 in 2004, and salaries ranged from $45,000 to $125,000.

Career Potential and Additional Information

This profession expects to grow at a faster rate than the average of all professions over the next decade. With the aging population and the rising costs of health care that are associated with health challenges such as smoking and obesity, the need for clinical and counseling psychologists is expected to have healthy growth.

You can obtain more information about a career as a clinical or counseling psychologist from the American Psychological Association. Their Web site is *www.apa.org*. Their address is 750 First Street NE, Washington, DC 20002-4242.

Chapter 9

Rehab Team Members

The rehab team is known for its participation after an event, such as injury or serious illness. However, as the trend toward preventative care continues to gain momentum, this role will continue to expand and change. For instance, physical, occupational, and speech therapists often work with patients who have suffered strokes. Medical social workers assist patients with emotional, financial, and social issues. Mental health counselors help with issues such as depression and mental illness, from day-to-day control to crisis intervention. Audiologists assess and treat hearing-related problems.

Physical Therapists

Physical therapists work to relieve pain, promote fitness, improve mobility, prevent disability, limit the amount of permanent disability, and restore function to individuals affected by illness and/or injury.

Duties, Activities, and Scope of Practice

The physical therapist examines and assesses patients for functional ability and loss through a series of tests, reviews medical history, and works with the physician to develop a plan to treat the individual. This can include treatment for an existing or potential problem related to an illness or injury.

Treatment plans can include one or all of the following: exercises to strengthen and stretch muscles, and to increase flexibility, range of motion, and endurance; electrical stimuli, hot or cold packs, massage, and ultrasound to reduce swelling and pain; traction or deep-tissue massage to reduce pain.

PTs work with patients to improve their mobility and range of motion, to reduce pain and swelling, and to improve balance, coordination, and endurance. They also instruct patients in the proper use of assistive devices such as canes, crutches, splints, braces, and wheelchairs or scooters.

Education and Training

Applicants to P.T. schools are often required to have logged a number of volunteer hours in a P.T. clinic or hospital department. The bachelor's degree should have included a strong science background in chemistry, biology, anatomy and physiology, and physics.

The master's degree program builds on this basic math and science background and includes courses in biomechanics, therapeutic procedures, neuroanatomy, and human growth and development. Clinical experience is included and is supervised by licensed physical therapists.

 Fact

A master's degree or doctoral degree in physical therapy is required to practice as a physical therapist, as is a license. According to the American Physical Therapy Association (APTA), there were 205 accredited schools of physical therapy in the United States in 2004.

Licensure/Certification

The Federation of State Boards of Physical Therapy administers a licensing examination for P.T.s in all fifty states and the District of Columbia. Many states require continuing education for renewal.

Work Settings and Salaries

About one-third of all physical therapists work in hospitals. Others work for P.T. offices, M.D.s, home health care agencies, skilled-nursing facilities, rehab centers, and outpatient care facilities. Many physical therapists hold more than one job. One in four works part-time.

The median salary for 2004 according to the U.S. Department of Labor was $60,180. Salaries ranged from $42,010 to $88,580.

Career Potential and Additional Information

Physical therapy jobs are expected to grow faster than the average for all jobs through 2014. As the population ages the need for physical therapists will expand. Technological advances will save the lives of more accident victims, as well as the lives of infants and children with severe disabilities, which will also increase the need for P.T.s.

For further information about physical therapy careers and educational programs, contact the American Physical Therapy Association. Their Web site is *www.apta.org*. Their address is 1111 North Fairfax Street, Alexandria, VA 22314-1488.

Occupational Therapists

The primary role for occupational therapists is to assist patients in maximizing their independence by improving their ability to perform activities of daily living (ADLs), such as grooming, bathing, eating, and dressing. They also help patients learn to function in their work environments. O.T.s work with patients who have disabling conditions. This can include mental, physical, emotional, or developmental disabilities. The disabilities can be temporary, in which case the O.T. will work with the patients to improve or return to their prior level of function and/or reasoning. If the disability is permanent, the O.T. will educate the patient and family members in adapting to the changes in their functional or cognitive abilities.

Duties, Activities, and Scope of Practice

O.T.s help patients maximize their independence by instructing them in exercises to improve function or reasoning, or in the use of adaptive equipment, splints and braces, or wheelchairs. The focus of the O.T. differs from that of a P.T., although there can be some overlap. O.T.s generally deal with activities of daily living such as eating, grooming, bathing, toileting, and dressing. They instruct patients in energy conservation and efficiency techniques in performing tasks.

Some O.T.s work with patients whose abilities to perform in their job may have been altered by an illness or injury. In these situations, the O.T., patient, and employer work together to make necessary adjustments in the work area to ensure that the patient can continue to be a productive employee. These might include ergonomic changes in the workstation, or installing ramps or grab bars to facilitate mobility.

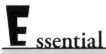

O.T.s often work in mental health facilities and drug and alcohol rehab centers to help patients who are mentally ill, emotionally disturbed, or otherwise impaired to adapt to daily life by teaching them skills such as time management, budget management, how to use public transportation, and homemaking.

When working in schools, the O.T. works with the student/patient as well as the school staff to ensure that the student can participate as fully as possible.

Education and Training

A bachelor's degree in occupational therapy is the minimum requirement for licensure at the present; however, by 2007, a master's degree will become the minimum requirement. The degree must be from an accredited school in order for the student to sit for the national certification examination.

O.T. programs include biological, physical, social, and behavioral sciences, as well as occupational therapy theory and skills. A minimum of six months of supervised clinical practice is required.

Applicants to O.T. programs should have some experience working or volunteering in the health care field.

Licensure/Certification

Graduates of an accredited program are eligible to sit for the national certification exam. Upon passing they are awarded the title of O.T.R. (occupational therapist registered). All fifty states and the District of Columbia regulate the practice of O.T.s.

Work Settings and Salaries

According to the U.S. Department of Labor, there were 92,000 jobs for occupational therapists in 2004. Of that number, one O.T. in ten held more than one job, and 25 percent work part time. The vast majority of O.T.s work in hospitals. Other employers include home health care services, outpatient care centers, public schools and private educational institutions, and skilled-nursing facilities.

The median salary reported for 2004 was $54,660, in a salary range from $37,430 to $81,600.

Career Potential and Additional Information

Federal legislation may impose limits on reimbursement of therapy and this will cause a temporary decline in the need for O.T.s. However, the aging population coupled with an increased need for O.T.s to help mainstream children with disabilities into public schools will provide reason for employment opportunities for O.T.s to grow faster than for the average of all professions through 2014.

For further information on careers in occupational therapy, contact the American Occupational Therapy Association. Their Web site is *www.aota.org*. Their address is 4720 Montgomery Lane, Bethesda, MD 20824-1220.

Speech Therapists and Language Pathologists

Communication disorders affect approximately 47 million people in the United States today. These can be caused by such things as birth defects and anomalies, hearing loss, emotional disturbances, or illness or injury. Speech and language pathologists work with patients to assess and treat speech, language, and voice disorders as well as swallowing difficulties.

Duties, Activities, and Scope of Practice

Speech, language, voice, and swallowing disorders stem from a variety of causes and affect people of all ages. These can include strokes, brain injury, developmental delays, birth defects, Parkinson's and Alzheimer's diseases, cerebral palsy, cleft palates, and cancers. S.T.s treat stuttering, voice quality problems such as a harsh pitch or hoarseness, and even cognitive impairments such as poor memory, attention deficits, and problem-solving issues from a stroke or other disabling disease. Those who wish to lose an accent would also work with a speech-language pathologist.

Children born with cleft palates and lips, deafness, or diminished hearing, or those who suffer from developmental delays or cerebral palsy, may experience communication disorders that will require assistance from a speech therapist.

Education and Training

Undergraduate work is done in the areas of biology, chemistry, physics, sociology, and linguistics. There are 239 accredited graduate schools of speech-language pathology. The courses include anatomy and physiology of the areas of the body affected by, and that affect, speech and language, hearing, and swallowing disorders. Also included in the curriculum are courses in development of speech; acoustics; the nature of speech, hearing, and swallowing disorders, psychology of communication; and treatment modalities for and correction of speech, language, and swallowing disorders. The programs also include supervised clinical practice.

Fact

There are forty-seven states that regulate the licensing of speech therapists. In all of those states, the minimum education requirement is a master's degree in speech-language pathology. Medicare and Medicaid require an S.T. to have a master's degree in order to be reimbursed for services.

Licensure/Certification

To practice, S.T.s must have a master's degree. To be certified, they must pass a national exam, which is offered through the Praxis Series of the Educational Testing Service. In addition to this test, the candidate must have had 375 hours of supervised clinical experience and nine months of postgraduate professional experience. The certification is a CCC-SLP (Certified Clinical Competence in Speech-Language Pathology). Thirty-eight states require continuing education for license renewal.

Work Settings and Salaries

S.T.s work in hospitals, skilled-nursing facilities, rehab centers, public and private schools, adult day care settings, and home health care agencies. Some work in private practice.

Those who work for schools may work a nine- or ten-month academic year. According to the U.S Department of Labor, the median income in 2004 was $52,410, and salaries ranged from $34,720 to $82,420.

Career Potential and Additional Information

Employment opportunities for S.T.s are expected to grow faster than the average for all professions through 2014. There are two factors that weigh heavily in this prediction. The population is aging and the baby-boom generation is entering the age range where more neurological disorders are likely to strike—such as strokes, Parkinson's, and Alzheimer's—affecting speech, hearing, and swallowing functions. The second factor is that federal law now guarantees special education and access to services for children with disabilities. Early diagnosis and treatment for speech, language, hearing, and swallowing disorders is essential for successfully maximizing improvement.

For more information about speech-language pathology jobs, contact the American Speech-Language-Hearing Association. Their Web site is *www.asha.org*. Their address is 10801 Rockville Pike, Rockville, MD 20852.

Respiratory Therapists

Respiratory therapists work with patients of all ages, from premature infants to the elderly. They evaluate and treat patients with acute and chronic respiratory and cardiopulmonary problems, such as asthma, COPD (chronic obstructive pulmonary disease), bronchitis, pneumonia, and congestive heart failure. They also work with patients who have suffered strokes or heart attacks, and drowning and overdose victims.

Duties, Activities, and Scope of Practice

Respiratory therapists evaluate patients for lung capacity and oxygen, CO_2, and pH levels to determine the appropriate interventions for the current breathing problem. They are trained to draw arterial blood samples for blood-gas analysis. R.T.s instruct patients and caregivers in the safe use of oxygen, ventilators, humidifiers, and aerosol machines. In addition to the use of this equipment, they instruct in cleaning and maintenance procedures.

E ssential

Respiratory therapists instruct patients in breathing exercises to help increase their lung capacity and relieve their symptoms. They perform chest physiotherapy to assist patients in clearing mucous from their lungs and respiratory system. This is most often used for patients with cystic fibrosis.

Education and Training

The minimum standard for R.T.s is an associate's degree in respiratory therapy; however, there are a growing number of R.T.s who have a bachelor's degree in respiratory therapy, as this offers them opportunities for more advanced practice.

The associate's degree is offered by community colleges and vocational schools, and the bachelor's through colleges and universities. Again, always be sure the program is accredited.

The curriculum of the R.T. program will include anatomy and physiology, with an emphasis on the cardiopulmonary system; chemistry; math; microbiology; pharmacology; anesthesiology; and cardiopulmonary diseases. Additionally they are trained in techniques such as airway management, CPR, management of ventilators, drawing and analyzing arterial blood gasses, and pulmonary function testing. They learn how to safely use oxygen and mixtures with other gasses.

As with other patient care careers, the R.T. training includes significant time spent in supervised clinical practice.

Licensure/Certification
Over forty states require licensure of respiratory therapists. Most employers require R.T.s to be certified as a C.R.T., which requires passing written and clinical exams after graduation from an accredited program. An R.T. can also become an R.P.T. (registered respiratory therapist) by passing another written and clinical exam.

Work Settings and Salaries
Most R.T.s work in hospitals or medical centers. Others work for medical equipment suppliers who supply oxygen and other respiratory care equipment to patients at home, home health agencies, and skilled-nursing facilities.

Health care is a 24-7 industry, especially in hospital settings; therefore, R.T.s may work any shift and will work some weekends and holidays.

The median salary in 2004 as reported by the U.S. Department of Labor was $43,140. Salaries ranged from $32,220 to $57,580.

Career Potential and Additional Information
Technological advancements that continue to improve and help to save the lives of premature infants will ensure a place for respiratory therapists, as these patients' lungs are immature and frequently problematic. The elderly are also vulnerable to cardiopulmonary diseases, and as the population ages, the need for respiratory therapists will grow. The need for R.T.s is expected to increase at a rate faster than for most occupations through 2014 according to the U.S. Department of Labor.

To find out more about becoming an R.T., contact the American Association for Respiratory Care. Their Web site is *www.aarc.org.* Their address is 9425 MacArthur Blvd., Suite 100, Irving, TX 75063.

Medical Social Workers

An important part of the rehab team is the medical social worker, whose job it is to help patients and their loved ones adjust and adapt to the changes and losses brought on by illness or injury. They work with patients and families of all ages. They assess for social, physical, and financial needs and assist patients in obtaining the care and assistance needed.

Duties, Activities, and Scope of Practice

M.S.W.s help the elderly find care at home or placement in an appropriate level of care. They help parents of infants and children with birth defects and chronic illness find help at home or at school. They involve child and adult protective services as needed in cases of abuse and neglect. And they offer counseling to help with emotional adjustment to loss and illness.

M.S.W.s assist with both short-term and long-term planning to adapt to the changes imposed by an illness, injury, or loss. M.S.W.s also work with mental health and substance abuse rehabilitation services to assist patients with counseling and ongoing support issues to promote wellness and prevent regression.

Education and Training

The minimum level of education for social workers is a bachelor's degree (B.S.W.), but more and more insurance reimbursement is dependent on a master's prepared social worker (M.S.W.). Those who wish to teach social work need to be prepared at the doctoral level. Programs are accredited by the Council on Social Work Education.

Licensure/Certification

All states require that social workers be licensed, certified, or registered. The Academy of Certified Social Workers offers certification to M.S.W.s who have two years of experience, pass a written examination, and are members of the National Association of Social Workers.

Question

What classes will I take to become a medical social worker?
The curriculum includes courses in behavioral sciences, human development, and social environment. Other classes involve social services, social welfare policy, and methods of social work. A significant portion of field experience is also included.

Work Settings and Salaries

Social workers are employed by hospitals and skilled-nursing facilities. They also work for home health care agencies, public health departments, crisis centers, mental health facilities, and in private practice. They can be on call for crisis intervention or on weekends and holidays as needed, but generally work forty hours a week.

The median salary in 2004 was reported to be $40,080. Salaries ranged from $25,390 to $58,740 according to the U.S. Department of Labor.

Career Potential and Additional Information

The job outlook for social workers will continue to be very favorable through 2014 due to the needs presented by an aging population as well as to technological advancements that save lives but pose lifestyle changes due to the nature of the illness or injury.

For further information about careers in medical social work, contact the National Association of Social Workers. Their Web site is *www.socialworkers.org*. Their address is 750 First Street NE, Washington, DC 20002.

Audiologists

Audiologists work with patients of all ages. When someone experiences hearing, balance, or other neural ear problems, they are usually referred to an audiologist for evaluation and treatment. They utilize computers, audiometers, and other equipment to measure the ability to hear sounds and at what level, the ability to distinguish between sounds, and the effects of the hearing or balance problems on the individual's lifestyle.

Duties, Activities, and Scope of Practice

The audiologist interprets the results of these tests and determines a course of treatment, which can include such things as hearing aids, cochlear implants, or just simple cleaning of the ear canal. They then tune the hearing aids or implants and instruct patients in their care and maintenance.

 Fact

Hearing and balance disorders can result from illness (especially when high fever or inner-ear infection is involved), or injury to the ear—both physical or from a loud noise or explosion. They can also result from birth defects, the use of certain medications, or simply aging. Premature babies may have poorly developed hearing systems, and are often prone to hearing problems related to the noise effects of incubators. Most states now require screening of newborns as well as mandate early intervention if problems are detected.

Audiologists also work with patients to improve hearing problems that don't respond completely to aids or implants. They teach lip-reading and other techniques to maximize communication. They may recommend amplifiers or light systems for such things as telephones, doorbells, and other alerting devices.

Education and Training

A master's degree is the current standard; however, by 2007 a doctoral degree will be required to seek certification. There are 107 accredited colleges or universities in the United States that offer programs in audiology. The curriculum includes English, math, communication sciences, chemistry, physics, biology, and psychology. The graduate courses include genetics, normal and abnormal communication, anatomy and physiology, pharmacology, ethics, and assessment, diagnosis, and treatment of the auditory, balance, and neural systems.

Licensure/Certification

Audiologists can become certified in two different manners. The first is by earning a CCC-A (Certificate of Clinical Competence in Audiology) from the American Speech-Language-Hearing Association. The candidate must have completed a graduate degree and 375 hours of supervised clinical experience, as well as complete a nine-month postgraduate internship and pass the Praxis Series Exam in audiology. This exam is administered by the Educational Testing Service.

The American Board of Audiology also certifies audiologists who have completed an accredited graduate degree, passed a national examination, and performed 2,000 hours of professional practice under the supervision of a certified audiologist within a two-year period.

All certified audiologists must apply for renewal every three years and must have completed forty-five units of continuing education in that three-year period. By 2007, all applicants must have a doctoral degree to become certified.

Work Settings and Salaries

In 2004 there were about 10,000 jobs for audiologists according to the U.S. Department of Labor. Most of those jobs were in hospitals, clinics, health care centers, physicians' offices, and outpatient care centers. Approximately one in seven jobs was in educational services, such as elementary and secondary schools.

Most audiologists work full-time and some cover weekend and evening hours to meet the needs of patients. Those who work in educational settings usually work an academic calendar year.

Salaries for those working in educational services were somewhat lower than for other audiologists. The educational median salary in 2004 was $53,000, and for others it was $56,000, according to a survey by the American Speech-Language-Hearing Association.

The U.S. Department of Labor reports salaries ranging from $34,990 to $75,990.

Career Potential and Additional Information

Many hearing, balance, and neural ear problems are related to aging, and as the population ages, the need for audiologists will continue to grow. Growth is expected to continue at a rate faster than the average for all occupations through 2014.

Educational systems are bound by federal law to provide access to special education and services for qualified students with disabilities. This will ensure a need for audiologists in the education system.

If you are interested in finding out more about careers in audiology, contact the American Speech-Language-Hearing Association. Their Web site is *www.asha.org*. Their address is 10801 Rockville Pike, Rockville, MD 20852.

Chapter 10

Assistants and Aides

This group of hardworking professionals carries the bulk of the direct hands-on care under the supervision of the nurses, dental hygienists, therapists, and pharmacists. The nursing aides perform bedside care, the dental assistants perform office and some chair-side care, the pharmacy techs count out the pills to fill prescriptions and assist pharmacists with other delegated tasks, the therapy aides perform specific activities and exercises with the patients as directed by the therapist, and the surgical techs work in the operating room with the surgical nurses.

Nursing Aides, Home Health Aides, P.C.A.s, and U.A.P.s

Nursing aides work with patients of all ages in a variety of settings such as hospitals, skilled-nursing facilities, residential facilities for the disabled, senior residential homes, patients' homes, and mental health facilities. Home health aides work with patients in their home on an intermittent basis; C.N.A.s (certified nursing assistants) who work in patients' homes are usually hired on an hourly basis and perform some housekeeping duties as well as patient care. P.C.A.s (patient care assistants) are C.N.A.s who have been given additional training by employers to assume more responsibilities in a specific facility. There is another group known as UAP (unlicensed assistive personnel) who receive on-the-job training (usually in hospitals or skilled-nursing facilities) to perform nursing-aide tasks. They are not licensed or certified. In some inpatient facilities, male nursing aides may also still be known as orderlies. (This term has its origin in the military and referred to a soldier assigned as an assistant to a military officer.) Orderlies typically help lift, transfer, and transport patients.

They also prepare patients for surgery by shaving the operative area, inserting catheters, and giving enemas.

Duties, Activities, and Scope of Practice

Nursing aides work primarily in facilities or patients' homes to assist with tasks such as answering call lights. They take vital signs, bathe patients, make beds, and assist with dressing and grooming, and transferring or walking. In some instances, they may change simple dressings (superficial wounds), insert catheters, suction tracheostomies utilizing clean-technique (a non-sterile technique that includes meticulous hand washing, clean gloves, and a clean environment; not used for treating surgical wounds and burns), assist with tube feedings, or remind patients (at home) to take medications.

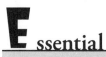

Nursing aides report to the supervising nurse any significant changes in condition or other statistics as directed by the nurse. Aides are not allowed to reassign duties or patients to another aide; they are not allowed to delegate. Only R.N.s can delegate and assign duties.

In facilities such as skilled-nursing homes, the C.N.A.s are the primary caregivers, and if family members are scarce, they may be the main contact that the residents have for long periods of time.

The types of duties aides typically perform meet these criteria:

- Constitute routine care for the patient
- Pose little or no hazard for the patient
- Have a predictable outcome
- Are similar from one patient to another
- Don't require the aides to assess, interpret, or make decisions

Education and Training

Nursing aides complete a program of seventy-fives hours of training in both classroom and clinical supervised care. They may then take a competency exam to obtain certification. Home health aides have additional training of up to seventy-five hours of classroom and clinical supervised care. They also take an additional competency exam. U.A.P.s are trained on the job. P.C.A.s are usually, but not always, trained on the job. C.N.A.s receive some additional on-the-job training in areas such as phlebotomy.

Licensure/Certification

Upon the completion of the nursing aide training, the aide is eligible to take a written and skills competency test to become certified. Then they are placed on the state's registry of nurses' aides. Home health aides complete a written and skills competency exam in twelve areas, including communication skills, documentation skills, taking and recording vital signs, basic nutrition, basic bodily functions, basic infection control, range of motion, and basics involving maintaining a hygienic environment in the home setting. The National Association of Home Care offers national certification for home health aides. P.C.A.s are usually C.N.A.s with additional training. U.A.P.s are not certified. None of the workers in this category are licensed.

Work Settings and Salaries

Nursing aides work in hospitals, skilled-nursing facilities, residential care facilities, and in patients' homes. Home health aides are specifically trained to assist patients at home, although they may also work as a C.N.A. in other facilities.

Many facilities rely on nursing aides to assume more responsibilities for patients in their creative attempts to improve working conditions for R.N.s in light of the nursing shortage. This is a physically and emotionally demanding job.

The median hourly income for C.N.A.s as reported by the U.S. Department of Labor for 2004 was $10.09. Hourly wages ranged from $7.31 to $14.02. Home health aides are usually said to earn slightly more, but the median hourly income in 2004 was reported to be

$8.81. Salaries were reported to be between $6.52 and $12.32 per hour. They are paid for the time spent in each patient's home. This may or may not include an allowance for mileage, but they are not paid for travel time from patient to patient.

Career Potential and Additional Information

Excellent opportunities will continue to exist in this field because of the increasing need posed by an aging population and the need to replace aides who have moved up the career ladder.

This is an entry-level position, and opportunities for advancement are limited. Home health aide positions are expected to grow faster than for C.N.A.s, P.C.A.s, and U.A.P.s due to an aging population requiring more assistance at home.

To find out more about nursing aide positions, contact your state board of nursing. You can locate your state board's information from the National Council of State Boards of Nursing. Their Web site is *www.ncsbn.org*.

For more information about becoming a home health aide, contact the National Association for Home Care (NAHC). Their Web site is *www.nahc.org*. Their address is 228 Seventh Street, SE, Washington, DC 20003.

Dental Assistants

The principal activity of the dental assistant is to assist the dentist in the care of patients. They differ from dental hygienists in that they do not perform teeth cleaning or other dental hygiene activities. Dental assistants perform a variety of duties involving direct patient and chairside care. They also perform laboratory and general office tasks.

Duties, Activities, and Scope of Practice

In the course of a day the dental assistant's duties may include any number of tasks related to direct patient care, such as retrieving records, making the patient comfortable in the chair, preparing the instruments the dentist will need for this patient, cleaning and sterilizing the equipment, taking and developing x-rays, handing instruments to the dentist during a procedure, suctioning the patient's mouth, preparing materials, and taking impressions of teeth and restorations.

 Fact

Dental assistants may make casts of the teeth and mouth from the impressions and make temporary crowns. They can clean and polish removable appliances. Office duties usually include making and confirming appointments, keeping dental records, ordering equipment, and possibly even sending out bills and receiving payments.

Education and Training

Most dental assistants now receive training from dental assistant programs at vocational schools, dental schools, and community colleges. However, some receive on-the-job training in the dentist's office. Formal training programs usually run about eleven months. Graduates receive a certificate or diploma. Community college programs are two years and offer an associate's degree. Some schools do offer accelerated programs, but most of these are not yet accredited. There are currently 265 accredited programs for dental assistants throughout the United States.

To enter a dental-assisting program, applicants must have a high school diploma or equivalent, and many programs require applicants to have taken courses in biology, chemistry, health, and use of computers. Office practice courses are also helpful.

The curriculum consists of laboratory and classroom education in biomedical sciences and dental-assisting theory, as well as clinical experience in dental-assisting skills and procedures.

Licensure/Certification

Most states regulate dental assistants and their duties and require licensing or registration. To become licensed or registered, the applicant must have completed an accredited program or have completed two years' experience as a dental assistant. They are then given either a written or practical exam depending upon the state's requirement.

Some states require additional education and licensing exams in areas such as radiology in order to take x-rays. A certification through the Dental Assisting National Board (DANB) is offered to those who have graduated from an accredited program or who have two years of experience as a dental assistant and then pass the certification exam. Thirty states recognize this certification. Annual recertification is necessary and requires continuing education.

Work Settings and Salaries

Dental assistants work in dental offices and clinics. Their work is generally performed chair-side or in the office setting. Most work thirty-five to forty hours per week, which may include some evenings or weekends as dentists flex their own schedules to meet the needs of their patients.

The median hourly salary in 2004 was $13.62, according to the U.S. Department of Labor. Salaries ranged from $9.11 to $19.97 per hour, and depend on the duties, qualifications, and experience.

Career Potential and Additional Information

This is an entry-level position and is often used as a stepping stone for those who want to become dental hygienists. Those who wish to advance often become office managers, move into teaching dental assisting, or work as sales representatives for dental supply companies.

As with most health care fields, the emphasis on preventative care is creating more of a demand for dental care. As technological advancements provide dentists with better tools for treating their patients, the need to delegate some of their responsibilities also creates a demand for dental assistants. An aging population adds to the need as well.

For more information on a career as a dental assistant, contact the American Dental Assistants Association. Their Web site is *www.dentalassistant.org.* Their address is 35 East Wacker Drive, Suite 1730, Chicago, IL 60601.

Therapy Aides and Assistants

Physical therapy assistants (P.T.A.s) and occupational therapy assistants (C.O.T.A.s) assist the therapists with treatments and exercises designed to improve the quality of life for patients who have experienced debilitating illnesses or injury or the effects of aging in general.

PT aides and O.T. aides generally assist with preparing the area for the treatment, keep therapy sites clean, perform office duties such as scheduling appointments, and assist patients to and from the therapy area. They can push patients in wheelchairs or provide assistance ambulating. They are not licensed or certified and are prohibited from performing any clinical tasks.

Duties, Activities, and Scope of Practice

P.T.A.s can administer massage, exercises, electrical stimulation, ultrasound therapy, paraffin baths, hot and cold packs, and traction. They perform these tasks under the direction and supervision of the physical therapist. They will also record the patient's response to these treatments and report the outcome to the therapist.

C.O.T.A.s work with occupational therapists to deliver a plan of care to help rehabilitate patients with physical, mental, and emotional issues. This will help patients to increase their independence in activities of daily living. C.O.T.A.s help to adapt devices and instruct patients in the adaptation of activities to meet their needs and improve their outcomes in working toward independent living. They teach patients how to transfer, how to stretch and limber their muscles, and how to conserve energy. And they ensure that the activities and exercises are being done correctly.

Education and Training

PT and O.T. aide positions are unlicensed and are usually on-the-job training positions. However, some more formal programs are being developed and run through adult schools and vocational schools. Most schools and employers require a high school diploma or equivalent.

To become a PTA or COTA requires an associate's degree from a community college. These are two-year programs, and typically the curriculum consists of math, biomedical sciences, and general-education courses the first year, and theoretical and clinical therapy courses the second year. The clinical courses are, of course, conducted under the direct supervision of a licensed therapist.

E ssential

Application to PTA or COTA programs is highly competitive, and applicants can improve their chances of acceptance by having completed algebra, biology, and chemistry courses in high school, as well as by accumulating volunteer work hours in the hospital, skilled-nursing facility, or therapy site.

Licensure/Certification

Upon graduation from an accredited school, the O.T. assistant can sit for the national certification exam from the American Occupational Therapy Certification Board and become certified. Most states regulate C.O.T.A.s, and they recognize this exam and certification process.

Not all states require licensing of P.T.A.s. Those that do have specific requirements that are available from the PT licensing board in each state.

Work Settings and Salaries

P.T.A.s and C.O.T.A.s are generally employed in hospital or skilled-nursing facilities or outpatient clinics or offices. Inpatient facilities generally utilize therapy services during the day shift and will often include weekends and holidays. Outpatient facilities quite often offer evening and weekend hours in addition to the normal eight-to-five schedule. Therefore these assistants may work a flexible schedule.

The median salary for P.T.A.s in 2004 was $37,890, and salaries ranged from $24,110 to $52,110 according to figures from the U.S. Department of Labor. For C.O.T.A.s, the median salary in 2004 was $38,430, and salaries ranged from $25,880 to $52,700.

PT and O.T. aides usually work in outpatient therapy facilities under the direct supervision of therapists. The PT aide salary ranged from $15,380 to $33,550 in 2004, with a median salary of $21,380. The O.T. aide salary ranged from $15,820 to $41,560, with a median salary of $23,150. Again, these are figures for 2004 as released by the U.S. Department of Labor.

Career Potential and Additional Information

The opportunity for these aides and assistants is expected to grow much faster than the average for all occupations through 2014. The aging population and the development of new technologies that save the lives of those who have suffered birth defects or debilitating illnesses and injuries will set the stage for a tremendous need for these workers.

As responsibilities trickle down from the primary practitioners to the therapists, so will the responsibilities of the therapists. This serves to maximize the efforts of all members of the health team in improving and maintaining the health care status of Americans over the next decade.

For more information on C.O.T.A.s and O.T. aides, contact the American Occupational Therapy Association. Their Web site is *www.aota.org*. Their address is 4720 Montgomery Lane, Bethesda, MD 20824-1220.

Information about P.T.A.s and physical therapy aides can be obtained from the American P.T. Association. Their Web site is *www .apta.org*. Their address is 1111 North Fairfax Street, Alexandria, VA 22314-1488.

Psychiatric Aides and Mental Health Assistants

Psychiatric aides or mental health assistants are nursing assistants who specialize in mental health and work with the mentally impaired or emotionally disturbed patients. This can mean working with adults in mental health wards or rehabilitation facilities for substance or alcohol abuse, or working with children with conditions such as autism or mental retardation.

Duties, Activities, and Scope of Practice

Psychiatric aides perform nursing aide duties such as bathing, grooming, and dressing patients, but they also participate with patients in socialization activities and interactions that provide both educational as well as recreational activities. They play cards or games, watch TV, and participate in group activities.

Psychiatric aides work closely with their patients and must be alert to potential violent outbursts and understand how to react to protect not only themselves but the patient and others as well. The patients are often uncooperative, disoriented, and even irritable or angry. Sometimes these patients are combative. This is especially true of children with emotional disturbances.

Psychiatric aides accompany patients on field trips and escort them to and from treatments and exams. The aides also observe the patients for behavioral outbursts or physical or emotional changes that are important for the staff of nurses, psychiatrists, and other mental health care team members to be aware of.

Education and Training

Psychiatric aides are first trained as nursing aides. Some states require additional training specifically in dealing with mental illness and behavioral issues. This is usually obtained on the job and is specific to the age group and/or types of mental or behavioral illnesses with which they work. Some vocational schools or adult education programs may offer formal psychiatric aide training. Mental health hospitals may also offer formal training.

Licensure/Certification

These health care workers are not licensed. Upon completion of their nursing-aide training they can sit for the certification exam that tests both written and practical areas.

Work Settings and Salaries

Psychiatric aides work in mental health settings, which can include hospitals, skilled-care facilities, rehab facilities for substance abuse, residential care facilities, and even prisons or other detention facilities such as Youth Authority. These are usually operated on twenty-four-hour schedules and require coverage for all shifts, including weekends and holidays.

The median hourly salary in 2004 as reported by the U.S. Department of Labor was $11.19. Salaries ranged from $7.63 to $16.74 per hour.

Career Potential and Additional Information

This profession is expected to grow at least as fast as the average for all occupations. As the population ages, there will also be an increased need for mental health services for the elderly.

It is an entry-level position and one that is both physically and emotionally demanding. The need for replacements will continue to present job opportunities. For some, this is a stepping stone to other more advanced opportunities in the field of mental health, such as nursing, psychology, and psychiatry.

There is no specific organization for psychiatric aides and mental health assistants. For more information about psychiatric aide positions, contact the American Psychiatric Association. Their Web site is *www.psych.org*. Their address is 1000 Wilson Boulevard, Suite 1825, Arlington, VA 22209-3901. Or contact the American Psychiatric Nurses Association. Their Web site is *www.apna.org*. Their address is 1555 Wilson Boulevard, Suite 602, Arlington, VA 22209.

Surgical Technologists

Surgical technologists are also known as Scrub techs, OR (operating) techs, and OR specialists. They assist in surgery under the supervision of the surgical nurses, surgeons, or other surgical professionals. Surgical techs are not nurses.

Duties, Activities, and Scope of Practice

The surgical tech participates in many activities involving the surgical process. They assist with prepping patients by performing duties such as washing and shaving the incision site and transporting the patient to the OR. They assist patients in transfer to the operating table and drape them appropriately for the surgery. They lay out the sterile trays of instruments for the surgeons. The set up and check out the equipment and all drapes, tools, and solutions that will be needed for the surgery.

They help the surgical team (the circulating nurses, surgeons, and anesthesiologists) during surgery by passing instruments, holding retractors, and counting sponges, needles, instruments, and supplies. They may also cut sutures and apply dressings.

After surgery they help to transport and transfer patients to the recovery room. Then they help clean and restock the surgical suite.

Education and Training

Surgical tech programs last from nine to twenty-four months and are offered by vocational schools, the military, hospitals, community colleges, and universities. There are now over 400 accredited programs that lead to either a certificate, diploma, or associate's degree. The programs are accredited by CAAHEP (the Commission on Accreditation of Allied Health Education Programs).

The curriculum includes both classroom and clinical experience. The classroom courses include anatomy and physiology, microbiology, pharmacology, and medical terminology. Students learn to sterilize instruments, prepare and utilize specialized equipment, and how to handle solutions, supplies, and special drugs used in surgery. They learn about infection control measures, standard precautions, and how to maintain a sterile environment (asepsis).

Licensure/Certification

Most employers prefer certification. Voluntary certification can be achieved in two ways. Graduates of accredited programs can sit for a national certification exam from either the Liaison Council on Certification for the Surgical Technologist or the National Center for Competency Testing. The former provides the title C.S.T. (certified surgical technologist), which must be renewed every four years by meeting continuing-education requirements. The latter is a TS-C (Tech in Surgery-Certified) and is renewed every five years by either continuing education or re-examination.

Work Settings and Salaries

Most surgical techs work forty hours a week and have some on-call responsibility. Their routine shifts may include evening and weekend hours. Surgical techs stand for long hours and must remain alert at all times during surgery. The median salary for 2004 according to the U.S. Department of Labor was $34,010. Salaries typically ranged from $23,940 to $45,990.

 Fact

About 70 percent of the 84,000 surgical technologists working in 2004 worked in hospitals. They mostly worked in operating rooms or delivery rooms. Others worked for outpatient surgical centers or for physicians or dentists who perform outpatient surgery in their offices.

Career Potential and Additional Information

The number of surgical procedures is expected to rise as the population ages and grows, and therefore the potential for employment for surgical techs is expected to grow faster than the average for all occupations through 2014. Hospitals will continue to be the primary employer.

Surgical techs have opportunities to specialize in certain areas, such as cardiovascular or neurological surgeries. They can also seek additional education and training and advance to roles such as surgical first assistant, who provides additional care and duties under the supervision of the surgeon, like suctioning, cauterizing, and closing wounds.

Surgical techs can advance up the hierarchy of surgical technologists and become supervisors or managers, or move into central supply or medical sales.

For more information about becoming a surgical tech, contact the Association of Surgical Technologists. Their Web site is *www.ast. org.* Their address is 6 West Dry Creek Circle, Littleton, CO 80120.

Pharmacy Technologists

Depending on various state rules and regulations, pharmacy technologists perform a variety of duties under the direct supervision of a registered pharmacist. They assist the registered pharmacist with filling prescriptions and labeling bottles so that the pharmacist has more time to spend with patients, consulting with physicians, and overseeing patient medication profiles.

Duties, Activities, and Scope of Practice

Pharmacy techs typically receive written and faxed prescriptions from practitioners and refill requests from patients. They prepare the prescriptions through the various methods required such as weighing, measuring, counting, or even mixing compounds. They fill and label the appropriate bottles or containers and give them to the registered pharmacist to check before giving them to the patient. They also price and file the prescriptions.

Sometimes the pharmacy tech is involved in delivering the prescriptions either to retail customers or to nursing stations in hospitals and facilities. In mail-order pharmacies they may be involved in preparing the prescriptions and packages for mailing after the pharmacist has checked the prescription.

Pharmacy techs also read patient charts in facilities and update patients' medication profiles.

They may prepare insurance forms, and stock and order prescription as well as over-the-counter items for the pharmacy. In a retail pharmacy they might also be expected to work with displays and patient education materials.

Education and Training

Many pharmacy technicians begin as pharmacy aides and learn this position on the job. However, formal education programs and certification are becoming more the norm. Programs are available through community colleges, vocational schools, the military, and some hospitals.

The curriculum includes classroom and laboratory work in subjects such as medical and pharmaceutical terminology, pharmaceutical math calculations, pharmacy recordkeeping, techniques, and ethics and laws. Students also learn about pharmacology, including medication names, actions, doses, and side effects. They must have strong English, reading, math, and spelling skills. Some programs offer internships.

Depending on the program, students earn a diploma, certificate, or associate's degree.

Licensure/Certification

The Pharmacy Technician Certification Board administers the National Pharmacy Technician Certificate Exam. At present it is strictly voluntary; however, many states as well as employers are beginning to require certification for pharmacy techs.

Candidates have to have a high school diploma or GED and have no felony convictions.

Certified pharmacy techs must renew every two years by completing twenty hours of continuing education, which must include at least one hour of pharmacy law.

Almost all fifty states have legislation governing the number of techs who can work under one pharmacist.

Work Settings and Salaries

In 2004, pharmacy techs held 258,000 jobs. Two-thirds of these jobs were in retail pharmacies. Others worked for hospitals, mail-order or Internet pharmacies, clinics, or the federal government.

Pharmacy techs work the same hours as pharmacists. Many pharmacies are open twenty-four hours or have on-call hours, so pharmacy techs could work shifts to cover evenings, weekends, and holidays to meet the needs of the patients.

The U.S. Department of Labor reports the median hourly wage for pharmacy techs in 2004 was $11.37. Wages ranged from $7.96 to $16.61 per hour.

Career Potential and Additional Information

This profession is expected to continue to grow faster than the average for all occupations through 2014 due to an aging and growing population that will require more medications in the future.

Further information about pharmacy tech positions can be obtained from two sources. The Pharmacy Technician Certification Board Web site is *www.ptcb.org*. Their address is 1100 15th Street, NW, Suite 730, Washington, DC 20005-1707.

The American Society of Health-System Pharmacists provides a list of accredited programs. Their Web site is *www.ashp.org*. Their address is 7272 Wisconsin Avenue, Bethesda, MD 20814.

Chapter 11

Other Therapists

Nontraditional therapists help patients adapt and adjust to physical, mental, and emotional changes that are the result of illness or injury. They also deal with issues such as pain, limited mobility, and losses. Many of these therapies also open avenues of communication for patients who are unable to effectively communicate in a verbal manner. Nontraditional therapists work with traditional practitioners and therapists to offer the patient a well-rounded approach to healing.

Art Therapists

Art therapists combine their artistic education with psychology to provide a medium for patients to express their emotions through a variety of arts-and-crafts activities and expose underlying problems to help heal the soul as well as the body.

Art therapists work with individuals, families, groups, and even whole communities if necessary to help them cope with illness, injury, trauma, abuse, or emotional disturbances.

Duties, Activities, and Scope of Practice

The highest concentration of art therapists in the United States is in the northeast section of the country. After 9/11, many art therapists were called in to help New Yorkers express their emotions and learn to cope with the tragedy and to heal.

Activities designed by art therapists stimulate socialization, encourage patients to express themselves, and help them to improve self-image as well as gain a sense of satisfaction and relaxation. Art therapy is useful for stress management and in helping patients improve their self-esteem.

Art therapists often work with psychiatrists, psychologists, and other health care team members to diagnose and develop a plan for the improved health status of the patient. Most of their patients are emotionally disturbed. Some are coping with physical changes, and others have mental disabilities or physical conditions that cause extreme stress such as cancer, asthma, HIV/AIDS, and post-traumatic stress syndrome.

 Fact

None of these nontraditional therapies is new. Most have been around for centuries, but in terms of being reimbursed by insurance and Medicare or Medicaid, they are relatively new. As such they offer exciting opportunities, but wait to be fully recognized.

Art-and-craft activities include drawing, painting, sculpting, and modeling. The therapist observes the patient during the creative process and then analyzes the finished product for clues as to behavioral issues hidden in the details, the colors, the proportions, and the aesthetic quality of the work. Art therapists also work in school settings with children who are emotionally disturbed to help them adapt and mainstream.

Education and Training

A master's degree is generally needed in this field. Undergraduate work should be done in commercial art, creative art, or art education. Behavioral and social science courses are also quite helpful at this level and are expanded on in the master's program. An art portfolio is a good idea.

The AATA (American Art Therapy Association) has accredited twenty-four graduate-level programs in the United States. The specific curriculum and exact degree name vary from one to another.

Licensure/Certification

The AATA offers registration and board certification to candidates who have graduated from an accredited program and provide the necessary credentialing materials to the board. These include a portfolio of slides or other electronic media showing artwork that meets quality standards, several letters of recommendation, and completion of the necessary internship and paid work experience.

The AATA assigns PCQs (professional quality credits) to each of the above categories, and when a candidate has acquired twelve PCQs they can become registered. Recertification is required every five years and requires 100 units of continuing education.

Work Settings and Salaries

Art therapists work with adults and adolescents or children on an equal basis. The largest numbers of therapists work in psychiatric hospitals in both long- and short-term facilities. Others work in schools, community mental health centers, skilled-nursing facilities, hospitals, substance abuse rehab facilities, and psychiatric clinics.

Full- and part-time opportunities are available. There are about 2,000 registered art therapists employed in the United States today, and about 3,000 more who have not achieved registration status.

Salaries vary depending on experience and credentials. The median income is approximately $28,000 annually, and the range of salaries is from $25,000 to $65,000 per year. Art therapists who have a doctoral degree can earn as much as $150 per hour.

Career Potential and Additional Information

It has taken awhile for this treatment to be recognized. In 1992, art therapy, music therapy, and dance therapy were all recognized in legislation that amended the Older Americans Act. This has opened doors to research and grant monies for expansion of these fields.

The growth of this field is expected to continue as the population increases and ages, and as new needs for alternative therapies arise.

Contact the Art Therapy Credentials Board for further information about the education and training necessary to become an art therapist. Their Web site is *www.atcb.org*. Their address is 3 Terrace Way, Suite B, Greensboro, NC 27403.

You can contact the American Art Therapy Association through their Web site at *www.arttherapy.org*. Their address is 5999 Stevenson Avenue, Alexandria, VA 22304.

Dance Therapists

To understand dance therapy, it is necessary to grasp the concept that the mind and body interact constantly. The mind and body both register pleasure and pain. Dance movements can express pain, anxiety, and depression involuntarily and help to diagnose physical and emotional conditions.

Dance movement usually makes a person feel happy and energized because it provides a diversion and keeps the person from dwelling on worries or physical ailments or pain. Emotional well-being is re-established. The purpose of dance therapy is to help restore emotional and physical health.

Duties, Activities, and Scope of Practice

Dance therapists are trained in dance as well as psychology. They are trained to observe and "read" a person's emotional and physical symptoms through their movements. They teach patients how to move to express their feelings and to improve their physical and emotional status.

E ssential

Patients of all ages can benefit from dance therapy. Children with emotional issues as well as physical coordination and even brain-damage issues can learn to communicate and express their feelings through the safety of repetitive movements. They can also learn to improve their balance and coordination through dance.

Adolescents and adults can learn to express their emotions and physical symptoms through dance movements, and work to improve their physical and emotional status. Many mental illnesses such as schizophrenia, psychotic depression, and personality disorders are diagnosed and effectively treated through dance therapy, in addition to traditional medical care.

Education and Training

To practice as a dance therapist, a master's degree is required. Undergraduate work should be done in dance and psychology. The master's curriculum focuses on psychopathology, kinesiology, human development, and movement observation, as well as dance and movement theory and practice. Choreography, improvisation, and teaching dance to children and adults is also recommended.

There are only about fifteen programs that offer a master's degree in dance therapy, and each awards a slightly different degree.

Licensure/Certification

The American Dance Therapy Association has established criteria for registration of dance therapists at two different levels. The first is the D.T.R. (dance therapist registered), which requires a master's degree that includes 700 hours of supervised clinical internship. The second is an A.D.T.R. (advanced dance therapist registered) for therapists who have met advanced criteria, including 3,600 hours of supervised clinical internship. This therapist is deemed fully qualified to teach or supervise dance therapists and to work in private practice.

Registration is not required, but it is quickly becoming the recognized standard, and it does open more doors to employment possibilities.

Work Settings and Salaries

This is a relatively new profession and has yet to be widely recognized. Therefore most dance therapists today work in large metropolitan locations. They usually work in psychiatric hospitals, both long- and short-term, residential care facilities, nursing homes, and psychiatric clinics and offices.

Data on salaries is limited, but the range appears to be from $27,000 to $65,000, depending on experience and training. Those with advanced training and registration will earn more.

Career Potential and Additional Information

This is a limited field at present and openings are not plentiful. As the field becomes more widely recognized for its work with emotionally disturbed individuals, the economy may well influence the promotion of this profession. Multitudes of Americans live on the streets or in mental health facilities due to emotional disorders, which could be helped through dance therapy.

As with art therapy, dance therapy was recognized in the legislation to amend the Older Americans Act in 1992. This has opened opportunities for research and grants for dance therapy. Several significant studies have been financed since then to successfully prove the effectiveness of dance therapy with patients who have experienced a head injury.

For more information, contact the American Dance Therapy Association (ADTA). Their Web site is *www.adta.org*. Their address is 2000 Century Plaza, Suite 108, 10632 Little Patuxent Parkway, Columbia, MD 21044-3263.

Music Therapists

Another of the up and coming nontraditional therapies is music therapy. Music has long been known for its soothing capacities, but recognition of its full potential as a therapy has yet to come. Research has shown that listening to music can reduce blood pressure, help individuals control anger, and improve attention span.

Mood changes affected by music represent the basis of music therapy.

Duties, Activities, and Scope of Practice

Music therapists work with individuals or groups to help restore and improve their physical and emotional well-being. The music can be instrumental, vocal, or a combination of both. Therapists use techniques such as biofeedback, relaxation, anger management, and stress reduction. They incorporate appropriate music to achieve the desired effects.

Fact

Music therapists can combine their therapy with other kinds, such as dance or art therapy, to help maximize the results. They teach patients to sing and to listen to music, and may even teach them how to play a musical instrument in order to incorporate the music into the treatment.

Patients of all ages can benefit from music therapy. Babies are soothed to sleep with lullabies, for example. Depression can be treated with music designed to be upbeat and engaging. The elderly can be encouraged to get up and move through music. Those with disabilities and brain injuries or illnesses affecting the neurological system, such as Alzheimer's, respond to music therapy.

Education and Training

Music therapy requires a college degree, and it is moving in the direction of requiring a master's degree, although few schools currently offer this program. The curriculum includes a bachelor's degree in music theory and courses in music therapy and behavioral sciences, as well as health and natural sciences.

Music therapy courses include both classroom theory as well as clinical application of the theory in combination with the behavior techniques learned in the study of behavioral and heath sciences, including psychology. For those who wish to work in public schools, courses in education are also required.

Licensure/Certification

Licensure is not required at this time. Certification and registration options are available to qualified candidates who complete the required internships and pass national exams. The Certification Board of Music Therapists bestows the MT-BC certification on those who demonstrate proficient entry-level skills. The certification must be renewed every five years either through 100 units of continuing education or re-examination.

The National Music Registry is a separate entity that bestows certification and registration credentials on qualified candidates who meet education requirements and demonstrate proficiency in the field.

Work Settings and Salaries

Music therapists work in a variety of settings including public schools, hospices, hospitals (general and psychiatric), residential care facilities, skilled-nursing facilities, and rehabilitation facilities.

According to the American Music Therapy Association, starting salaries in 2004 ranged from $23,000 to $28,000. Salaries for experienced music therapists averaged $32,000 per year.

Career Potential and Additional Information

Success in working with the elderly as well as with special-education children has sparked an interest in music therapy. As the population ages and increases and Americans turn to more alternative healing approaches, the field of music therapy will continue to grow. Currently there are about 5,200 music therapists in the United States. Grant and research monies that have come about through legislation to amend the Older Americans Act have also affected the popularity of this up and coming profession.

Contact the American Music Therapy Association for more information on this health care profession. Their Web site is *www .musictherapy.org*. Their address is 8455 Colesville Road, Suite 1000, Silver Spring, MD 20910-3392.

Recreation Therapists

Recreation therapists are also known as therapeutic recreation specialists. This group of professionals works with individuals and groups to improve their emotional, mental, and physical health through medically approved activities. These activities include arts and crafts, music, drama, dance, sports, and games. Community outings and field trips are also part of this form of therapy.

Duties, Activities, and Scope of Practice

Recreation therapists work with patients who have mental, physical, and/or emotional disabilities from illness and injury. Their focus is to improve their patients' health status and quality of life, to promote independence, and to help patients achieve a lifestyle that improves their sense of self-worth. These goals are achieved through the fun and excitement of social interventions that are tailored to the immediate and long-term needs of each individual.

E ssential

A recreation therapist observes the patient and works with the health care team members to assess the patient's needs. He then individualizes the interventions to meet the immediate and long-range needs of the patient.

Recreation therapists use techniques of arts and crafts, sports, games, and so on to help patients learn to adapt to their limitations. These limitations may be imposed by an illness or injury, such as a stroke that has left the patient paralyzed on his dominant side. In this instance, the therapist would teach the patient to use his nondominant hand to perform tasks. Patients who need socialization are encouraged to play group games and sports.

For relaxation or stress management, the therapist would utilize stretching and limbering activities.

Education and Training

Entry-level positions in this field require a bachelor's degree in therapeutic recreation, or recreation with an emphasis on therapeutic recreation. There are approximately 140 bachelor's degree programs available to prepare students to become recreation therapists. Some schools also offer master's and doctoral degrees.

The curriculum includes anatomy and physiology, abnormal psychology, medical terminology (including psychiatric terminology), assessment, treatment, and program planning. It also includes courses in professional ethics, the use of adaptive equipment, technology and devices, and the characteristics of disabilities and illness. The programs also include supervised clinical experience, usually in a hospital setting.

Licensure/Certification

Most employers prefer to hire certified recreation therapists. The National Council for Therapeutic Recreation Certification offers certification to candidates who have a bachelor's degree, complete 480 hours of internship, and pass a written competency examination.

The American Association of Rehabilitation Therapy offers registration to recreation therapists who are members of their organization, have worked for two years in a health care facility as a therapist, and submit college transcripts and two letters of recommendation.

Work Settings and Salaries

In 2004, there were 24,000 jobs for recreation therapists. About two-thirds of the jobs were in hospitals or nursing facilities. The rest were in residential care facilities, substance abuse facilities, juvenile detention facilities, prisons, assisted living and residential care facilities for seniors, and mental health facilities.

Most therapists work full-time and may work weekends and holidays to meet the needs of the patients. In 2004, salaries ranged from $20,130 to $51,800, and the median salary was $32,900 according to figures from the U.S. Department of Labor.

Career Potential and Additional Information

This profession is relatively new and is expected to grow more slowly than the average for all occupations. The shift away from inpatient care and toward outpatient care will be a factor as well. More than two-thirds of the therapists working in 2004 worked for inpatient facilities looking to contain costs and reduce services, such as hospitals.

Fact

As more outpatient facilities, such as adult day care and short-term mental health facilities, begin to see the positive effects of using recreation therapists, this portion of the profession will begin to grow along with the population.

For more information on a career as a recreation therapist contact the American Therapeutic Recreation Association. Their Web site is *www.atra-tr.org*. Their address is 1414 Prince Street, Suite 204, Alexandria, VA 22314-2853.

Horticulture Therapists

Horticulture therapists use the beauty of nature and the process of planting seeds, nurturing the plants, and reaping the benefits from the final products to help build patients' confidence, improve their self-esteem and attitudes, encourage sociability and communication, improve problem-solving and motor skills, and give them a sense of accomplishment. This is the premise and foundation for horticulture therapy. In 1879, the Pennsylvania Friends Asylum for the Insane built the first greenhouse used for horticulture therapy.

Duties, Activities, and Scope of Practice

Horticulture therapists work with patients in a variety of settings such as hospitals, rehabilitation centers, convalescent care centers, and mental health facilities. They are experts in the benefits of gardening for medical as well as psychological purposes. These therapists teach patients to plant seeds and care for and nurture plants, flowers, and shrubs. This gives the patient an opportunity to become the caregiver, to have a purpose and a renewed sense of ability.

The horticulture therapist assesses patients for their abilities, both physical and cognitive, and designs a program around their needs to improve their well-being and promote health. They tailor the program to the specific needs and abilities of the patient and continue to assess these as they progress toward the set goals.

Horticulture therapists work with individuals as well as groups to teach them new skills and abilities designed to help them realize their owl potential for independence and wellness.

Education and Training

A bachelor's degree in horticulture therapy is the present standard. Five schools in the United States offer this degree, and three of them also offer a master's degree. Kansas State University pioneered this field and now offers several of their courses online.

The curriculum for this degree includes agriculture and horticulture, as well as sociology, psychology, behavioral sciences, and horticulture therapy. Clinical internship is also included in the curriculum.

Question

How does horticulture therapy work?
Reaping the harvest of fruits, vegetables, and flowers and selling them for profit teaches skills and also provides a sense of purpose and ability. Enjoying the beauty of the flowers and the taste of the fruits and vegetables also helps to improve attitudes, reduce stress, and alleviate depression.

Some schools offer certificates and elective courses in horticulture therapy, but a bachelor's degree is not currently offered. A strong background in biology and some experience with landscaping or working in nurseries or greenhouses is recommended for students seeking a degree in horticulture therapy.

Licensure/Certification

There are no licensing laws for horticulture therapists. The American Horticultural Therapy Association (AHTA) offers two professional classifications for horticulture therapists. The H.T.R. (horticulture therapist registered) is a designation for therapists who hold a bachelor's degree in horticulture therapy and who have worked in the field for one year (2,000 hours). The H.T.M. (master horticulture therapist) is the designation given to therapists who have a master's degree in horticulture therapy and who have worked full-time in the field for four years (8,000 hours).

Work Settings and Salaries

Horticulture therapists work in a variety of settings, including general, rehabilitative, and psychiatric hospitals. They also work in special-education programs in public schools, juvenile detention facilities, prisons, residential care facilities for various disabilities as well as for seniors, substance abuse centers, and training centers for those with disabilities.

Salaries range from $28,000 to $35,000. A 2004 survey that included both full- and part-time horticultural therapists listed the average salary as $31,000.

Career Potential and Additional Information

Because this group of therapists does not work primarily in hospitals, the field should experience a rapid growth over the next decade. It is still a relatively new field and has proven to be quite effective in helping the elderly and the disabled.

Further information about this profession is available from the American Horticultural Therapy Association. Their Web site is *www.ahta.org*. Their address is 3570 East 12th Avenue, Suite 206, Denver, CO 80206.

Massage Therapists

Massage therapy is another of the nontraditional approaches to health care and wellness, but it has been around for centuries. Today, other practitioners such as nurses, nurse practitioners, and chiropractors have studied massage therapy and are incorporating the medical benefits of massage therapy into their practice.

Massage therapy can be used for pain relief and control, stress reduction, rehabilitation of sports and other injuries, and improving circulation, which helps to remove waste products from the body.

Duties, Activities, and Scope of Practice

There are over eighty different types of massage in which a therapist can specialize. Some of the most common are Swedish massage, deep-tissue massage, sports massage, reflexology, and acupressure. The type and length of massage depends on the needs and the physical condition of the patient.

Massage therapists work by appointment. Most massages are thirty minutes to one hour long. The patient or client is interviewed at the beginning of the session to determine his health status, medical history, and desired effects of the massage.

 Fact

Massage therapists use oils, lotions, and creams to rub the patient's muscles. The patient is covered with a sheet or blanket, and only the portion of the body being worked on is exposed. As the massage progresses, the therapist alters and adjusts the approach or concentration on specific areas to meet the needs of the client.

Education and Training

Education and certification laws vary from one state to another, and often within the state. In 2004, however, thirty-three states passed legislation to regulate massage therapy by requiring formal education and a certification exam. Check with your state and locality to determine requirements.

There are about 1,300 massage therapy schools and programs in the United States. Only about 300 are accredited, and if your state requires certification, you will most likely need to have attended an accredited program. The curriculum consists of anatomy and physiology, kinesiology, ethics, business and legal practice, pathology, and hands-on massage therapy techniques. Additional modalities may be taught in elective courses.

Licensure/Certification

Thirty-six states and the District of Columbia regulate massage therapy. Other states may regulate massage therapy through city or county governments. The National Certification Board for Therapeutic Massage and Bodywork (NCBTMB) offers nationally recognized certification. The basic requirements to sit for this test are to have graduated from an accredited program or a program that includes 500 hours of training. Proof of training is required if it is not from an accredited program. Their Web site is *www.ncbtmb.com*.

The credential has to be renewed every four years and requires 200 hours of massage and 48 credit hours of continuing education.

Work Settings and Salaries

The median hourly wage for 2004 as reported by the U.S. Department of Labor was $15.36, which includes gratuities. Wages ranged from $7.16 to $32.21 per hour, including gratuities. Gratuities for massage therapists working in hospitals or other clinical settings are not commonplace. Therapists who work in private practice or for health spas, hotels, and salons do make gratuities, and salaries can weigh heavily on the tips.

E ssential

Massage therapists can be found working in chiropractic centers, physicians' offices, and fitness and recreation centers. Due to the high physical demands of the job and the time needed between clients, massage therapists generally work fifteen to thirty hours per week, and this is considered to be full-time.

Career Potential and Additional Information

This field is expected to grow faster than the average for all occupations over the next decade. The benefits of massage therapy for an aging population will cause it to grow in popularity. Health care providers are just beginning to recognize the benefits of massage therapy to supplement and complement traditional therapies in the treatment of certain illnesses and injuries. Businesses are discovering the advantages of hiring massage therapists to provide in-house massages as an employee benefit.

To find out more about this profession, contact the American Massage Therapy Association. Their Web site is *www.amtamassage .org*. Their address is 500 Davis Street, Suite 900, Evanston, IL 60201.

Chapter 12
Adjunct Team Members

This group of health care workers provides a set of services necessary to help in the process of diagnostics and running of medical offices and clinics. They are involved both directly and indirectly in the day-to-day care that helps improve the quality of life and outcomes for the patients.

Phlebotomists

Phlebotomists are employed by clinical laboratories—either freestanding or as part of a clinic, hospital, or other health care facility. They draw blood samples from patients either by venipuncture or by finger stick according to the type of sample needed for specific diagnostic tests.

Duties, Activities, and Scope of Practice

The phlebotomist receives and reads the order from the practitioner and assembles the needed equipment to obtain the specific blood sample from the patient. Patients can be all ages, from newborns to the elderly. Not all veins are created equal, and some require a great deal of patience and skill to draw from. Some patients are less likely to be cooperative, such as babies or small children, and this requires the phlebotomist to be skilled as well as patient.

After samples are drawn, the phlebotomist carefully labels the samples with all necessary patient identifying information and delivers the blood samples to the laboratory to run the ordered tests.

Education and Training

A high school diploma or GED is required. Phlebotomists can be trained on the job or through programs at community colleges or vocational schools. The curriculum includes anatomy and physiology, collection and handling of specimens, infection control and safety, quality assurance, professional standards and ethics, as well as supervised hands-on experience in drawing samples from patients of all ages.

Currently the National Accrediting Agency for Clinical Laboratory Sciences (NAACLS) has accredited more than fifty phlebotomy courses. See their Web site for more information at *www.naacls.org*.

Licensure/Certification

Some states require licensing or registration, and some are changing their rules. This information will be available from your State Department of Health or occupational licensing boards. The National Credentialing Agency for Laboratory Personnel (NCP) offers certification to candidates who meet their criteria. More information is available from their Web site at *www.nca-info.org*. Periodic recertification is available to those who meet continuing education and employment criteria.

Work Settings and Salaries

Phlebotomists work in a variety of settings such as hospitals, clinics, physicians' offices, and commercial laboratories. Most work forty-hour weeks, but in some sites the schedules may include early morning, evening, weekend, and even on-call hours. In hospitals, twenty-four-hour coverage is usually available, meaning all shifts, including weekends and holidays, have to be covered by staff.

 Fact

The median hourly salary for 2004 according to the U.S. Department of Labor was $11.13 for hospital phlebotomists, $10.57 for those working in private clinics, and $10.50 for those who worked in physicians' offices. The current salary range is from $18,000 to $26,000 annually.

Career Potential and Additional Information

This position is an essential one, and therefore the continuing job outlook is good. In fact, this position may even grow faster than average for all occupations over the next decade. As the population ages, the chances of disease and illness increase, and this increases the need for essential medical personnel. This is an entry-level position and many phlebotomists use it as a steeping stone to other careers in laboratory work or other health care careers, so the need for replacements is ongoing.

For more information about careers in phlebotomy, contact the American Health Care Association. Their Web site is *www.ahca.org.* Their address is 1201 L Street NW, Washington, DC 20005.

Clinical Laboratory Technicians and Technologists

This group of professionals can be known by a variety of different terms, including clinical laboratory scientists, medical technologists, medical laboratory technicians and technologists, and medical scientists. They perform the laboratory tests that are crucial to the identification, diagnosis, and treatment of diseases.

Duties, Activities, and Scope of Practice

The technicians have lesser degrees and therefore perform at a lower level of responsibility and diagnostics than the technologists. The primary function of this group is to analyze blood and other bodily fluids, tissue samples, cultures, and cellular structure to identify bacteria, parasites, microorganisms, and disease. They also test for drug levels, count cells, and match blood samples for transfusions. This information is used in analyzing the success of treatments, the presence of disease, and the need for other treatments.

Technological advancements have allowed technicians and technologists to become more specialized and to spend more time analyzing data than in the precise process of such things as hand-counting components of cells.

Education and Training

Technicians typically have completed an associate's degree, and the technologists at least a bachelor's degree, in clinical or medical laboratory science. The curriculum includes biology, chemistry, and math, as well as theory and laboratory experience in hematology, immunology, microbiology, and clinical chemistry. The program also includes an internship in supervised clinical practice. There are approximately 275 accredited courses today. The National Accrediting Agency for Clinical Laboratory Sciences (NAACLS) oversees this accreditation.

Those who want to pursue an avenue of teaching or research need to have a master's degree.

Licensure/Certification

Many states require licensing, and this information is available from the State Department of Health or occupational licensing boards. Certification is available from several agencies. The oldest is the Board of Registry of the American Society for Clinical Pathology (ASCP), which has its own set of criteria for education and experience before a candidate can sit for the examinations. Their Web site is *www.ascp.org*.

Other agencies offering certification include the National Credentialing Agency for Laboratory Personnel (*www.nca-info. org*), and American Medical Technologists (*www.amt1.com*). The International Society for Clinical Laboratory Technology (ISCLT) no longer provides examinations.

Work Settings and Salaries

The U.S. Department of Labor reports that clinical laboratory technologists and technicians held more than 300,000 jobs in 2004, and more than half of these jobs were in hospitals. Others held jobs in physicians' offices, medical and diagnostic laboratories, ambulatory health care centers, and some in educational services.

The median salary for technologists in 2004 was $45,730, with salaries ranging from $32,240 to over $63,000. Technicians earned a median salary of $30,840 in 2004. Their salaries ranged from $20,410 to over $45,000.

E ssential

You can find advancement in this profession through education and specialization opportunities. There is also a lot of room for advancement for those who wish to learn to operate and maintain new technological equipment as it emerges.

Technologists and technicians work forty-hour weeks, but the hours can vary depending on the setting. In hospitals, technologists and technicians work twenty-four hours per day, and therefore these professionals may work any shift, and their hours will include weekends and holidays. In smaller, independent laboratory settings, the hours may vary as well and can include on-call responsibilities for after hours and weekends/holidays in case of emergencies.

Career Potential and Additional Information

The outlook for those seeking employment in these laboratory careers is expected to continue to grow faster than the average for all occupations. This is due in part to the fact that the number of jobs already exceeds those seeking employment. The needs of a growing and aging population who will require more medical services will also increase employment opportunities in this field. Technological advances will create new tests that are more sophisticated and complex.

Additional information on careers in clinical laboratory fields is available from the American Society for Clinical Laboratory Science. Their Web site is *www.ascls.org*. Their address is 6701 Democracy Blvd., Suite 300, Bethesda, MD 20817.

EKG Technicians

Cardiovascular technicians who specialize in electrocardiograms, Holter monitors, and stress testing are known as EKG technicians. There are several other categories of cardiovascular technicians, and you can learn more about these professions through the Alliance of Cardiovascular Professionals. All of these professionals assist physicians in diagnosing cardiovascular and peripheral vascular diseases by performing noninvasive examinations and tests.

Duties, Activities, and Scope of Practice

EKG technicians utilize a device that measures and traces electrical impulses that represent cardiovascular activity. They attach a set of electrodes according to the type of EKG ordered. These electrodes are attached to a combination of the chest, arms, and legs and then manipulated by a set of switches to measure the activity and obtain a reading. They print out this reading for the physician, who interprets it to make a diagnosis.

Holter monitoring is an advanced part of the EKG technician's skills. This involves placing electrodes on the patient's chest, and a portable EKG monitor on the patient's belt. The patient keeps this on for twenty-four or more hours while performing normal activities to help the physician diagnose such issues as heart rhythm disorders or problems with pacemakers. The EKG tech removes the tape at the set time from the Holter monitor and places it in a scanner to be read. Then the tech prints out a report from the scanner for the physician to analyze.

 Fact

EKGs are part of the standard tests performed prior to surgery and are usually performed as part of an annual physical for patients with a history of cardiovascular disease or routinely after middle age.

The third aspect of the EKG technician's duties is administering a treadmill stress test. The technician first obtains a medical history, then attaches the EKG monitor and obtains an at-rest baseline reading as well as a blood pressure reading. The patient begins to walk on the treadmill as the tech monitors the patient and the heart performance. Gradually the speed, and sometimes the incline of the treadmill, is increased so that the tech can monitor the heart's response to the increase in exertion. The tech provides the physician with a written report and printout from the test to analyze.

Education and Training

A high school diploma or GED is required. EKG technicians usually receive on-the-job training by an EKG supervisor or a cardiologist. This training typically lasts eight to sixteen weeks and is in basic EKGs only. Community colleges and vocational schools also offer a one-semester program to educate EKG technicians who wish to perform Holter monitoring and stress tests. Most employers prefer to train those who are already employed in the health care field, such as nursing assistants, L.P.N.s, or medical assistants in EKG technology. Others are usually cardiovascular technology students who wish to work part-time in the field to gain experience.

Licensure/Certification

Currently there are no licensing or certification requirements for EKG technicians.

Work Settings and Salaries

EKG technicians work primarily in hospitals and physicians' offices. Those who work in hospitals may work any of the shifts to cover twenty-four-hour availability and/or have on-call responsibility to cover weekends and holidays. Those who work for physicians will cover hours as set by the physician. The median income for 2004 was $38,690, and salaries ranged from $21,790 to $50,130.

Career Potential and Additional Information

As hospitals train more nursing aides to perform EKGs, the need for EKG technicians will decrease somewhat over the next decade. However, for those who are also trained in Holter monitoring and stress tests, the job outlook is much more favorable. To advance in the field or to have better job prospects and job security, it is advised to consider additional fields of cardiovascular technology.

More information about EKG technicians as well as other cardiovascular technologists and technicians is available from the Alliance of Cardiovascular Professionals. Their Web site is *www.acp-online. org*. Their address is P.O. Box 2007, Midlothian, VA 23112.

Perfusionists

Perfusionists operate heart-lung machines, which maintain life during periods when these organs are not functioning, such as during organ transplantation or coronary bypass surgery. This machine removes carbon dioxide and infuses oxygen into the blood of anesthetized patients during these surgeries.

Duties, Activities, and Scope of Practice

The perfusionist operates the heart-lung machine during complicated surgeries or emergencies. This machine is used for extracorporeal (outside the body) circulation to sustain life while the heart and/or lungs are not functioning.

The perfusionist also helps with the procedure by salvaging the patient's blood prior to the procedure. In response to the fear of AIDS and the shortages of blood supplies, many patients choose to donate their own blood over a period of time, ideally several weeks prior to the procedure, to minimize the need for replacement with donor blood.

Perfusionists are also trained to use other technology such as cell-savers, which use centrifugal force to remove the plasma, damaged platelets, and saline left in the heart-lung machine so that it is not returned to the body after the surgery.

They are also trained in ECMO (extracorporeal membrane oxygenation), which is a procedure used for premature infants in respiratory distress or for certain post-op heart patients, especially those awaiting organ transplants. By attaching the patient to a heart-lung machine, the physician buys time for transplant candidates awaiting an organ, for premature lungs to develop, or other healing to take place. The perfusionist must be present during this procedure to monitor the patient and operate the machine.

In other circumstances, such as other organ transplants or other surgeries where rapid infusion of lost blood is needed, or to replace low blood volume with warmed blood, a perfusionist and the heart-lung machine are utilized to help maximize healing and minimize the traumatic effects on the body.

Education and Training

In the early days of perfusion, nurses and respiratory therapists usually received on-the-job training in the procedures. Today it is a freestanding field. The Commission on Accreditation of Allied Health Education Programs (CAAHEP) accredits the formal education programs for perfusionists.

Alert

The programs are few and admission is competitive. Almost all programs require a bachelor's degree as a prerequisite. Some require some sort of medical background such as nursing, respiratory therapy, or medical technology.

The curriculum is usually one to two years, depending on the program and/or the applicant's background. The curriculum includes anatomy and physiology, pathology, chemistry, pharmacology, and courses in the heart-lung bypass for adults as well as infants and children. It also includes study of heart surgeries and respiratory emergencies. Use and special applications of the perfusion equipment and technology and necessary aspects of long-term support of extracorporeal circulation are also covered extensively. Supervised clinical applications of perfusion are also a vital part of the education for perfusionists.

Licensure/Certification

Certification is available from the American Board of Cardiovascular Perfusion (ABCP). The candidate must meet educational and clinical experience requirements, and pass an oral and written exam. Certified perfusionists may use the title CCP (certified cardiovascular perfusionist).

Work Settings and Salaries

Perfusionists work long hours and have on-call responsibilities for emergencies. The job is highly stressful, as it involves situations of life or death and requires attention to detail, constant alertness, and making quick decisions. Perfusionists work in hospitals and medical centers, usually in large cities.

The American Society of Extra-Corporeal Technology (AmSECT) reports the starting salary for perfusionists in 2004 was $58,000 to $61,000, and for those with ten or more years of experience, salaries can range from $85,000 to $100,000 annually.

Career Potential and Additional Information

There were about 3,700 perfusionist working in 2004 according to AmSECT, and there is a shortage of perfusionists. This presents tremendous growth opportunities over the next decade.

For further information about a career as a perfusionist, contact the American Society of Extra-Corporeal Technology (AmSECT). Their Web site is *www.amsect.org*. Their address is 2209 Dickens Road, Richmond, VA 23230.

Medical Assistants, Front Office Workers, and Medical Secretaries

These health care workers are generally the first people you encounter in physicians' offices and other ambulatory or intermediate care settings such as clinics or urgent care. They are multiskilled and perform many duties, both clerical and clinical.

Duties, Activities, and Scope of Practice

Medical assistants perform a variety of functions in order to keep things running smoothly in their particular health care setting. These can include answering phones and scheduling appointments, receiving patients and copayments, ordering supplies, and stocking cabinets. In addition to these responsibilities, medical assistants may also help to obtain patient medical histories, take height and weight measurements as well as vital signs, and prepare patients for examinations.

They may also be trained to draw blood samples, perform routine tests, and take EKGs. They may assist the physician in procedures and examinations, apply dressings, and provide necessary instructions to patients regarding tests, medications, and treatments.

Medical assistants also maintain examination rooms and waiting rooms in a neat, clean, and orderly fashion. They sterilize instruments and dispose of contaminated supplies.

Education and Training

A high school diploma or GED is required. The majority of medical assistants are trained in formal programs offered by community colleges and vocational schools. Programs are accredited by the Commission on Accreditation of Allied Health Education Programs (CAAHEP). Community college programs offer an associate's degree and take two years to complete. Vocational schools and other programs offer certificates or diplomas and are about one year in length.

 Question

What courses are included in the associate's degree program?
The curriculum includes medical terminology, biology, anatomy and physiology, transcription, computers, accounting, and record keeping. There is also instruction in laboratory techniques, use and maintenance of medical equipment, and clinical procedures.

Programs also cover written and oral communication, medical law and ethics, business correspondence, insurance procedures, and billing. Supervised clinical practice and externship are also part of the curriculum.

Licensure/Certification

Certification or registration is completely voluntary but does improve the hiring capabilities and often increases the salary for medical assistants.

Medical assistants can be certified by the American Association of Medical Assistants (AAMA) or the American Medical Technologists (AMT). The AAMA requires the candidate to have graduated from an accredited program and pass a written competency exam. Those who successfully complete this process become certified and can use the title C.M.A.

The AMT offers registration to medical assistants who have completed an accredited program or an armed-forces training course and pass the certification examination. High school graduates who received on-the-job training and have five years' experience as a medical assistant can also apply to take the AMT exam and become registered.

Work Settings and Salaries

Salaries vary depending on education, experience, duties, the volume of the physician's practice, as well as geographic area. The median salary for 2004 as reported by the U.S. Department of Labor was $24,610. The salary range was between $18,010 and $34,650.

Medical assistants work primarily in physicians' offices, either for physician groups or those in private practice. They may also work in clinics, urgent-care facilities, and other intermediate care facilities.

Medical assistants work forty-hour weeks, but hours depend on the hours physicians work. Some work evening, weekend, and sometimes holiday hours to accommodate the needs of patients.

Career Potential and Additional Information

Medical assisting is expected to grow faster than any other occupation over the next decade. This is due in part to the cost constraints from insurance and other reimbursement, forcing physicians to eliminate nurses in their offices and to consolidate responsibilities of their staff. The growing and aging population will have an increased need for medical services, and therefore the outlook for medical assistants, especially those formally educated and certified, will continue to grow.

For further information on a career as a medical assistant, contact the American Association of Medical Assistants. Their Web site is *www.aama-ntl.org*. Their address is 20 North Wacker Drive, Suite 1575, Chicago, IL 60606-2903.

Orthotists and Prosthetists

The orthotist evaluates patients' needs and then designs, makes, and fits braces or other strengthening devices to assist patients with disabling conditions of their limbs or spine. The prosthetist designs and makes prosthetic devices, otherwise known as artificial limbs, for patients. They also teach patients how to use them and care for them and to care for the body part to which the devise is attached.

Duties, Activities, and Scope of Practice

An orthotic is a device to help strengthen or straighten a weakened limb or spine. A prosthetic is designed to take the place of a missing limb. These can be very simple devices or they can be very complex and sophisticated. Technological advances in materials as well as inventions that replicate functions of the limbs and spine have brought about tremendous advances in the field and promise to continue to do so.

The orthotist follows an order from a physician or consults with the physician to design and fabricate the orthotic. Then the orthotist fits and adjusts the orthotic to fit and function appropriately. He instructs the patient in use and care of the orthotic and keeps records of the patients and devices. As new technologies develop, the orthotist will often contact the patient to offer new and more modern devices.

Fact

Prosthetic devices can require adjustments periodically, and the patient then consults with the professional for refitting. If problems result, such as ulcers from rubbing on the device, the orthotist or prosthetist can pad or adjust the devise to reduce pressure and refer the patient to the physician for treatment and follow up.

The prosthetist works with patients of all ages who are missing parts of or whole limbs. The prosthesis attaches to the stump and replaces the missing limb. With the advent of myoelectrics, the prosthetic can now mimic (with some very exact degrees of precision) the function of the missing limb. This electromechanical technology utilizes electrical signals from the contraction of muscles in the limb to signal a motor in the prosthesis to turn or contract.

Computer technology is now available to the orthotist and prosthetist to aid in the design and production of orthotics and prostheses. The computer measures the limb or portion of the spine needing the device, and the professional takes casts of the stump or limb to make and/or sculpt a model for the device. The appropriate materials are selected next, and the information is all fed into a computer that runs the machine that sculpts the device or limb.

The prosthetist also keeps records of patients and devices and updates patients periodically.

Education and Training

A bachelor's degree is required. The degree can be in the field of orthotics or prosthetics, or in some other field. If the degree is in another field, the candidate has to complete CAAHEP-accredited training in orthotics or prosthetics. This training takes one to two years, and a certificate is awarded.

Undergraduate preparation includes biology, physics, anatomy and physiology, psychology (especially of the disabled), chemistry, biostatistics, mechanics, biomechanics, properties of materials, mechanical drawing, orthotic and prosthetic techniques, and metalworking, as well as supervised clinical experience and training.

Many study both fields and can be certified in both fields.

Licensure/Certification

Certification is not required but does offer improved employment and salary options.

The American Board for Certification in Orthotics and Prosthetics (ABC) administers the Practitioners Certification Exam, which is a three-part exam to test for competency. Continuing education is required for periodic recertification. Contact the ABC for further information. Their Web site is *www.abcop.org*.

Work Settings and Salaries

Prosthetists and orthotists work in privately owned facilities, hospitals, and rehabilitation facilities. The median salary for 2004 was reported to be $57,323 by the U.S. Department of Labor.

Career Potential and Additional Information

This profession is expected to grow well into the next decade. Employment will be limited by funding for hospitals and other health care facilities. Exciting technological advancements make this an important field for highly skilled professionals interested in helping those who have loss of limbs and associated disabilities.

For more information on a career as an orthotist or a prosthetist, contact the American Orthotic and Prosthetic Association. Their Web site is *www.aopanet.org*. Their address is 330 John Carlisle Street, Suite 200, Alexandria, VA 22314.

Veterinarian Assistants and Technicians

Veterinarians employ assistants and technicians to assist them in the care of animals in much the same way that nurses or medical assistants help physicians in the care of patients. The technicians typically have more formal education and the assistants receive on-the-job training.

Duties, Activities, and Scope of Practice

The duties of the assistant and technician may include the following: receiving animals for examination or care, including emergency care, weighing animals, taking temperatures, performing laboratory tests and collecting specimens, changing dressings, holding animals during examinations, administering medications, and preparing animals for surgery, helping anesthetize them, and observing them postoperatively. They also instruct owners in care and treatments to be done at home.

Education and Training

Assistants can receive on-the-job training, but most technicians are formally trained through programs at community colleges or vocational/trade schools. Bachelor's degree programs are also available in veterinary technology, but most technologists perform the same duties as technicians and the programs are not as popular. Those who wish to work in the area of research need to pursue a degree in laboratory animal science.

Programs should be accredited by the American Veterinary Medical Association (AVMA).

E ssential

The curriculum for a degree in laboratory animal science consists of biological and behavioral sciences related to animals, chemistry, math, pharmacology for animals, as well as supervised clinical experience working with animals and learning testing procedures in laboratory sciences. It also includes study of veterinary office practices, use and care of equipment, and sterilization of instruments.

Licensure/Certification

All states regulate technicians to ensure competency through a written, oral, and practical exam, but each state is different. Most recognize the National Veterinary Technician (N.V.T.) exam that all graduates of an accredited program are eligible to take.

Work Settings and Salaries

Veterinary assistants and technicians work for veterinarians in clinics and animal hospitals, animal shelters and humane societies, boarding kennels, and zoos. Depending on the facility, assistants and technicians may need to be available twenty-four hours a day, so they have to cover various shifts. Others work set hours, which can include weekends and evenings, to meet the needs of the animal owners. Part-time and full-time options are available.

The U.S. Department of Labor reports a median hourly salary of $11.99 in 2004. The salary range was from approximately $8.51 to $17.12 hourly for full-time technicians.

Career Potential and Additional Information

Pet owners are becoming more affluent and also consider their pets a part of the family, so they are more willing to spend money to take care of their pets. This is helping to increase the need for veterinary technicians and will continue to do so over the next decade. As technology advancements improve the quality of care and the ability to save and extend lives of animals, more veterinary services will be needed as well.

There is no official professional organization for veterinary assistants and technicians, but more information on these careers is available from the American Veterinary Medical Association. Their Web site is *www.avma.org*. Their address is 1931 N. Meacham Road, Suite 100, Schaumburg, IL 60173-4360.

Chapter 13

Administrative Team Members

When people think about the health care delivery system, they usually think about doctors, nurses, therapists, and other members of the delivery team, and not about the administrators. However, careers for health care managers and executives are expected to continue to grow rapidly. Because the health care industry is facing budget shortfalls and skyrocketing costs, effective management is essential. Like the members of the delivery team, administrators in all areas of health care need to promote wellness and constantly improve the quality of care and outcomes for the patient.

Health Care Administrators

Health care administrators run the business side of the health care team. They can be hospital directors, nursing home directors, or home health directors, all of which will be covered later in this chapter. Health care administrators also run health care businesses such as physicians' practices for individuals or small to large groups or corporations, clinics, urgent-care facilities, outpatient surgery, managed-care settings, and independent practices for therapists and counselors. Executive management positions are not necessarily ones that new grads will walk right into. Entry-level positions exist in areas such as finance, human resources, marketing and public relations, and patient care services.

Duties, Activities, and Scope of Practice

The duties will vary from job to job, but most will entail overseeing or directly handling business matters, such as managing patient care services, finances, facilities, materials and operations, and personnel; purchasing capital outlays and other equipment; managing public affairs; and public relations and marketing.

Budgets and operations for health care facilities can range in the millions of dollars. Managers develop budgets and evaluate performance and cost-effectiveness. They develop and implement policies, procedures, objectives, and business strategies. They may also supervise a staff of assistants who manage one or two of these areas. Improving quality of care and patient outcomes as well as the efficiency of the delivery system, while controlling costs, is a huge challenge that health care administrators face.

Education and Training

Health information managers, who manage the security and maintenance of medical records, require at least a bachelor's degree from an accredited program in health information technology or medical records administration.

In some instances medical and health care managers are clinical managers who have risen to this level of responsibility. In addition to their clinical training, these managers usually also have a business degree, often a master's degree in business administration (M.B.A.).

For nonclinical managers, the standard credential is a master's degree in business administration, health services administration, long-term care administration, health sciences, or public health. In some small offices or facilities, an entry-level position could be obtained with a bachelor's degree in any of these areas, but a master's is usually required for advancement.

Licensure/Certification

Health information managers are required to have an RHIF certification (Registered Health Information Administration). This is obtained from the American Health Information Management Association.

Managers in long-term nursing facilities require licensing. Certification is available for other levels of health care managers, but is not required.

Work Settings and Salaries

Health care administrators usually work long hours. Those who manage facilities that operate continuously, such as hospitals, have to be on call to respond to problems at any time.

Salaries vary depending upon the responsibilities and the facilities or practice being managed. The U.S. Department of Labor reports a median salary of $67,430 for 2004. The range of salaries was from $41,450 to $117,990.

Career Potential and Additional Information

The outlook for this profession over the next decade is that it is expected to grow faster than the average for all occupations. As the health care industry continues to expand and diversify, many more job opportunities in the field of management will emerge and diversify as well. Positions in physicians' offices and management groups for physicians as well as home health care are expected to grow the fastest.

For more information about careers in health care administration, contact the American College of Healthcare Executives. Their Web site is *www.healthmanagementcareers.org*. Their address is One N. Franklin Street, Suite 1700, Chicago, IL 60606-4425.

For small medical group management careers and certification, contact the Medical Group Management Association. Their Web site is *www.mgma.org*. Their address is 104 Inverness Terrace East, Englewood, CO 80112-5306.

Hospital Directors

Hospital directors oversee the functions of the hospital and may have several directors underneath them to assist in this process. In small community or rural hospitals, however, they may not have many other directors or assistants.

Duties, Activities, and Scope of Practice

Hospital directors need to have an understanding of the needs of the patients, the medical staff, the nurses, the support staff, the technologists, and the general community in which the hospital resides. Their job is to meet the needs of all of these groups and to soothe the needs not yet being met. Recruiting and retaining staff, especially nursing staff, is a huge challenge for hospital directors and will continue to be over the next decade.

Directors have to have an understanding of available state-of-the-art medical care and technology as compared to what their hospital offers. And, of course, they have to understand the financial aspects of the hospital. They are ultimately responsible for the finances, personnel, patient services and care, materials and equipment, purchasing, and public affairs and relations. There may be other personnel, such as a director of nursing or a public relations administrator, who perform these different functions, but the ultimate responsibility lies with the hospital director.

Education and Training

A master's degree in health care administration or business administration has become the standard for hospital directors. Excellent communication skills, both written and spoken, are recommended. These programs usually include a one-year internship in a health care setting.

Undergraduate degrees in business or health care administration are recommended; however, some programs encourage degrees in liberal arts or in health care, such as nursing or physical therapy.

The curriculum of the graduate program includes such courses as hospital organization and management, accounting, budgeting, strategic planning, human resources management, health care economics, health information technology, laws and ethics, biostatistics, and epidemiology.

Licensure/Certification

Licensure is not required.

Work Settings and Salaries

Graduates of accredited health care administration programs generally begin their careers at an entry-level or midlevel position and work their way up to hospital director. Those who have been in the position for a number of years earn substantial salaries, in the $100,000 to $200,000 range. The U.S. Department of Labor reports a median income for directors of general medical and surgical hospitals for 2004 as being $71,280.

 Fact

Entry-level positions usually earn $35,000 to $60,000 per year, and some midlevel positions can expect earnings up to $100,000 depending upon responsibilities, financial status of the hospital, and geographic location. Large urban hospitals typically pay better than small community hospitals because of their financial status.

Hospital directors work long hours and may have to travel extensively, especially if they work for a hospital corporation with many hospitals that requires corporate meetings or events. If the hospital holds fundraising events, events to support associated charities, or participates in community events, the director(s) will be expected to attend. In the event of emergencies or any crisis affecting the hospital, the director will be expected to be available.

Career Potential and Additional Information

For all health care administrative positions, hospitals will continue to employ the most managers of the next decade. However, because the trend is to encourage outpatient services whenever possible (to contain skyrocketing health care costs), the number of *new* jobs is expected to be slower than for outpatient settings.

Competition for high-level positions is keen because of the high salaries and the prestige of the position.

For more information on careers as a hospital director, contact the American College of Healthcare Executives. Their Web site is *www.healthmanagementcareers.org*. Their address is One Franklin Street, Suite 1700, Chicago, IL 60606-4425.

Nursing Home and Long-Term Care Directors

Nursing home and long-term care directors may work for an individual facility or for a corporation that owns many facilities. They might also work for the corporation and oversee several facilities.

Duties, Activities, and Scope of Practice

Similar to the hospital director, the nursing home and long-term care director has the ultimate responsibility for the facility and its operations. The director oversees patient services, personnel, finances, facilities and operations, marketing, and public relations.

Education and Training

A bachelor's degree in nursing home administration is required. A master's degree in health care administration is recommended.

Licensure/Certification

All states and the District of Columbia require nursing home and long-term care directors to be licensed. This requires completion of at least a bachelor's degree in nursing home administration from an accredited program, a one-year internship, and passing a comprehensive written examination. The National Association of Boards of Examiners of Long Term Care Administrators administers the licensing test known as the *NAB*. This is a computer-based test. Some states also require a state test.

Alert

Continuing-education requirements must be met to renew licensure each year. Specific requirements can be obtained from your state board of examiners, but typically range from twenty to fifty hours of continuing education. In addition, some states require administrators to complete an Administrator-in-Training (AIT) program, which is approximately 1,000 hours or six months of additional training.

Work Settings and Salaries

Directors of nursing homes and long-term care facilities are on call for all situations, twenty-four hours a day. They work forty to fifty hours a week on a regular basis, and that may include rotation of weekends and holidays and some evening hours to meet the needs of patients' family members.

Some directors run more than one facility for a corporation and will rotate time spent in each. Others work in the corporate offices and direct services for more than one facility from there.

The median salary reported for 2004 by the U.S. Department of Labor was $60,940.

Career Potential and Additional Information

As the population ages, there will be an increasing need for nursing homes and long-term care facilities. This means this field will continue to grow over the next decade.

For more information about these careers, contact the American College of Health Care Administrators. Their Web site is *www.achca.org*. Their address is 300 N. Lee Street, Suite 301, Alexandria, VA 22314.

Home Health Care Directors

As trends in health care move more toward outpatient care and away from hospital-based care, home health care will continue to expand. Helping patients transition home from hospitals has long been a focus of home health. Now the focus is on keeping patients at home and preventing or diminishing hospitalizations.

Duties, Activities, and Scope of Practice

As with all health care administrators, home health care administrators have to stay on top of changes in reimbursement, regulations, billing, and other conditions of participation with federal agencies such as Medicare and Medicaid. Home health care has been subjected to multiple changes in recent years.

Home health care administrators also deal with patient services, strategic planning, personnel, finances, materials management, operations, and relationships with the medical community (practitioners, hospitals, skilled-nursing facilities, community agencies, etc.), and must have a clear understanding of the home health care delivery process.

They usually have a team of assistants handling each of these areas, but in small agencies all these responsibilities may fall on the administrator.

Education and Training

The industry standard is a master's degree in health care administration or an M.B.A. Administrators need to have a clear understanding of health care economics, certification processes from Medicare and state health departments, other legal and regulatory issues, information management, quality and risk management, public relations and marketing, biostatistics, and epidemiology.

Licensure/Certification

Currently there is no required license or certification. The National Association for Home Care and Hospice (NAHC) is promoting a program for certification of home care and hospice administrators to set standards for professionals. There have been many issues of fraud and abuse in Medicare-certified home care agencies in the past twenty-plus years that have brought about many changes in regulations and procedures. Certification of administrators could help to contain these issues and protect the consumer. For further information about the certification program, visit NAHC's Web site, at *http://nahc .org/CHCE/about.html.*

Work Settings and Salaries

Home health care administrators work long hours and must be on call for emergency issues. Almost all home health care is provided on a continuous basis through after-hours, on-call systems. Home health agencies can be for-profit or nonprofit. They can be freestanding or part of a hospital system.

 Fact

The median salary for home health administrators in 2004 was $60,320 according to statistics from the U.S. Department of Labor. Many for-profit agencies are owned by administrators, and salaries for owner/administrators can be much higher.

Career Potential and Additional Information

Home health care is expected to grow much faster than the average for all occupations over the next decade. Medicare has periodically placed moratoriums on certification of new agencies in the past; however, the number of home health agencies is continuing to expand to meet the needs of an aging population and of the health care industry, which is moving toward a focus on outpatient settings for care.

For more information on a career as a home health care administrator, contact the American College of Healthcare Executives. Their Web site is *www.healthmanagementcareers.org.* Their address is One Franklin Street, Suite 1700, Chicago, IL 60606-4425.

Or contact the National Association for Home Care and Hospice (NAHC). Their Web site is *www.nahc.org*. Their address is 228 Seventh Street, SE, Washington, DC 20003.

Directors of Quality Assurance and Performance Improvement

Quality directors monitor the quality of the patient care and develop performance improvement plans to improve the quality of patient care. As a part of this process they are also in charge of risk management issues. State and federal regulations have demanded the improvement of patient services and outcomes. Quality directors have to take these regulations into consideration and adapt programs to help their facility comply with them and improve the outcomes for their patients.

Duties, Activities, and Scope of Practice

Quality directors take into consideration the factors that affect the quality of patient care, including staffing issues, the types and adequacy of patient services available, the level of care, the risk issues, and the effectiveness of the present quality-control program.

They also need to keep abreast of regulatory changes from the state and federal government as well as any accrediting agency, such as JCAHO (Joint Commission on the Accreditation of Healthcare Organizations). These changes need to be implemented according to timelines presented by the agency, and the facility needs to establish a level of proof that these changes have been implemented and are understood and followed by appropriate staff.

The director analyzes the quality program for success and failure and works with the facility or agency managers to make and implement modifications as needed. The quality director educates staff as to the changes needed as well as the reasons for them and reports to the administration on the successes and failures.

Education and Training

As with other health care administration roles, a master's degree in health care administration is becoming the standard for quality directors in many health care settings. The graduate degree could also be an M.B.A. Either way, the course of study should have an emphasis on health care policy and ethics.

A bachelor's degree is the minimal requirement in this field and is usually in nursing or medical records/health information. Specialization in the quality assurance/risk management department can lead to a supervisory role and eventually a position as director of quality improvement.

Licensure/Certification

There is no requirement for licensure or certification. Health care information managers who aspire to this position will have already attained the RHIA (Registered Health Information Administration) status.

Voluntary certification is available from the Healthcare Quality Certification Board. Their Web site is *www.cphq.org.* Recertification is done every two years and requires thirty units of continuing education.

Work Settings and Salaries

In general the quality assurance director will work a normal forty-hour week, except during periods of pressing needs such as annual reports or in the event of scheduled or unscheduled surveys from JCAHO or regulatory agencies. At these times, overtime may be accrued as needed.

Essential

All health care facilities such as hospitals, home health agencies, clinics, and other ambulatory care settings are regulated by federal and state agencies and will need a Quality Assurance Department. Depending on the size of the facility or agency, it could be a solo role or a whole staff.

Salaries generally range from $35,000 to $70,000, depending on the size of the facility or agency as well as the responsibilities and education level of the director.

Career Potential and Additional Information

Quality assurance and performance improvement are mandated by state and federal regulations for health care facilities and agencies; therefore, roles for quality directors and staff will continue to grow over the next decade.

For more information about quality in health care contact the National Association for Healthcare Quality. Their Web site is *www .nahq.org*. Their address is 4700 W. Lake Avenue, Glenview, IL 60025.

Geriatric Case Managers

Helping seniors and others with disabilities maintain their independence and live at home is the goal and purpose of geriatric case managers, also known as geriatric care managers.

Duties, Activities, and Scope of Practice

Geriatric case managers assist clients in a variety of ways. In order to maintain their independence and a healthy lifestyle, many seniors need assistance. Adult children are often far away and working full-time. Living with extended families is not the norm in this country today. Although families are still the main support system for seniors, the availability is limited.

Geriatric case managers oversee many aspects of their clients' lives depending on their needs. The case manager makes frequent visits to clients' homes to make sure they are managing their life. This includes checking to see that rent and utility bills are being paid, that they have adequate and appropriate food and water and are eating properly, that their home is safe, orderly, and sanitary, that they have their medications and are taking them as directed, and that they are being seen by their physician and dentist routinely.

If the client needs assistance with bill paying and financial resources, the case manager may assist the client or make arrangements for payments to be made by a family member or other reliable source. The case manager may also need to make arrangements for housekeeping services and transportation, and offer assistance in setting appointments for medical care. They may need to make arrangements for social services to assist with securing necessary health care, food delivery, shopping, medications, and transportation.

Question

What other things do geriatric case managers do?
If the client needs additional help or supervision in the home, the case manager arranges for this. Case managers could arrange for home health care to assess home safety and provide any skilled nursing or therapy needed to improve the client's ability to remain at home, especially following an episode of illness.

Generally the case manager is screened and hired by an adult child or other family member and reports back to that person.

Education and Training

Geriatric case managers require a bachelor's degree, and in some instances a master's degree is preferred. The degree is usually in psychology, social work, nursing, or gerontology. Courses in business, ethics, and general law are recommended.

Licensure/Certification

Some states require geriatric case managers to be licensed or certified. They should be bonded and belong to the professional organization.

Work Settings and Salaries

Some geriatric case managers are self-employed; others work for hospitals, nursing homes, rehabilitation facilities, assisted-living facilities, private geriatric case management companies, home health agencies, or social service offices. They visit clients in their homes, in hospitals, and in nursing homes. Generally visits are made during a standard workweek, but occasionally there may be a need for extended hours, weekends, holidays, or emergency visits.

Salaries range from $25,000 to $55,000, depending on responsibilities and the employer.

Career Potential and Additional Information

Geriatric case managers will be greatly needed to meet the needs and requirements of an aging and growing population.

For more information about geriatric case management opportunities, contact the National Association of Professional Geriatric Care Managers. Their Web site is *www.caremanager.org*. Their address is 1804 N. Country Club Road, Tucson, AZ 85716.

Chapter 14

Affiliated Team Members

Others involved in health care include those who assist in emergencies; help to develop medical equipment; train clients to use exercise, diet, and equipment to promote wellness and recover from illness and injury; and help to record medical information and to communicate and educate through words, illustrations, and photographs.

Paramedics and E.M.T.s

Emergency medical technicians (E.M.T.s) and paramedics are dispatched to emergency calls to assist with accidents, injuries, and sudden illnesses. These are typically calls placed to the 911 system. The paramedic is an E.M.T. with advanced training in life support measures and procedures.

Duties, Activities, and Scope of Practice

Upon arrival at the scene, the first thing paramedics or E.M.T.s do is to assess the scene to ensure it does not pose any threat of additional danger to the victim, to others, and to themselves. They evaluate the situation, assess the patient's vital signs, and determine the nature and extent of the patient's condition, illness, or injury. They obtain a history or eyewitness account of the events, and they take a medical history from the patients or others if possible.

They provide basic first aid and then contact their base for instructions from a physician or specially trained nurse. Further care is provided in the field by the E.M.T. or paramedic, and the patient is transported to the hospital for further care and treatment.

Upon arrival at the hospital, the E.M.T. or paramedic reports the patient's status (vital signs, treatment provided, and response) to the emergency room physician or nurse. They may stay at the hospital to help staff attend to the patient.

Education and Training

To become an E.M.T. you must be eighteen years of age, have a high school diploma or GED, and have a valid driver's license. There are four levels of emergency responders:

- First responder
- E.M.T.-1 (basic)
- E.M.T.-2 or -3 (intermediate)
- E.M.T.-4 (paramedic)

The first responder is the most basic level. These are usually police and firefighters or other emergency workers who have been trained in CPR and basic first aid.

The E.M.T.-1 is trained to assist patients at the site of an accident and provide first aid. They can assess patients and manage respiratory, cardiac, and trauma emergencies. The E.M.T. training is 110 hours of training in emergency medical care. It includes CPR, handling emergencies involving ingestion of toxic chemicals and substances, cardiac arrest, bleeding, fracture, soft-tissue injuries and trauma, shock, internal injuries, and childbirth.

The E.M.T.-2 and 3 (or intermediate E.M.T.) has more advanced training of about thirty-five to fifty-five hours and can start and administer IVs and oral and IV drugs, interpret EKGs, insert endotracheal tubes (intubate patients), use the defibrillator, and manage shock. Some states offer this training as a specialization in either cardiac care or shock/trauma.

The E.M.T.-4, or paramedic, has had E.M.T. basic or intermediate training and has 700 to 1,000 hours of continuous employment, hospital experience, and a supervised field internship. This program typically lasts approximately two years, and the graduate earns an associate's degree in applied science.

Licensure/Certification

After completing E.M.T. basic training, the applicant can take a written and practical exam from NREMT or state agencies and become registered. Registration is required to advance to any other E.M.T. level.

Fact

All fifty states require E.M.T.s to be certified. Most states require registration or that candidates pass a state certification exam. All states require re-registration every two years. Candidates must be employed as an E.M.T. and complete continuing-education requirements.

Paramedics with accredited training can take the NREMT exam to become certified. Re-certification is required and requires continuing education.

Work Settings and Salaries

E.M.T.s and paramedics work for fire or police departments, hospitals, private ambulance companies, and public ambulance companies. They work between forty-five and sixty hours a week in most instances. Emergency response workers are available twenty-four hours a day, so E.M.T.s work shifts to cover all hours. They can also be on call for extended hours.

According to the U.S. Department of Labor, the median salary in 2004 was $25,310. Salaries ranged from $16,090 to $43,240.

Career Potential and Additional Information

Opportunities for E.M.T.s and paramedics are expected to grow faster than the average for all occupations thorough 2014. An aging population presents an increased possibility of injuries and other medical emergencies. The highest growth is expected to be with private ambulance services. Competition for jobs with fire and police departments will be stiff due to the potential for better job benefits, such as a pension after retirement.

For more information about a career as an E.M.T. or paramedic, contact the National Association of Emergency Medical Technicians. Their Web site is *www.naemt.org*. Their address is P.O. Box 1400, Clinton, MS 39060-1400.

Biomedical Engineers

Biomedical engineers take ideas and concepts from physicians, scientists, and therapists and convert them into equipment, instruments, devices, treatments, and techniques to help diagnose and treat patients, to solve problems, and to improve quality of life.

Duties, Activities, and Scope of Practice

There are four general categories of biomedical engineers: generalists, rehabilitative, clinical, and medical.

The generalists apply general principles of engineering to normal and abnormal (diseased or debilitated) anatomy and physiology. They are usually involved in improving and removing pollutants from the biological environment and protecting plants and animals from environmental factors.

Rehabilitative bioengineers are involved in developing devices for people with disabilities. These include communication devices, orthopedic devices, and electrical stimulation of nerves and paralyzed muscles.

Clinical bioengineers use technology and concepts to improve clinical systems and health care delivery processes. They maintain and test medical instruments and equipment and train staff in their safe and appropriate use.

Medical bioengineers utilize engineering concepts to develop new instruments and diagnostic devices and technologies, to develop new biomaterials, and to invent new techniques, computer systems, services, and other equipment. They also develop new artificial joints, prosthetics, and organs.

Education and Training

A bachelor's degree in biomedical engineering is required for entry-level positions in this field. Graduate degrees are preferred, especially doctoral degrees.

The curriculum includes mathematics, including algebra, trigonometry, and calculus. Biomedical engineering courses such as systems and design, biomedical computers, bioinstrumentation, biomechanics, biomaterials, biothermodynamics, and engineering biophysics are required.

Licensure/Certification

A license as a P.E. (professional engineer) is encouraged and in some instances required. Certification is available for clinical bioengineers from the International Certification Commission for Clinical Engineering and Biomedical Technology. This requires a degree, three years of hospital-based employment in a specialty area, and passing a written examination.

Work Settings and Salaries

There are a wide variety of work settings for biomedical engineers. Most are in large cities. Hospitals, laboratories, research facilities, undersea and space agencies, NASA, the EPA (Environmental Protection Agency), and private companies that produce medical devices are the major employers of biomedical engineers.

The broad areas of employment, education, and responsibilities represent the vast differences in salaries as well. In general, salaries range from approximately $45,000 to over $100,000.

Career Potential and Additional Information

The National Institutes of Health has recognized that the demand for biomedical engineers far exceeds the number of qualified engineers available. They also recognize the vital contribution to the health care industry that these professionals make. It has formed the National Institute for Biomedical Imaging and Bioengineering (NIBIB) to promote research and encourage the recruitment of high school students into bioengineering programs.

You can find out more about biomedical engineering opportunities from the Biomedical Engineering Society. Their Web site is *www.bmes.org*. Their address is 8401 Corporate Drive, Suite 140, Landover, MD 20785.

Medical Illustrators and Photographers

Medical illustrators and photographers combine their artistic skills with their scientific knowledge to document and help bring medical science to life for students, scientists, practitioners, and others.

Duties, Activities, and Scope of Practice

Both of these professions involve many different aspects of health care, from education to forensics, and from a microorganism to the entire human body. Illustrators and photographers create end products to be included in such sites as textbooks, journals, pamphlets and brochures, reports, and presentations, and for television and the Internet.

Essential

The work of medical illustrators and photographers can be used for documentation purposes, demonstration, and in the design of artificial body parts, limbs, and even organs. The drawings and photographs can be of a single cell, an anatomical illustration, or the documentation of an entire procedure such as an autopsy or a surgical or dental procedure.

Medical illustrators and photographers have to have an understanding of and ability to use a variety of media, including drawing and photography, videography, sculpting and modeling, graphical design, and computer-aided processes.

Some illustrators and photographers do specialize in a particular medium or medical specialty, but the majority of these professionals are open to all aspects of their field.

Education and Training

There are five accredited schools of medical illustration in the United States today, and all five offer master's degrees, which is the industry standard. Each school accepts only a small number of applicants each year (six to twelve students), so competition is stiff. The curriculum includes courses in human anatomy, neuroanatomy, histology, and pathology, as well as illustration techniques. These include such areas as pen-and-ink drawing, watercolor, acrylics, gouache, and airbrush techniques. Most candidates have undergraduate degrees in either art or biological studies with an emphasis on art electives.

Medical photographers have to have at least an associate's degree in biomedical photography, which includes all aspects of still ands video photography, as well as using equipment such as microscope cameras. They also have to understand how to use computer software designed for use with photos and videos.

Licensure/Certification

There are no licensing requirements for medical illustrators or photographers. Certification for medical illustrators is entirely optional.

The BioCommunications Association (BCA) offers a voluntary certification exam for photographers through its Board of Registry. This exam consists of three parts: written, oral, and practical. Those who pass can use the title RBP (registered biological photographer).

Work Settings and Salaries

Medical illustrators usually work for medical schools and other teaching facilities and research programs. They may also work for hospitals, clinics, dental and veterinary schools, medical publishers, and pharmaceutical companies. Some freelance, and others may work for organizations that employ large groups of medical artists and photographers.

The average salaries as reported by the Association of Medical Illustrators range between $40,000 and $45,000, but can be as high as $75,000 for experienced illustrators.

Salaries for medical photographers range with the job requirements and responsibilities, but according to available data, salaries range from $25,000 to $45,000.

Career Potential and Additional Information

These are both growing fields in the health care industry. Communication is essential to health care, and visual media enhances communication and documentation. Visual media also improves education and research efforts. The role of illustrators and photographers in health information is just developing and presents tremendous opportunities as well. As technology advances in techniques and equipment used by illustrators and photographers continue, so will the uses in the health care field.

For more information about opportunities in the media fields of medical illustrators and photographers contact the Health and Science Communications Association. Their Web site is *www.hesca .org*. Their address is 39 Wedgewood Drive, Suite A, Jewett City, CT 06351-2428.

The Association of Medical Illustrators' Web site is *www.medical -illustrators.org*. The Web site for the BioCommunications Association is *www.bca.org*.

Medical Writers

Medical writers are also known as biomedical communicators, biomedical writers, or health science writers or communicators. Writers and editors who also have an interest or education in health sciences have tremendous opportunities to share their skills and abilities in a variety of publications and media.

Duties, Activities, and Scope of Practice

Medical writers can write for medical professionals or the general public. The responsibilities will change depending on the audience. For the medical profession, the writer is usually delivering facts and statistics and must be very detail-oriented and specific. For the general audience, the medical writer interprets information and presents it in a language that can be understood by those who don't understand medical terminology.

Medical professionals—such as physicians, dentists, nurses, and other scientists—usually write research reports and most medical textbooks. Medical writers may assist with these as ghostwriters or editors.

Medical writers may write television or radio health news reports, drug package inserts for pharmaceutical companies, or technical instructions for the use and maintenance of medical equipment. They may translate medical and scientific discoveries for professionals as well as for laymen. They may also write for publications for hospitals, clinics, and other facilities, or patient teaching materials, or question-and-answer columns for newspapers.

Education and Training

Education requirements can vary depending on the job. Usually a minimum of a bachelor's degree is needed, but in many cases advanced degrees are required. Some employers may want a degree in a health science with a minor in journalism or English, and others may require the opposite. Competency in the use of computers as well as publishing software is also often a requirement.

Licensure/Certification

The American Medical Writers Association offers a program called the Core Curriculum. This program consists of instruction in six areas designed to improve the skills of the medical writer. These areas are editing and writing, audiovisuals, pharmaceuticals, freelancing, teaching and public relations, and advertising. The AMWA awards certificates to those who successfully complete the courses.

They also offer advanced certificates to those who complete advanced curriculum courses and meet employment requirements.

Work Settings and Salaries

Many medical writers freelance, and others work directly for magazines, journals, newspapers, television, and radio. They write for textbook publishers, medical equipment and pharmaceutical companies, Web sites, and medical schools, hospitals, clinics, and physicians.

The salaries are as varied as the opportunities and can range from $25,000 to over $100,000 per year, depending upon employer, education, and experience.

Career Potential and Additional Information

Advances in technology and new discoveries in medical science happen almost every day and need to be communicated to the health care profession as well as to the general public. The Internet makes information available almost as soon as it happens and opens many avenues for disseminating the information. The need for medical writers and researchers in all areas will continue to grow, but the competition for jobs (especially the highest paying and most prestigious) will continue to be stiff.

To find out more about becoming a medical writer, contact the American Medical Writers Association. Their Web site is *www.amwa.org*. Their address is 40 West Gude Drive, Suite 101, Rockville, MD 20850-1192.

Alert

Certified Athletic Trainers

This profession was first recognized in 1990. Athletic trainers should not be confused with fitness or personal trainers, who are not members of the health care team. Athletic trainers, on the other hand, are. Athletic trainers help to treat and prevent injuries for patients of all ages. They work with athletes of all stages, from children just learning to play a sport to professional athletes. They also work in industry to help workers prevent and rehabilitate injuries.

Duties, Activities, and Scope of Practice

Some, but not all, athletic trainers who work with sports teams in high schools, colleges, and universities are also required to be teachers.

Athletic trainers work under the supervision of or in coordination with a physician and in conjunction with other health care workers to treat and rehabilitate musculoskeletal injuries such as sprains, strains, contusions, and fractures. They also work with players to prevent injuries by instructing in proper fitness, conditioning, nutrition, and general health.

Teams hire athletic trainers to be present during training, practice, and competition to assess and provide first aid for injuries as well as to work with players to prevent injury. They may have to make quick decisions that can affect the health or career of the athlete as well as the outcome of the competition. In all instances they need to advocate for the patients and not necessarily the outcome of the competition, which may not be the most popular action at the time.

They will help the players warm up properly, massage sore muscles, and apply ice to players leaving the field, such as to a pitcher's arm and shoulder.

They also work in business and industry to help workers prevent on-the-job injuries through proper body mechanics, conditioning, and general health. They are also on-hand in case of an injury to provide immediate treatment.

Education and Training

The undergraduate education curriculum includes anatomy and physiology, nutrition, exercise physiology, kinesiology (study of human muscular movement), physics, pharmacology, pathology, health education, psychology of coaching, and chemistry. They must also complete a CPR course and remain certified. Clinical practice in a supervised setting is also part of the program.

As of 2004, a bachelor's degree in athletic training from an accredited program was required to meet certification requirements for forty-three of fifty states. According to the National Athletic Trainers' Association, 70 percent of athletic trainers have a master's or doctoral degree. Those who work in high schools and are required to teach will have to have a teaching credential as well.

Licensure/Certification

The National Athletic Trainers' Association (NATA) is the certifying agency. Candidates must have at least a bachelor's degree in athletic training and 800 hours of experience. The exam measures clinical skills, basic knowledge, and decision-making skills. Recertification requires continuing education. Those who pass the examination become certified athletic trainers and may use the designation ATC.

Some states require licensure. Check with your state government for information.

Work Settings and Salaries

The U.S. Department of Labor reports that there were about 15,000 jobs for athletic trainers in 2004. Of those, about one-third worked in health care, either for hospitals or in offices of physicians or other health care practitioners. Another one-third worked for public or private schools, mostly high schools, colleges, and universities. Others worked for professional sports teams or in business and industry. A small number worked for recreational sports or fitness centers.

The jobs with professional sports teams are highly competitive and generally require a commitment to work the most hours per week. Athletic trainers work long and mostly irregular hours. Those who teach may also have very long workweeks.

Salaries depend on the job, including responsibilities and experience. The median salary for 2004 was $33,940. Salaries ranged from $20,000 to over $53,000 per year. Most included benefits, and some included payment for continuing-education requirements.

Career Potential and Additional Information

This career is expected to grow faster than the average for all occupations over the next decade. Positions are expected to grow in elementary and middle schools but may require teaching responsibilities as well.

As the population ages and technology advances, the demand for skilled health care workers will continue to grow. Athletic trainers will be needed to help meet these needs. Demands for trainers interested in preventing and treating musculoskeletal injuries in an aging population will grow faster than the demand for trainers for professional teams. These positions are and will continue to be highly competitive because the turnover of trainers is low.

For further information on careers in athletic training, contact the National Athletic Trainers' Association. Their Web site is *www .nata.org*. Their address is 2952 Stemmons Freeway, Dallas, TX 75247.

Medical Transcriptionists

Medical transcriptionists produce documents for medical records from dictation provided by practitioners and other health care providers regarding such issues and events as x-ray and imaging reports, surgical reports, admission and discharge summaries, medical histories and physical examinations, autopsy reports, consultation findings, letters of referral, and progress notes.

Duties, Activities, and Scope of Practice

Medical transcriptionists listen to dictations and type up the reports for verification and signature of the dictating health care professional. These documents eventually become part of the patient's medical records. Therefore medical transcriptionists have to understand and abide by rules of patient confidentiality.

The medical transcriptionist receives dictations in several modes. They can be via digital or analog recording devices or over the Internet. With the advent of speech recognition software, the transcriptionist may even receive a draft report derived from this software that needs proofreading and proper formatting. As this technology becomes more sophisticated, medical transcription will evolve as well.

Medical transcriptionists need to have a good understanding of medical terminology, anatomy, pathology, and medical procedures. Resource materials are available online and in print. Experienced transcriptionists will be able to spot any inconsistencies or mistakes and refer to the practitioner for correction.

Different practitioners and facilities will possibly have different formats to follow for their documents. Medical transcriptionists need to be able to adapt to the changes accordingly.

Education and Training

Postsecondary training for medical transcriptionists is available through distance-learning programs, vocational schools, and community colleges. Employers prefer to hire those with formal training and either a certificate or an associate's degree in medical transcription.

The curriculum includes medical terminology, English grammar and punctuation, anatomy, and legal issues of health care documentation. Supervised on-the-job experience is also often included in these programs. Those with prior medical experience, such as nurses, nursing aides, medical secretaries, etc., often find medical transcription to be an alternative career.

Licensure/Certification

Certification is not required but demonstrates competency. Voluntary certification is available from the American Association for Medical Transcription (AAMT) for those who pass their certification exam. Recertification is given every three years to those who complete the required continuing-education credits.

Work Settings and Salaries

According to the U.S. Department of Labor, approximately 105,000 medical transcriptionists were employed in 2004. About 40 percent worked for hospitals, 30 percent in physicians' offices, and others worked in a variety of settings, including those who were self-employed with a home-based business. Some of the other settings included medical laboratories, outpatient care centers, clinics, and therapy offices. Those working in settings other than home-based businesses usually worked forty-hour weeks. Those who were self-employed worked more irregular hours and often part-time on weekends, evenings, or on call.

Salaries vary with the employer. Those who were self-employed tended to earn more but had no benefits and higher expenses. The median salary according to the U.S. Department of Labor for 2004 was $13.64 per hour. Hourly salaries ranged from $9.67 to $19.11.

Career Potential and Additional Information

The outlook for medical transcriptionists is very good for the next decade. This profession is expected to grow faster than the average for all occupations. Two factors influence this. One is the growing and aging population, which is expected to seek more medical services that will need to be documented. The other is the need to create accurate electronic medical records that can be shared by providers, third-party payers, consumers, and health information systems.

For further information about careers in medical transcription, contact the American Association for Medical Transcription. Their Web site is *www.aamt.org*. Their address is 100 Sycamore Avenue, Modesto, CA 95354-0550.

Chapter 15

Other Health Care Workers

The following group of health care workers performs essential functions that help support others in the practice of health care. They help to ensure that health care is provided in a safe environment, that health care providers are up to date with the latest information and education, and that actions are accurately documented and health records are maintained and readily accessible.

Environmental Health Specialists

The health and safety of everyone depends on environmental health specialists, also known as sanitarians, who enforce government regulations regarding food, water, waste, and sewage. They are also concerned with hazards presented by such things as radioactive contamination and the pollution in the atmosphere. These scientists also work to discover what conditions make people sick and how to prevent the spread of illness.

Duties, Activities, and Scope of Practice

In the health care environment, the safe disposal of medical waste comes under the control of environmental health specialists. Some of the areas concerned here include the safe disposal of sharps such as needles and syringes, soiled dressings, blood and bodily fluid samples, and the chemicals and radioactive products needed for x-rays and other diagnostic tests.

Entry-level sanitarians perform inspections and report findings. The more experienced sanitarians are involved in consulting services and educating clients as well as the general public.

Fact

Safe food and water supplies in health care settings are a vital aspect of public health. Sanitarians oversee the safety of water, food, sewage, and waste in all public arenas to help protect the public health and ensure safety for all.

Education and Training

A bachelor's degree in environmental engineering or environmental health is required. Many new and evolving positions in this field require advanced degrees.

The curriculum includes chemistry, physics, biology, microbiology, mathematics, biostatistics, environmental health and studies, communication, epidemiology, and behavioral sciences. It also incorporates fieldwork.

Licensure/Certification

Most states require certification, but requirements vary. Contact your state government agency for specifics. Certification and registration testing and credentialing are offered through the National Environmental Health Association.

Work Settings and Salaries

The majority of these professionals work for state and local public health departments. Others work in the private sector, such as for private hospitals and clinics, and for the public through uniformed services such as fire and police and homeland security agencies.

Salaries vary as much as the workplace and job responsibilities, but the general range is between $25,000 and $50,000 and can exceed $100,000 in some instances.

Career Potential and Additional Information

As terrorism, flu pandemic threats, and biohazards continue to be front-page news, the need for more environmental health scientists will continue to grow very rapidly. The public's growing concern with global-warming effects and pollution of the planet as well as the atmosphere will keep these professionals busy for many years to come. Technology advances and changing threats will continue to bring changes to the roles these professionals play and how they conduct research and perform their jobs.

For more information about career potential as an environmental health scientist, contact the National Environmental Health Association. Their Web site is *www.neha.org*. Their address is 720 S. Colorado Blvd., Suite 970-S, Denver, CO 80246-1925.

Genetic Counselors

Over fifty years ago, when James Watson and Francis Crick made their Nobel Prize–winning discoveries about how DNA stores and passes on hereditary information, they opened up a whole new world of health care considerations. The Human Genome Project has continued this, and today the world of genetics is one of the most fascinating sciences. Genetic counselors help others understand this information and how it applies to their specific situations.

Duties, Activities, and Scope of Practice

Geneticists can now identify literally hundreds of genetically transmitted diseases and conditions. The genetic counselor works with patients who need more information about genetic disorders affecting themselves, their family members, and even their unborn child.

Genetics can help to predict the occurrence of diseases and conditions in patients of all ages. They can also predict the possibility of disease or conditions for couples with family histories of these diseases should they decide to have children.

Question

Education and Training

Genetic counselors need to have a bachelor's degree and at least two years of graduate study, which is usually a master's degree in human genetics. They should have had biology, molecular and Mendelian genetics, chemistry, psychology, probability, and statistics in their bachelor program. The master's program should include courses in biochemistry, anatomy and physiology, bioethics, human genetic laboratory studies, medical genetics, issues in clinical genetics, and clinical counseling. Fluency in a foreign language is also recommended.

Licensure/Certification

Licensure and certification are not required. Certification is available and denotes competency. Over 70 percent of genetic counselors are certified. The examination is given by the American Board of Genetic Counseling. Their Web site is *www.abgc.net*. Recertification is required every ten years.

Work Settings and Salaries

Genetic counselors work primarily in medical centers that are usually associated with universities where the genetic testing is performed. Most work in obstetrics or pediatrics. Others work in specialty clinics and centers where adults and children are treated for genetic disorders.

This is a relatively new and growing profession, and the salaries vary tremendously depending upon geographic location, genetic disorders, and responsibilities. Salaries are reported to range from $18,000 to over $75,000 per year. Mean salaries were in the $40,000 range throughout the country.

Career Potential and Additional Information
This is a relatively new profession, and the opportunities are expanding along with the findings of the Human Genome Project. One hundred percent of the graduates in genetic counseling are working in the field. This represents the demand for these professionals as well as the wide acceptance of these counselors as respected members of the health care team.

For more information about careers in genetic counseling, contact the National Society of Genetic Counselors (NSGC). Their Web site is *www.nsgc.org*. Their address is 233 Canterbury Drive, Wallingford, PA 19086-6617.

Health Information Administrators
Health information is an exciting and growing field. Events such as Hurricane Katrina emphasized the need for secure electronic medical records that can be accessed by professionals all across the country—and possibly around the world. Health information administrators plan, develop, and supervise the systems that will make this possible. This is just part of the administrator's responsibilities.

Duties, Activities, and Scope of Practice
Health records keep track of the medical history of a patient and can and should eventually span from birth to death and include all information gathered from every medical contact and experience. Hospitals and medical facilities use the data in medical records to facilitate planning and evaluate performance. Public health officials use the data to study health trends. Researchers use the information to help support and develop new methods for treating and diagnosing illnesses.

Processing, organizing, and maintaining medical records come under the supervision of the health information administrator. They devise systems to assist medical professionals to access and analyze the information from medical records for these purposes. They design methods to ensure confidentiality is maintained while allowing access to the information. They may also assist in the collection and analysis of the data.

 Fact

Health information administrators supervise the medical information technicians and coding specialists to ensure standardization of information, and to make certain that the data-collection process meets with the legal and ethical requirements of the institution.

Health information administrators also review the information in the records to help medical staff analyze the quality of care being delivered. Administrators also develop policies and procedures for processing information for insurance companies, legal issues, and patient requests for copies of their medical documents.

Education and Training

A bachelor's degree in medical record administration or health information management is the minimal requirement in this field, and a master's degree is recommended for those who wish to advance to executive levels. Programs should be accredited by the Commission on Accreditation of Allied Health Education Programs (CAAHEP).

The curriculum includes liberal arts, biology, statistics, fundamentals of medical science, medical terminology, anatomy and physiology, classification of diseases, medical ethics and law, computer science, health information administration, and methods of research. Programs also include supervised practice in an accredited health care setting.

Licensure/Certification

Health information administrators are required to be registered. The registration examination is given by the American Health Information Management Association (AHIMA). This is a one-day written examination. Those who pass become registered health information administrators and use the initials RHIA. Continuing education is required for renewal every two years.

Work Settings and Salaries

Health information administrators work primarily in hospitals and other ambulatory care settings such as clinics and urgent-care facilities. Others work in physicians' offices, long-term care centers, and mental health facilities. Some work for insurance companies, and others teach or work as consultants.

Salaries depend upon responsibilities and geographic location, but in general range from $30,000 to $50,000. Managers typically earn more, as do consultants. Executives can earn upwards of $100,000 per year.

Career Potential and Additional Information

This is a growing field that will face many changes as technology advances and electronic medical records become the norm. The field is expected to grow faster than average for all occupations over the next decade. The growing and aging population will require more medical care, which is expected to create enormous quantities of records to be managed.

For more information about careers in health information management contact the American Health Information Management Association (AHIMA). Their Web site is *www.ahima.org*. Their address is 233 North Michigan Avenue, Suite 2150, Chicago, IL 60601-5800.

Medical Coding Specialists

Diseases are classified in numerical sequences for identification and data collection purposes. This is somewhat similar to the Dewey decimal system of classifying books in a library. This system is used for information purposes and for billing third-party payers. Medical procedures are also coded for the same purposes.

Duties, Activities, and Scope of Practice

Coding specialists review medical records and assign numeric codes for the diagnoses identified and procedures performed. The codes are known as ICD-9 (International Classification of Diseases, Ninth Revision) codes and CPT (Current Procedural Terminology) codes.

The coding specialist may need to make a determination as to the primary diagnosis being treated in an episode of illness, and assign codes to other diagnoses in a specific order according to rules set out in the ICD-9 coding regulations.

The CPT codes are more specific to billing third parties for procedures performed by providers such as practitioners, laboratories, and diagnostic centers. ICD-9 codes are used for reimbursement from Medicare and Medicaid and some other third-party payers when reimbursement is related to the diagnosis.

Education and Training

A high school diploma or GED is required. Coding-specialist training is part of the curriculum for a health information technician program that leads to an associate's degree in health technology. Most coders obtain their AA degree. The curriculum includes medical terminology, disease processes, and pharmacology, in addition to learning how to apply ICD-9 and CPT codes.

The American Health Information Management Association offers seminars and workshops in medical coding.

Licensure/Certification

Certification is not mandatory, but is becoming the standard. Candidates who have completed coding training can sit for the exam given by AHIMA to become certified coding specialists (CCS).

Work Settings and Salaries

Most coding specialists work in hospitals, but many work in practitioners' offices, long-term care settings, ambulatory care centers, home health agencies, and insurance companies.

Salaries range from $20,000 to $25,000 per year.

Career Potential and Additional Information

HIPAA (Health Insurance Portability and Accountability Act) regulations require the use of codes to improve standardization of information, help promote the possibility for electronic medical records, and protect the privacy and confidentiality of health care records.

Essential

An aging and growing population will require more medical care and result in the creation of considerable amounts of medical records, which will need to be coded for reimbursement, electronic access, data collection, and research. This will continue to create a need for medical coding specialists. This occupation will grow fast over the next decade.

More information about medical coding specialists is available from AHIMA. Their Web site is *www.ahima.org*. Their address is 233 North Michigan Avenue, Suite 2150, Chicago, IL 60601-5800.

Health Information (Medical Records) Technicians

A new entry is made in patients' medical records each time they receive care. In an inpatient setting such as a hospital or long-term care facility the records will be separate from those maintained in practitioners' offices or other outpatient ambulatory care settings. Each record will contain information about the patient's complaint and symptoms, the diagnostics (test and x-ray results and reports), the diagnosis, treatments, and outcomes.

Duties, Activities, and Scope of Practice

The medical records or health information technician assembles the patient's information and ensures that all portions of the chart are complete and signed by the appropriate team member, such as the physician, nurse, or therapist. If the records are computerized, the technician ensures that all information is entered correctly and is complete.

They make sure that each portion of the chart is correctly identified and that all forms are complete and signed appropriately. In some instances the technician may participate in the tabulation and analysis of patient data to ensure quality is maintained, to improve patient care delivery, or to control costs. Technicians then follow procedures and systems established by the RHIA (Registered Health Information Administrator) to ensure the records are maintained, secure, and easily accessible.

Education and Training

Employers prefer to hire health information technicians who are registered. This requires a minimum of an associate's degree in health information from an accredited program. The Commission on Accreditation for Health Informatics and Information Management Education (CAHIIM) accredits these programs.

The curriculum includes general-education courses plus medical terminology, anatomy and physiology, computer science, the legal aspects of health information, coding, quality improvement, database management, statistics, and abstraction of data.

Licensure/Certification

Graduates of accredited programs can sit for the certification examination given by AHIMA. Those who pass may use the credentials RHIT (registered health information technician). Recertification is done every two years and requires continuing education.

Work Settings and Salaries

Medical records technicians usually work forty hours per week. Some overtime may be required occasionally. In hospitals, the medical records department must be accessible twenty-four hours a day, and therefore technicians may work day, evening, or night shifts, and some weekends and holidays.

Health information technicians also work in ambulatory care settings, long-term care facilities, and public health departments.

 Fact

According to the U.S. Department of Labor, the median income in 2004 for health information medical records technicians was $25,590. Salaries ranged from $17,720 to over $40,000 and largely depended on education, credentials, and settings. Those working in hospitals tended to make more money.

Career Potential and Additional Information

There is expected to be an enormous amount of medical records produced in the next decade due to an aging and growing population that is expected to require much more medical care and services. Therefore the U.S. Department of Labor expects this profession to grow faster than the average for all occupations over the next decade.

To find out more about becoming a medical records health information technician, contact the American Health Information Management Association (AHIMA). Their Web site is *www.ahima.org*. Their address is 233 N. Michigan Avenue, Suite 2150, Chicago, IL 60601-5800.

Medical Librarians

Medical librarians are also known as health sciences librarians and health information professionals. This career encompasses far more than just cataloging medical books and other literature. They work with computers and set up and maintain networks, they develop Web pages, and they assist with research for other health care professionals to use to write papers.

Duties, Activities, and Scope of Practice

Medical information is an exploding field. Medical librarians are specially trained information specialists in health sciences information. They are responsible for procuring and cataloging new books, journals, and other media sources for their library. This can be a challenging proposition with over 8,000 professional journals to choose from. In 2004, there were over 3,000 new books published for the medical field alone, and over 1,000 other media selections from which to choose.

Depending on the size of the library in general, as well as the number of students, educators, staff, and researchers who need to access the information, a facility's medical library can be quite large. And if it's small, the choices may be even more critical.

Medical information professionals have to organize, categorize, and maintain the information as well as make it accessible. In doing so they will need to make use of other media to help promote and disseminate the information available. These specialists will also have to be available to assist the medical professionals in researching the available literature as well as online sources to find critical information for the diagnosing and treatment options of their patients.

Education and Training

Health information professionals need a master's degree in library science with an emphasis on health sciences. Although certification is not required it is highly recommended. In order to become certified, the candidate has to have a degree from an accredited program. The American Library Association is the accrediting agency.

Licensure/Certification

Certification is not required. However, the Medical Library Association (MLA) offers four levels of certification that signify competency. Membership in the Academy of Health Information Professionals (AHIP) is also highly recommended. More information is available from MLA. Their Web site is *www.mlanet.org*. They also have a list of ALA-accredited schools.

E ssential

Work Settings and Salaries

Medical librarians work for hospitals, pharmaceutical companies, federal and state agencies, health maintenance organizations (HMOs), research centers, and professional medical associations. They also work in schools of medicine, nursing, pharmacy, veterinary medicine, and allied health. Over 60 percent of the medical libraries are in hospitals, and 12 percent are in professional schools.

Salaries range from $30,000 to $65,000 per year.

Career Potential and Additional Information

It has been estimated that in the last ten years more health literature has been published than in all previous years combined. This trend is not expected to change, and with the Internet, information will only continue to explode. This creates a tremendous need for information professionals to organize and categorize the information to improve the access.

Cost-containment issues facing hospitals may influence the number of jobs available, but highly qualified candidates should have no problem finding jobs.

For more information about careers in medical library science, contact the Medical Library Association. Their Web site is *www.lanet .org*. Their address is MLA Professional Development Department, 65 East Wacker Place, Suite 1900, Chicago, IL 60601-7298.

Chapter 16

More Health Care Roles

Here are a few more health care professionals whose contribution is important to the well-being of patients. The traditional health care field, continues to expand and grow literally every day. There are many more opportunities and avenues to explore in the health care field, and even more will be created over the next decade. Technology advances in diagnostics, treatments, and cures will provide the growing and aging population with health care options well into the next few decades.

Opticians

Dispensing opticians fit, adjust, and dispense contact lenses and eyeglasses according to the prescription written by the ophthalmologist or optometrist. They assist clients in selecting contacts and glasses frames to fit their specific needs as well as style. Some opticians help to fit optic prosthetics, such as artificial eyes or cosmetic shells, that help to conceal defects in the eye.

Duties, Activities, and Scope of Practice

The optician takes measurements of the patient's face to assist in the design and fit of eyeglasses. This includes measuring the distance between the pupils, measuring the surface of the eye and the lens, and determining the length for the earpiece. They suggest appropriate frames based on the type of lens needed, the weight of the lens, and the facial features of the patient. They may also suggest special coatings or tints. They then write an order for the ophthalmic laboratory technician to grind the lens and adjust the frames. When the glasses are ready, the optician makes any necessary adjustments to ensure the glasses fit properly. The optician also instructs the patient in proper wear and care of the glasses.

For contact lenses, the optician measures the corneas and writes an order for the lens manufacturer, or fits the patient with the appropriate lenses from stock according to the prescription from the optometrist of ophthalmologist. This is sometimes a painstaking process. Opticians also instruct patients in the insertion removal, and care of the contact lenses.

Education and Training

A high school diploma or GED is required. Some employers offer on-the-job training and apprenticeship programs that can last from two to four years. Community colleges offer an associate's degree in optical fabrication and dispensing. Some vocational and technical schools offer diplomas or certificates. Not all programs are accredited. Twenty-one states require an optician to be licensed, which often means they have to attend an accredited school.

An average curriculum includes courses in optical math and physics, which require an understanding of algebra and geometry. Students also study how to use precise measuring devices and optical tools, and how to fit and adjust glasses. Some learn to grind lenses. They also learn office management skills and sales techniques.

Courses in the fitting of contact lenses are usually offered by lens manufacturers, by some medical schools, and through professional organizations.

Licensure/Certification

Licensure is required in twenty-one states. Specifics vary by state, but most require a written and practical exam. Relicensure usually requires continuing education.

Certification denotes competency. It is voluntary but recommended. The American Board of Opticianry administers two exams. The first attests to entry-level competency. It is the National Opticianry Competency Examination. The second is an advanced certification in ophthalmic dispensing. Advanced opticians can then take the Master's in Ophthalmic Optics Program.

Fact

Work Settings and Salaries

Opticians work in large or small retail optical stores, optical laboratories, hospital eye clinics, and offices with optometrists and ophthalmologists. Often opticians open their own retail business. Most opticians report working a forty-five-hour workweek. Those who work in retail stores may also work weekends and evening hours.

The U.S. Department of Labor reports that in 2004 the median salary for opticians was $27,950. The range for salaries was $17,390 to $45,340. Those who worked in offices of optometrists and ophthalmologists earned the most.

Career Potential and Additional Information

With an aging population there will be an increasing need for glasses over the next decade. The outlook for opticians is that the profession is expected to grow about as fast as the average for all occupations. Technological advancements in materials for glasses and contact lenses will spur the demand as well.

For more information about a career as an optician, contact the American Board of Opticianry. Their Web site is *www.abo.org*. Their address is 6506 Loisdale Road, Suite 209, Springfield, VA 22150.

Patient Representatives and Health Advocates

Patient representatives are also known as health advocates, patient advocates, and ombudsmen. Historically they worked primarily in

, out now they work in other health care arenas as well to .ot patients and their families deal with health and medical issues and to advocate for the patient.

Duties, Activities, and Scope of Practice

This is a relatively new career and the duties may differ from one employer to another. The basic premise is to improve the outcomes for the patient as well as improve patient satisfaction with the care provided.

Hospitalization in particular is a stressful situation to all involved. Patients and family members experience a sense of loss of control and independence. They often do not understand a lot of what is happening and feel they have no rights or options. This is not true. Patients have rights as well as responsibilities. Most institutions adhere to the American Hospital Association's "Patients Bill of Rights" or one that their state has adopted. A list of these rights is given and/ or read to patients upon admission to the facility. Hospitals are in competition for patients and have a vested interest in making sure their patients understand their rights and are satisfied with the level of care they receive.

Question

How do patient advocates improve patient outcomes?
They assist patients and families in understanding and dealing with policies, procedures, and personnel in hospitals, clinics, and other ambulatory care settings. They also help patients to understand their diagnosis, treatment, and procedures. Health advocates listen to patients, intervene if there is a dispute or problem, and educate patients (and the general public) about health care issues and patients' rights and responsibilities.

Education and Training

Sarah Lawrence College in New York has the only formal master's degree program in health care advocacy. However, many colleges and universities offer courses in health care advocacy. Ombudsman programs are available through many government or private programs across the country to assist the elderly in understanding their health care options.

Because this is such a new profession, many employers have very different expectations for the education and training of the professionals they hire. It is fairly standard, however, that employers expect health care advocates to have a bachelor's degree in some area of health care or social services, and those who have studied health care advocacy as part of their curriculum will have an advantage.

Courses of study and experience recommended by the National Society for Patient Representation and Consumer Affairs include human relations, communication, conflict negotiation, medical terminology, supervision, and management. Other useful courses include microeconomics, social and behavioral sciences, and a foreign language such as Spanish.

Licensure/Certification

There are currently no licensing or certification requirements or programs, but in keeping with the rest of the health care industry, trends indicate that there will be some in the future.

Work Settings and Salaries

Health care advocates primarily work in hospitals, but other ambulatory care settings are beginning to utilize them as well. This can be particularly true in areas where English is not the predominant language of the consumer.

Advocates may also work in nursing homes, residential care facilities for the disabled as well as the elderly, ambulatory care centers for the physically or mentally disabled, and schools. Some advocates work for disease-related foundations, and some are political lobbyists.

Salaries vary greatly from one employer to another and with geographic locations. Salary studies have reported incomes ranging from $20,000 to $60,000, depending upon education, experience, and type of employment. Some advocates work as independent contractors and consultants, and their fees vary greatly as well.

Career Potential and Additional Information

Several factors will influence the job outlook for health advocacy. Cost-containment efforts may reduce staffing in some hospitals, but many consider health advocates vital to their survival and ability to attract patients in an era when patient consumerism is increasing. An aging and growing population presents many more issues between patients and institutions. Combine all this with the fact that a proactive approach to health care is demonstrating a tremendous savings in the long run, and health care advocacy looks to be a strong and growing field well into the next decade.

You can find more information about this emerging profession from the Society for Healthcare Consumer Advocacy of the American Hospital Association. Their Web site is *www.shca-aha. org/shca-aha/index.jsp*. Their address is One North Franklin, 31 North, Chicago, IL 60606.

Radiology Technologists and X-ray Technicians

Radiology technologists encompass x-ray technicians as well as the technologists who perform CAT, or CT, scans and MRIs (computer tomography and magnetic resonance imaging). All of these diagnostic tests provide practitioners with a view inside the body to help detect and diagnose or rule out illness, disease, debility, and injury.

Duties, Activities, Scope of Practice

These are specialists trained to perform diagnostic tests, which can include administering a variety of injectable as well as ingestible dyes and other contrast media, and develop images. They should not be confused with the radiologist, who is the physician who reviews and interprets the findings and gives an expert opinion as to a diagnosis.

E ssential

Following the precise prescription of the practitioner, radiology technologists prepare patients, explain procedures, ensure the equipment is set properly at the right angle, height, and exposure, prevent exposure to other parts of the body, and finally take the image and develop the films.

To protect themselves from unnecessary exposure to x-ray, magnetic, and radio waves, radiology technologists wear lead shields and stay behind barriers when actually exposing the radiation or magnetic and radio waves.

Education and Training

Training for these positions is available from hospitals, colleges and universities, and vocational/technical schools. The armed forces also offer training. Most hospitals, however, prefer to hire those with formal training. The formal training can range from one to four years, and the student receives a diploma, associate's degree, or bachelor's degree depending upon the program. The associate's degree is the most common.

Most formal programs are accredited by the Joint Review Committee on Education in Radiologic Technology.

The curriculum includes classroom and clinical study of anatomy and physiology, principals of imaging, patient care and positioning, medical terminology, radiation physics, radiobiology, pathology, and radiation protection. Additional courses are required for CT scanning and MRI technology.

Licensure/Certification

As of 2003, thirty-eight states licensed radiologic technologists and technicians. Registration is voluntary and available from the American Registry of Radiologic Technologists. Most employers prefer to hire registered radiologic technologists and technicians. Candidates must graduate from an accredited program and pass an examination. Every two years they must complete twenty-four units of continuing education in order to renew their registration.

Work Settings and Salaries

Most radiology technologists and technicians work for hospitals. Others work for private diagnostic imaging laboratories, urgent care, or clinics, in offices of physicians and dentists, and for other ambulatory care facilities. In hospitals all shifts as well as weekends and holidays have to be covered, so technologists and technicians may work day, evening, or night shifts, and some weekends and holidays.

The median salary for 2004 as reported by the U.S. Department of Labor was $43,350. Salaries range from $30,020 to $60,210.

Career Potential and Additional Information

Some employers report a shortage of qualified radiologic technologists and technicians. This profession is expected to grow faster than the average for all occupations through the next decade. Those who are multiskilled in x-ray, CT, and/or MRI technologies will have the best opportunities for employment as hospitals try to contain costs by using few individuals with more skills than more individuals with fewer skills.

For more information about careers in radiologic technologies contact the American Society of Radiologic Technologists. Their Web site is *www.asrt.org*. Their address is 15000 Central Avenue SE, Albuquerque, NM 87123-3917.

Ultrasound Technicians and Sonographers

Sonography utilizes sound waves to generate an image that can be analyzed to determine or rule out a diagnosis. It is most well known for its use in obstetrics and the ability to visualize the fetus at varying points during a pregnancy. However, sonography is useful in many other specialties, such as abdominal, breast, brain (neurological), and vascular studies. Cardiovascular sonography and echocardiography is another specialty that requires additional training.

Sound waves are bounced off of the organs, and the reflections or echoes that are returned are converted into an image that reveals data about the contour, composition, and structure of parts of the body such as organs, vessels, nerves, and systems. Sonograms reveal information about these structures as well as any abnormalities, like tumors, cysts, and blockages.

Duties, Activities, and Scope of Practice

The sonographer takes a brief medical history from the patient and then prepares the patient by explaining this safe and relatively noninvasive procedure. The sonographer positions the patient and drape for privacy as needed, exposing only the area they need to access. The equipment is selected according to the tests ordered and is set to the appropriate levels. A gel is applied to the skin, and the sonographer presses a transducer unit onto the skin. While viewing the images on a monitor screen, the sonographer moves the transducer slowly to obtain an image of the entire area.

The sonographer has to have a clear understanding of such things as normal and abnormal function and shape of the bodily structures being studied. They also have to be able to recognize obstructions and the often subtle difference between pathological and healthy tissues. Sonographers need to be discreet and leave final diagnosis and discussion to the physician.

Newer technology allows the sonographer to produce a video-like image for the physician to review. However, still images are also captured from the equipment, and the sonographer identifies key elements. They will take measurements and calculate values to report to the physician along with their own preliminary analysis.

Education and Training

Training is available from hospitals, vocational schools, colleges and universities, and the armed forces. Programs are from one to four years in length and offer certificates for the one-year, associate's degrees for the two-year, and bachelor's degrees for the four-year programs. Accredited programs are approved by the Commission on Accreditation of Allied Health Education Programs (CAAHEP).

Formal classroom education as well as supervised clinical experience is provided at all levels. The one-year programs are only open to allied health care professionals, such as R.N.s, respiratory therapists, or radiology technologists. Some other programs also only accept candidates who are allied health professionals.

The curriculum includes anatomy and physiology, histology, medical ethics, pathology, and psychology. It also includes acoustical physics, principles of ultrasound, operation, calibration, and quality controls of the equipment, imaging and display techniques, and the biological effects of ultrasound.

Specialization programs are typically one year long, in addition to the basic education, and cover the anatomy, physiology, function, and pathology of the organ systems involved for such areas as obstetrics and gynecology, neurology, and breast and abdominal sonography.

Licensure/Certification

There are no requirements for licensure or certification at the current time. Employers do show a preference for hiring professionals who have demonstrated their competency by obtaining registration. Registration is available through the American Registry for Diagnostic Sonography (ARDMS). Candidates must have completed an accredited program and satisfied requirements of employment in the field. They must pass an exam covering the general principles and instrumentation involved in sonography. They also have to pass an exam specific to the specialization. Registered sonographers may use the designation R.D.M.S. (registered diagnostic medical sonographer). More information is available from their Web site: *www.*

ardms.org. Recertification is done every three years and requires thirty hours of continuing education.

Work Settings and Salaries

Sonography does not involve radiation, so the effects of ionization are not an issue. Most sonographers work in hospital settings and therefore may need to work day, evening, or night shifts, and some weekends and holidays. They may also have to be on call.

Others work in offices of physicians, medical diagnostic and imaging laboratories, clinics, and other ambulatory care settings.

The median salary as reported by the U.S. Department of Labor for 2004 was $52,490. Salaries typically ranged from $37,800 to $72,230 per year. Those with other allied health credentials typically earned more than those without.

Career Potential and Additional Information

Sonography technology is evolving rapidly primarily because of its safe and noninvasive properties. Some of this will be slowed by cost-containment measures, but it will continue to be a fast-growing occupation. With shifts toward outpatient services, growth is expected to be more rapid in these areas than for hospitals. Overall, opportunities for sonographers are expected to grow faster than the average for all occupations over the next decade.

More information about careers in medical sonography is available from the Society of Medical Sonography. Their Web site is *www* *.sdms.org.* Their address is 2745 Dallas Parkway, Suite 350, Plano, TX 75093-8730.

Electroneurodiagnostic Technologists

Electroneurodiagnostics is the field devoted to studying the nervous system. Technologists in this field monitor, record, interpret, and study the brain and other components of the nervous system utilizing highly specialized and technical tests and instruments. With advances in technology, this field now encompasses far more than just electroencephalography (E.E.G.); however, it remains the primary focus, as it studies the functionality of the brain.

Fact

These technologists may also be known as E.E.G. technologists, E.N.D. (electroneurodiagnostic) technologists, evoked potential technologists, sleep (polysomnographic) technologists, nerve conduction technologists, and intraoperative neurophysiologic technologists. E.E.G. technicians are being phased out, and in many cases this term now refers to technologists waiting to take registration exams.

Electroencephalography is used to record brain wave activity to help diagnose stroke, trauma, infectious disease, tumors, and other medical conditions such as Alzheimer's. It is also used to determine brain death. Evoked potential studies monitor visual, auditory, and somatosensory (sensations such as pain, touch, temperature) systems. Nerve conduction studies study the peripheral nerves and the response to stimuli. Polysomnography studies nighttime sleep patterns, and intraoperative neurophysiologic monitoring is the monitoring of the brain, spinal cord, and other nervous system components during surgery.

Duties, Activities, and Scope of Practice

The E.N.D. is responsible for recording the activity of the brain or other components of the nervous system according to the test ordered by the physician. E.N.D.s obtain a brief medical history from the patient, then explain the procedure and prepare and position the patient. They apply the appropriate combination of electrodes and instrument controls and conduct the test.

During the testing they observe the patient's behavior, respiration pattern, and cardiac and neurological data. They are trained in what normal and abnormal activity looks like and how to record the data. They are also trained in how to respond to any medical emergency that might come up during the testing.

When the test is complete, they remove the electrodes and debrief the patient. They will then send a report to the physician or encephalographer describing the events during the testing, as well as a tracing of the electrical activity.

Education and Training

Prior to 2005, on-the-job training was allowed for entry-level positions in this profession. That standard has now changed and an associate's degree is required. CAAHEP accredits many programs through community colleges and vocational schools. Bachelor's degrees are also available through many colleges and universities.

In addition to general-education courses, the curriculum includes neurology, neuroanatomy, anatomy and physiology, and neurophysiology, in addition to the use of the diagnostic equipment and instrumentation. Classroom education as well as supervised clinical practice is standard.

Licensure/Certification

There is currently no licensure requirement for E.N.D. technologists, but they can become registered and demonstrate competency through examination. The American Board of Registration for Encephalographic and Evoked Potential Technologists (ABRET) administers the examination to those who have met education and employment requirements. Those who pass may use the designation R. E.E.G. T. (registered E.E.G. technologist). ABRET also offers examinations in evoked potentials and intraoperative neurophysiologic testing.

Work Settings and Salaries

E.N.D.s work primarily in hospitals. Often they only work the day shift and rotate being on call for evening and night emergencies, weekends, or holidays. Those who perform sleep studies have to be available at night. Some work in the offices of neurologists and neurosurgeons.

The American Society of Electroneurodiagnostic Technologists reports the average salary in 2003 for E.N.D.s was approximately $45,000. Salaries range from $30,000 to $70,000 per year, depending on experience, education, and location.

Career Potential and Additional Information

This field is expected to grow as the population ages and requires more studies into the activity of the neurological system. New and advanced technology in this field will open more opportunities as well.

For more information about careers in the field of electroneurodiagnostics, contact the American Society of Electroneurodiagnostic Technologists (ASET). Their Web site is *www.aset.org*. Their address is 6501 East Commerce Avenue, Suite 120, Kansas City, MO 64120.

Chapter 17

Alternative Medicine and Wellness

Current trends in health care toward being proactive and emphasizing the patient's responsibility for their own health care status have renewed an interest in alternative medicine. There has also been a trend of dissatisfaction with traditional medicine and traditional practitioners over the past few years. The skyrocketing costs alone have driven many away from traditional medicine. As a result there has been a renaissance of sorts for wellness and alternative approaches to health care.

The Controversy

Alternative medicine and wellness is not accepted by everyone. There is, in fact, a great deal of skepticism and even charges of quackery about many of these fields. What needs to be remembered is that alternative medicine and wellness do not offer cures in the same way that traditional allopathic medicine does. If a licensed alternative medicine practitioner is touting a cure, then indeed there should be skepticism, and a second opinion should be sought. Remember: If it sounds too good to be true, it probably is.

Most of the controversy arises from unlicensed practitioners who prey on the feelings of helplessness and desperation of patients and family members in reaction to illness, especially when it is life-threatening. In some instances this is a moneymaking scheme, and in others the healer truly believes he or she can heal or cure the patient.

Alternative medicine does offer drug-free options for symptom control, such as pain management and allergy relief. However, bringing out-of-control symptoms under control is not the same as providing a "cure." When symptoms continue to be controlled, the appearance of the disease can be so well controlled that it does actually abate for a period of time. This does not mean that the disease is cured, and follow-up examinations should never be ignored.

E ssential

Many traditional practitioners—such as physicians, physician assistants, chiropractors, R.N.s and nurse practitioners, veterinarians, and dentists—have explored alternative medicine and wellness as adjunctive therapy to their own traditional practices and have become certified in the practices and treatments. Board certification is available in many areas.

More traditional, licensed practitioners have been able to use alternative approaches such as acupuncture and reflexology as adjunctive therapy to help their patients attain symptom control, particularly in the area of chronic pain.

The federal government established the National Center for Complementary and Alternative Medicine (NCCAM), which is a branch of the National Institutes of Health (NIH). Their Web site is *www.nccam.nih.gov.*

State laws governing the licensing of alternative medicine practitioners vary. Some states don't license alternative medicine practitioners, and not all alternative medicine practices are licensed. In general, to become licensed in an alternative medicine practice, the candidate must have at least a master's degree from an accredited college or university and pass a state examination. Other conditions may apply. Most states have an Office of Complementary and Alternative Medical Therapies that oversees licensing. Check with your state government for specifics.

Otherwise, the alternative medicine "experts" are simply considered counselors. They can't diagnose or prescribe. As counselors, they may make recommendations based on opinions and give advice or provide noninvasive treatments, but they are not licensed practitioners.

Basic Tenets of Alternative Medicine

How the practitioner views the body is the primary difference between traditional and alternative medicine. While traditional medicine takes the approach of viewing the body as a conglomeration of systems and organs, alternative medicine sees the body as a whole.

Alternative medicine practitioners focus on bringing harmony to the body and establishing balance. They include the body, mind, and spirit in this process, and focus on preventing illness in the first place. Alternative medicine relies on herbal and holistic remedies and treatments such as massage and acupuncture. Practitioners also council patients on lifestyle changes needed to promote wellness and decrease their risk of illness.

The basic tenets of alternative medicine include:

- Harmony of body, mind, and spirit promote health and wellness and reduce the risk of illness.
- Illness is caused by imbalances in the body as a whole.
- The root of the illness must be addressed in order to effectively treat and cure an illness. Treating symptoms alone will not cure a disease.
- Optimal health is achieved only when the treatment plan is individualized to the specific strengths and weaknesses of the patient.
- The practitioner is an educator with the responsibility to teach patients how to live a healthy lifestyle and how to care for themselves and remove obstacles that prevent them from achieving good health.

Empowering patients to take a proactive approach to their health and wellness instead of relying on medical professionals to cure them has always been a premise of alternative medicine and is one that traditional Western medicine has recently adopted.

Students of alternative medicine will find many overlapping areas of science and philosophy. Anatomy, physiology, biology, chemistry, physics, and math are the basic foundation of both alternative and traditional medicine and should be taken in undergraduate work.

Acupuncturists

Acupuncture is one of the three oldest practices of health care, following faith healing and herbology. It has been practiced for over 3,000 years, and it is only a part of the vast practice of medicine known as traditional Chinese medicine (TCM). According to Chinese medicine, vital energy, or *qi* (pronounced "chee"), flows along the pathways or meridians in the body. When the energy flows freely and is unimpeded, a balance is maintained and wellness is preserved.

The word *acupuncture* literally means "needle piercing," and the practice involves the use of very thin, solid needles. The needles are placed through the skin, just deep enough to hold them in place, and into one of more than 2,000 points along the pathways or meridians.

 Fact

The body's balance of energy is composed of two inseparable and opposing forces called yin and yang. Yin represents cold, slow, and passive principles. Yang represents hot, active, and excited principles. Yin and yang are not opposite, but rather complementary, as one flows into the other, such as day turning into night, and night into day.

If the flow of energy is impeded or blocked, the balance is affected. The acupuncturist takes a careful history and classifies the issues into yin and yang. The needles are placed into appropriately chosen acupuncture points along the meridians to help improve the flow of energy and reinstate the yin/yang balance.

In terms of Western medicine, it is believed that acupuncture regulates the nervous system, which allows for the release of endorphins and immune system cells that aid in the alleviation of pain. Other studies have shown that acupuncture may alter brain chemistry. This results in the release of neurotransmitters and neurohormones that affect portions of the central nervous system. This leads to changes in involuntary bodily functions, such as immune reactions. It can also alter blood pressure and body temperature.

Education and More Information

Allied health care professionals can train in acupuncture through accredited programs, which involves 300 hours of training, including 100 hours of clinical practice. Physicians can apply to the American Board of Medical Acupuncture to become board certified in acupuncture.

Patients often report being either energized by the acupuncture (an increase in yang) or relaxed by it (an increase in yin). This follows the principles of traditional Chinese medicine of treating yang symptoms with yin and vice versa.

Others seeking to become acupuncturists must graduate from an accredited school with a master's degree in acupuncture and Asian medicine in order to be licensed by their state. Most accredited programs include an internship of about 400 hours of closely supervised work with professional medical practitioners.

More information about careers in acupuncture is available from the American Academy of Medical Acupuncture. Their Web site is *www.medicalacupuncture.org*. Their address is 4929 Wilshire Boulevard, Suite 428, Los Angeles, CA 90010.

Reflexologists

Reflexology is another alternative medicine practice. It can be traced back to ancient Egypt and Asia. Pictorial evidence of the practice is said to be found in the physician's tomb in Egypt and dates back to 2300 B.C. There are several forms of reflexology, such as foot, hand, and ear, but foot reflexology is perhaps the most common in recent times. Podiatrists (see Chapter 7) often study this practice and incorporate it as an adjunct therapy.

Reflexologists utilize a detailed mapping of the foot to identify and treat an imbalance of energy flow to other parts of the body such as organs and tissues. It has been shown to be effective in the treatment of acute as well as chronic conditions, such as migraines, back pain, sleep disorders, digestive disorders, infertility, hormonal imbalances, and stress-related conditions. In general the right foot corresponds to the right side of the body and its organs, and the left foot to the left side; however, there can be some crossover.

The reflexologist takes a detailed history of health and lifestyle. Based on the information collected, select pressure points in the feet are massaged to restore the flow of qi (vital energy). Treatments usually last about an hour. Responses can usually be linked to the yin or yang energy flow that was enhanced by the treatment. Feedback about the response generated is essential to ongoing treatments.

Education and More Information

Reflexology training by itself can be from 100 to 1,000 hours of study. Vocational schools and schools of massage or other healing arts typically offer reflexology courses. Graduates of accredited programs can apply for national certification from the American Reflexology Certification Board (ARCB). Licensure regulations vary from state to state and may fall under the category of massage therapy modalities (see Chapter 11).

Those who want to seriously practice alternative medicine may also wish to pursue a master's degree in alternative medicine and combine the reflexology training into their practice.

The curriculum will include learning Chinese medical language and symbols, traditional herbal remedies, basic acupuncture techniques, as well as interviewing techniques and how to identify the problems and choose treatments. Again, these programs require about 400 hours of internship with traditional medical practitioners.

Fact

Reflexology was introduced to the Western world in 1913 as "zone therapy," which was further developed into reflexology in the 1930s. It's known as a complementary therapy that is also based on the principles of qi, or vital energy, and the theory of harmony and health.

More information about careers in reflexology is available from the Reflexology Association of America. Their Web site is *www.reflexology-usa.org*. Their address is 4012 Rainbow, Suite K-PMB #585, Las Vegas, NV 89103-2059.

Homeopaths

Homeopathy is an alternative approach to healing using the body's own vital force to restore balance after health problems have developed from the disruption of that energy. The name comes from the Greek words *homeo*, which means "similar," and *pathos*, meaning "suffering" or "disease." Homeopathy has been practiced in the United States since the early nineteenth century. It was developed in Germany.

Treatments are individualized to the patient and take into consideration the whole patient, including the symptoms, the emotional and mental status, and the lifestyle of the patient. Therefore, two people with the same symptoms could be given very different remedies.

Homeopathic remedies are derived from plants, minerals, and animals and are regulated by the U.S. Food and Drug Administration (FDA) in the same manner as are nonprescription, over-the-counter medications. This means they can be purchased without a prescription. New OTC drugs are required to go through rigorous testing for safety before they can be marketed. This however, is not true for homeopathic remedies. Remedies are expected to meet legal requirements, including labeling that details ingredients, dilution, safety information, and the ailments they can be used for. They also have to meet standards for packaging, purity, quality, and strength.

Alert

Homeopathic treatment is based on the premise that like cures like. It involves giving the patient extremely small doses of substances (called remedies) that if given to healthy people in large doses would cause the same illness as the one being treated. The remedies are expected to stimulate the body to use its own defense mechanisms and self-healing properties to treat and/or prevent illness.

Homeopaths compile data regarding the patient's medical history and lifestyle, and then recommend remedies based on their findings and from looking at the whole person. They evaluate feedback from the patient about responses to the treatments and continue or modify the approach until wellness is re-established.

Some patients report feeling worse initially, and homeopaths interpret this as the body temporarily exacerbating symptoms in the process of stimulating the self-healing process to restore health.

Education and More Information

Most homeopaths are also medical practitioners, so they are able to diagnose and/or prescribe. These include M.D.s, nurse practitioners, physician assistants, naturopaths, dentists, veterinarians, and chiropractors. It also provides them a license under which to practice medicine in only three states. Those already holding a degree in allied health care take continuing-education courses specific to the practice of homeopathy.

Otherwise, homeopaths can practice as long as they don't represent themselves as doctors. They may counsel patients and give advice, but they may not diagnose or prescribe. Education for these homeopaths can vary from two days to four years. As with other alternative medicine options, a master's degree in holistic medicine or alternative medicine gives great credence to the homeopath, who can become certified by the National Center for Homeopathy (NCH).

The American Institute of Homeopathy (AIH) provides more information about careers in homeopathy. Their Web site is *www .homeopathyusa.org*. Their address is 801 N. Fairfax Street, Suite 306, Alexandria, VA 22314.

Naturopaths

Since ancient times, naturopathic practitioners and healers have used the philosophy of Hippocrates that "nature is the healer of all diseases." They use such natural products and treatments as herbs, water, nutrition, sunlight, fasting, massage, and manipulation of tissue to stimulate the body's own healing powers.

In the 1970s, patients began to become dissatisfied with traditional medicine and the beginnings of the skyrocketing costs of health care. Many Americans began to look at alternatives to traditional medicine as a means to promote wellness and prevent illness. Naturopaths and other alternative medicine providers began to gain in popularity again.

Naturopaths also believe in the principle of holistic medicine that the entire entity must be treated, and balance and harmony restored, in order to treat illness and promote wellness. They also combine many of the other alternative treatments such as acupuncture, massage, and traditional Chinese medicine into their practice. And when necessary they will refer the patient to a traditional allopathic medical practitioner.

As true physicians, naturopaths may diagnose and prescribe treatment, although they do not utilize traditional medicines in their practice.

Education and More Information

Naturopathic physicians (N.D.s) have the highest level of education for naturopathic practitioners. They usually have a bachelor's degree in pre-med, but it is not required. Then they attend a four-year graduate program in a naturopathic medical school. They take all of the same basic courses as traditional medical students, such as medical sciences and conventional diagnostics. In addition, they study holistic medicine, which includes courses in traditional Chinese medicine, homeopathic medicine, acupuncture, clinical nutrition, botanical medicine, hydrotherapy, naturopathic manipulative therapy, psychology and counseling, minor surgery, and pharmacology.

 Fact

In the early part of the twentieth century there were thousands of naturopathic physicians in the United States, and a number of naturopathic medical schools. These physicians were treating thousands of patients nationwide, but by the 1950s, with the advent of miracle drugs such as antibiotics, most patients turned to allopathic medicine for treatments and cures.

Schools for naturopaths are accredited by the Council on Naturopathic Medical Education (CNME). Additional training in acupuncture and home birthing are also available to N.D.s who wish to specialize.

N.D.s take board certification examinations from the North American Board of Naturopathic Examiners (NABNE), and in the twelve states that so far license naturopaths, they must also pass the NPLEX (Naturopathic Physicians Licensing Examination Board) examination. Many other states are investigating licensure for naturopaths, mostly because a growing portion of the public is demanding alternatives and wants to have the option of preventative medicine and wellness. The American Association of Naturopathic

Physicians (AANP) is strongly advocating for the licensing of NPs in all fifty states.

You can get more information about careers in naturopathic medicine from the American Association of Naturopathic Physicians. Their Web site is *www.naturopathic.org.* Their address is 4435 Wisconsin Avenue NW, Suite 403, Washington, DC 20016.

Other Alternative Healers

Other alternative healers may conjure up an idea of faith healers and those who sell snake oil, but there are many other legitimate areas of alternative medicine to be considered. These include but are not limited to other massage therapies such as Reiki. There is also acupressure, which is similar to acupuncture except that pressure points are accessed and no needles are used. Another choice is biofeedback, which uses machinery to train the patient to recognize and respond to signals from the body to help improve health. Herbology is the study of using herbs for medicinal purposes.

Ayurveda is another form of Asian alternative medicine derived in ancient India. It is based on finding and maintaining harmony between the five basic elements of earth, wind, fire, water, and space. These are all represented as different elements in the body, and a balance is required to maintain health.

There are many other options to explore for traditional as well as nontraditional health care careers. They may just be an important adjunct to other traditional allied health care treatments. It is also important to understand that all health care careers require lifelong learning.

The Internet has brought information into the homes of your patients and clients. A little knowledge can be dangerous, and it is a challenge all health care professionals face. One of the issues with homeopathy, for instance, is that patients have access to the remedies without having to seek the advice of the homoeopathist. It is important for all traditional and alternative health care professionals to have an understanding or at least an awareness of the options and alternatives their patients may be using, as well as the fact that there are options to be considered.

E ssential

One of the reasons patients have sought out nontraditional medicine is that they have been dissatisfied with professionals who are closed-minded and often secretive. Patients want to be in control of their health status and treatment options. They want to be proactive and promote wellness. Having access to information has been an important step in this process.

You can read more about any of these and other alternative health care options by searching the Internet. Stay abreast of the options and changes in the health care field.

Chapter 18

Other Issues to Consider

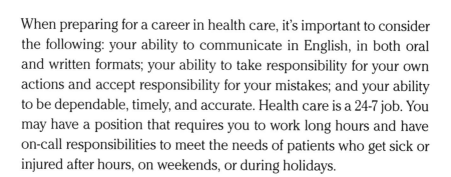

When preparing for a career in health care, it's important to consider the following: your ability to communicate in English, in both oral and written formats; your ability to take responsibility for your own actions and accept responsibility for your mistakes; and your ability to be dependable, timely, and accurate. Health care is a 24-7 job. You may have a position that requires you to work long hours and have on-call responsibilities to meet the needs of patients who get sick or injured after hours, on weekends, or during holidays.

The Importance of Communication: Oral and Written

Communication is one of the most vital components in health care. You will not only have to be able to communicate your ideas, but you will also need to be able to understand and listen to your patients in order to learn about their complaints and issues.

You need to be able to speak clearly. Many times you will need to think on your feet and respond quickly and accurately. You might be barking orders during a resuscitation effort, or you may be calling in a new prescription to the pharmacy. Not only do you need to have a clear and accurate understanding of what you are communicating, but the listener on the other end of the defibrillator paddles or the telephone needs to be able to understand you.

Written communication also needs to be accurate. Legibility is important. Many avenues are being used, and new ones explored, especially in the technology department, to eliminate issues with the physician's notoriously illegible scribble. You must be able to document your findings, your actions, and the outcomes. This means you need to be able to write something similar to a short story or essay about your experience with the patient at each given time. Sometimes it will be very short, and other times it must be detailed and even lengthy. The documentation is important so that the person coming in after you has a clear picture of the diagnosis or identified problem, the care given, and the response or outcome.

If English is not your first language, you may need to take a course or two to improve your skills. There are many "English as a second language" (ESL) courses available from community colleges or community adult schools. Some courses concentrate on either oral or written language skills, so be sure to take the ones most pertinent to your needs.

Alert

All health care documentation is part of a legal record and could be subpoenaed at any given time in the future. Remember: If it's not documented, you didn't do it! Your documentation is your proof. It can also be evidence against you, so you must always be accurate and truthful, even if you made an error.

In the event that writing just isn't your strong suit, there are remedial courses or courses in subjects such as business English that can teach you how to write things in clear, specific, and concise terms.

A speech class will be beneficial as well to ensure that you can speak clearly, and that you get over the fear of speaking in front of a crowd. There may never be a need to address a large audience, but in the event of an emergency, timidity in calling out instructions in front of strangers simply will not work.

If your patient has something to tell you, you must stop talking and listen! Reiterate what you think you heard and ask questions if you don't understand. Never assume anything, and always get verification. Verification and validation of the patient's feelings, concerns, and observations is important to achieve effective communication, as well as to diagnose and treat the issues at hand.

E ssential

Effective communication includes being a good listener as well as a good speaker. Communication is a two-way process. The first lesson in this process is to understand that you cannot listen if you are speaking. And when you are speaking you must have the undivided attention of the listener.

Honesty and the Ability to Take Responsibility

Health care professionals deal with life and death issues. Accuracy is essential to success. Despite all of the best efforts, there will be times when mistakes happen. When they do, it is important that all efforts are turned to righting the error, and never to trying to cover it up. The timely reporting of the error can be extremely important to the successful correction. There is not room for excuses. Just take action and make efforts to solve the problem and prevent it from happening again.

Mistakes and even near misses are avenues for learning. Avoiding errors in the first place is always best, but when they do happen, learn from your mistakes and grow from the experience.

Staffing shortages, such as those nurses face in many areas, can often lead to mistakes. This adds to the job stress, and it becomes a vicious cycle.

Working to solve these shortages by enforcing nurse-to-patient ratios or to address the patient acuity and to reduce some of the responsibilities are areas where some progress is being made to reduce errors.

Technological advances are being used to address the problem of errors as well. For example, using barcodes to identify and match patients to their medications can help to avoid costly medication errors. But this is successful only if the process is followed. It is essential that health care team members take this issue seriously and develop and maintain a strong work ethic steeped in honesty and a commitment to always strive for accuracy.

 Fact

Sometimes errors can involve a situation that is very uncomfortable, such as learning of a mistake that someone else made and having to confront them and/or to report it to your supervisor. The patient's well-being must be the top priority, and every mistake must be reported upon discovery.

It is possible the error may just be an omission in the charting, but this is an error nonetheless. This is usually an easy one to correct, and unless it has caused the patient harm, such as in the form of having something repeated, it usually has little or no impact on the patient's condition. Simple correction of the omission can be done following the facility's rules for doing so.

The rule that *if it isn't charted, it wasn't done* is a standard by which every health care worker must live. The chart can be amended as long as the person doing so has full memory of what transpired, but omissions should always be avoided in the first place and certainly never become the norm.

Honesty is an essential characteristic for health care workers, and the ability to accept responsibility is just as important. Mistakes happen; no one is perfect. While no one wants to make mistakes, and sometimes they can be costly ones, it is important to be able to accept responsibility and not to look for someone else to blame.

Learn to examine what went wrong and how to prevent it from ever happening again, and move on. This process moves toward healing and finding solutions. In order for this to happen, however, you must be able to accept responsibility for the error as well as for finding a solution or correction. This is an uncomfortable situation for everyone, and not all people are able to do this. Consider carefully how you would react and whether this is something you could learn to do. If you always look to blame someone else for your mistakes, or don't believe you ever make mistakes, then perhaps health care is not the career choice for you.

Dependability, Accuracy, and Timeliness

Health care is a team effort. For that team effort to be the best it can be, everyone has to pull his or her own weight. There are no superstars, and there is no I in "team". Most health care positions are physically and emotionally demanding and highly stressful. When the team is well oiled and runs smoothly, it is much easier to cope with these demands and stressors. For that to happen, each team member has to set dependability, timeliness, and accuracy as priorities.

This means you need to have a strong work ethic. You must always be willing to show up for shifts as assigned, be on time, and stay until your shift has ended and your work is complete. You also have to put forth your very best effort to be accurate at all times.

If you routinely call in "sick" to do other things, such as go skiing or spend time with your friends, you may want to think again about taking on a career in health care.

E ssential

People don't suddenly get well because it's the weekend or you want to see your child play basketball. They don't wait until the fireworks have all gone out on the Fourth of July before they have that heart attack. And sometimes they do call you in the middle of the night to ask you what size hat they should buy for their newborn!

Timeliness is important even more so in some fields than others. In some cases, such as for nurses in hospitals, each shift reports off to the next. It is vital to arrive on time to get the report (or conference) as it is given and to have an opportunity to discuss any concerns without imposing on the staff that is leaving to go home. If you are late, you may miss important information or an opportunity to speak with a patient's nurse or aide before he leaves. You will also burden your coworkers with having to cover your patients until you arrive. Always remember to treat team members as you would like them to treat you. Don't impose unnecessarily. Life happens, but be considerate.

Accuracy and attention to detail are also essential characteristics for all health care workers. For example, if you are a medical illustrator, it would be important to get the right name for the right organ. If you are a medical assistant, your patient won't be happy if you schedule the appointment for 2 P.M. and then write on their appointment card that it's at 2:30 P.M.

If you are giving medications, it is important that you give the correct medication to the correct patient at the right time and then record the correct dose, time, route, and response. Timely documentation ensures that the patient isn't given another dose.

Health Care Is Not a Nine-to-Five Job

If you work in a field of health care that doesn't involve patient care, you might be able to work a set schedule and possibly avoid working holidays, weekends, or evenings. For those involved in direct care, you're going to have to adjust to a lifestyle that doesn't revolve around banker's hours.

Health care is needed twenty-four hours a day, 365 days a year. Health care professionals are expected to meet the needs of patients. Whether you are the practitioner on call or the home health aide, you may be expected to deal with the needs of a patient in the middle of the night, on Christmas morning, or even on your birthday. You might be the pharmacist in the all-night pharmacy who gets the call at 3 A.M. to fill a prescription for a two-year-old with the croup.

Think about your own experiences in visiting your physician, having x-rays or blood drawn, or making a trip to urgent care or the ER. You usually have to wait, and sometimes way beyond your appointment time, or for several hours in an emergency room.

On the professional side of this scenario, everyone involved in the health care setting, from the receptionist to the practitioner, is going to be affected by the delays and the unexpected. In hospital settings, it's not uncommon for the unexpected to happen just before the end of your shift!

Alert

Health care is not predictable. When you finally get to see the physician, you want her full attention and to be her first priority. In order to give 100 percent to all patients, she may have to spend a little more time with one person, and that sets everything back for the day. Sometimes an emergency happens and everything has to get rescheduled.

Unlike your friends who work in other industries, you won't find yourself taking two-hour power lunches. You most likely won't have a job where you can leave for a while and come back and finish up your day's work by staying late. In some cases you might be the only ranking professional (such as the R.N.) available, and find that you cannot even take a bathroom break until another R.N. comes to relieve you.

It's important to understand the extent of your responsibilities as a health care worker before you enter the profession. If you want to be a doctor just for the money and the prestige, you'll quickly find yourself overwhelmed and very unhappy with the schedule you're required to keep and resenting the sacrifices you have to make. This is one of the biggest reasons many health care workers leave the profession in their first three years. And it's one of the reasons for the tremendous shortages in some health care fields such as nursing.

Another reason for some of these shortages stems from the fact that years ago, women who wanted to work outside the home had few choices. They became secretaries, teachers, or nurses. Today there are many career choices for women in the health care field alone. Many women as well as men look for positions that offer them the best opportunities for flexible schedules.

Future challenges for those seeking to solve staffing shortages involve solving some of the issues of flexibility. Creative solutions are needed. Those employers who cannot learn to think outside the box and insist on following the same rules and schedules that they always have will find themselves dealing with continued staffing shortages and retention issues.

Working Within Your Scope of Practice

As a health care professional, you will most likely have a license, certification, and or/job description that is defined by a Practice Act and/ or scope of practice to which you are expected to adhere. Although many of the health care workers will have studied similar curriculum in the course of their education, a physical therapist is not a nurse, a social worker is not a speech therapist, and a chiropractor is not a neurosurgeon.

In this same light, a physical therapy aide is not a physical therapist, and a nurse's aide is not a nurse. The medical assistant in the physician's office cannot diagnose or prescribe. Sometimes these lines get fuzzy if the aide is enrolled in a program to advance to become a physical therapist or nurse, or the medical assistant is about to graduate from medical school. But the bottom line is that even though you may have been trained in how to do something more complex, you are not yet licensed to perform these tasks, and your job description does not entitle you to perform them. You may only perform duties in the scope of practice for the specific job you are doing at that particular moment.

Each state will have its own Practice Act for your particular field. For instance, physical therapists may be allowed to change dressings on wounds in some states and not in others, even though they have been trained and educated to do so. It is important to understand and to stay informed about the licensing, Practice Acts, and scope of practice changes for your field in your geographic location. This information is available from your state government as well as the licensing board and your professional organization.

Alert

Licensing agencies are set up to protect the public from those who are not qualified or are no longer licensed or qualified to practice in a given area. As a consumer, you will appreciate the fact that your doctor is qualified to diagnose your problem and prescribe the treatment, whereas another health care worker is not.

You should never assume that an employer is up to date on all of the Practice Acts. If you receive a request to perform something you aren't certain is within your scope of practice, consult the experts. Check with your state's Practice Act. Most are available online at your state government's Web site.

If you have never performed the specific duty being requested, you must also speak up so that you are appropriately supervised and/or checked off on the skill before performing it alone.

Confidentiality and HIPAA

Patients have a right to privacy and confidentiality. This encompasses many things, from protecting their dignity to maintaining the confidentiality of their medical history and present diagnosis. In examining a patient, and often in treating them as well, there will be a need for them to remove clothing. They have the right to not be exposed unnecessarily to anyone. They also have the right to discuss health care issues in confidence.

Health care professionals are expected to honor these rights at all times. There may be points at which information must be shared. For example, TB is a communicable disease that must be reported to public health officials, and in some instances to other individuals who may have been exposed. Sexually transmitted diseases must be reported to public health officials as well as to all potentially exposed partners. However, there are rules to follow in doing so in order to protect the rights of those involved.

There are laws governing confidentiality, and they vary greatly from state to state. For instance, in California, it is illegal to transmit any information on the HIV status of a patient. The diagnosis may not be coded on medical records but may be listed in the medical history.

 Fact

In 1996, Congress passed legislation known as HIPAA. This is the Health Insurance Portability and Accountability Act. The original intent was to protect individuals from losing their health insurance or from having pre-existing clause limitations placed on their health insurance coverage if they left or changed jobs. The other intent was to provide the federal government with the power to intervene in issues of fraud and abuse in the health care industry.

It took five years for HIPAA to take effect, and two more years to become mandatory. As of April 2003, all health care facilities must comply with the rulings. You most likely have received notifications about your HIPAA rights, or have noticed changes in the way business is conducted. For instance, many pharmacies now have you stand way back from the counter when dropping off or picking up prescriptions so that you won't overhear information about another customer.

Another intention of HIPAA is to set in motion the process for establishing Electronic Health Records (EHR). This would create a national database of medical records that could be accessed by professionals when needed. The need for this type of access was recently pointed out in the aftermath of Hurricane Katrina, when masses of individuals were relocated without access to their medications, prescription information, and medical records. Patients didn't know their diagnoses and/or the names of their medications to even begin to assist in the process.

Confidentiality is an important aspect of health care. It's a challenge sometimes not to share the fact that you are treating a celebrity. It is also important to understand that you cannot share information about a patient with their family members or friends without the patient's consent. The ability to keep secrets and honor confidentiality is an important characteristic for all health care professionals.

Medical Malpractice Issues

Medical science is not an exact science, but most laypeople believe it is. Health care workers of all levels have fed into this myth for many thousands of years. Doctors have had God complexes, and patients have believed that their physicians are perfect and superhuman since the time of Hippocrates—that is, until something goes "wrong." Sometimes it is indeed an error. But sometimes everything humanly possible was done to the best of everyone's ability and it just didn't help.

Any major change can represent a loss of some sort. Loss produces grief. One of the five stages of grief is anger. When that anger escalates and is directed at specific people, oftentimes it is the health care workers who receive the brunt of it. All too often in our litigious society that brunt is in the form of a malpractice action.

Health care workers and facilities carry large malpractice insurance policies. In some instances the facility's policy covers the employees, such as nurses, therapists, aides, and other health care workers, throughout the facility. Professional organizations often offer additional coverage as a perk to members. Some insurance companies also offer group rates for individual coverage through ads in trade journals. For those who work in private practice or as independent contractors, such as for home health agencies or clinics, an individual policy is a must.

Alert

Malpractice actions are usually brought against those with the deepest pockets, such as the hospitals and other facilities and the physicians. But many times the "wealth" is spread to include any and all who participated in the care. This is often the case when there was an event or action that was indeed an error.

In some instances malpractice coverage has become so costly that physicians have closed their practices. These costs have contributed immensely to the skyrocketing costs of health care. Congress has considered many different forms of legislation to limit liabilities and payouts from malpractice issues in order to curb this trend.

Humanizing patient care as well as placing the responsibility for health status and outcomes on the patient's shoulders have helped to reduce the impact of medical malpractice issues.

Health care workers can help to further this cause by demanding excellence from themselves and their peers, and yet steering clear of egos and the attitude that they are infallible and omnipotent. Taking responsibility for their actions and correcting errors also play a big part in reducing the litigious climate. Patient education and effective communication are also important keys to lowering the risk of malpractice issues.

Chapter 19

Finding a Job

Before you complete your education, you should be scoping out prospective employers. Many health care educations include clinical experience and internships. This time should be used wisely to begin to get a clear picture of not only the profession, but the type of employment setting you would be interested in working in, as well as the ones you would not. Devise lists of the pros and cons of not only this particular employer, the managers, and management system, but of the type of work setting itself.

The Job Search

In many instances health care students can graduate from school and go to work for the same place where they did much of their clinical studies. Nurses, for example, frequently do this. Not only have you had an opportunity to observe firsthand the function of a particular setting, but the facility has had an opportunity to get to know you as well. Often it is the facility that does the recruiting of students.

Look Close to Home

In some instances you might not have the choice of whether or not to work in a hospital. In other instances there may be many options. And sometimes a year's experience working in a hospital setting first may be required or highly recommended. For many health care professions the hands-on clinical training takes place in a hospital setting. Should you not be recruited or not have had an opportunity for clinical practice, there are many places to job search.

Alert

Don't forget the most obvious starting point, which is the school where you trained. Many times employers send their job listings to schools before they post them elsewhere. Schools often have out-placement counselors and centers to help students find their first jobs. This is usually true of vocational and technical schools and is often part of their marketing plan for their programs.

Locate facilities near your home or where you want to work, and contact the Career Center or Human Resources Department to determine openings. You may be able to find a Web site for the facility and learn about job openings online. You may also wish to send a cover letter and copy of your resume for them to consider and keep on file for future openings.

Professional Publications

Professional journals usually have listings from at least some of the major players in your field. If they don't list an opportunity for someone with your qualifications, there will be contact information listed and you can call or send a letter of inquiry. You can find copies of professional journals in your school library or in medical school libraries. Most are also accessible online. There may be a fee involved, or they may send you a sample issue to consider for subscription. See Chapter 21 for more information on professional associations, many of which publish the professional journals or will have references to them. You can also find information about trade journals from your local library. Ask the librarian to help you locate the *Magazine Industry Market Place*. This reference book is updated yearly and available in libraries.

Additional Resources

Other sources for locating jobs in the medical field include employment agencies and executive recruiters, through networking, and your professional organization.

There are several major health care job search companies online. These include:

CareerBuilder Health Jobs
✎*www.healthcare.careerbuilder.com*

Health Care Jobs Online
✎*www.hcjobsonline.com*

Hospital Jobs Online
✎*www.hospitaljobsonline.com*

J. Allen and Associates (physician job search)
✎*www.NHRphysician.com*

MedCAREERS
✎*www.medcareers.com*

Medzilla
✎*www.medzilla.com*

Monster Health Care
✎*www.monsterhealthcare.com*

Yahoo! Hot Jobs/Health Care
✎*www.hotjobs.yahoo.com/healthcarejobs/*

Resumes and Cover Letters

Once you have located the job opportunities you wish to pursue, you will need to build and write your resume and a cover letter, which introduces you and explains your interest in the available position(s).

These are very important documents. You should keep copies and update your resume on an ongoing basis. This is particularly important so that you keep a record and documentation of professional experiences as well as ongoing education.

E ssential

Your resume is your opportunity to list your accomplishments so far. Perhaps you had to have some experience in the health field in order to get into your chosen education program. That will be as important to entering the field as it was to the education requirements. It demonstrates that you have some firsthand knowledge of the health care field.

Your educational accomplishments are important as well. Where did you rank in your graduating class? Did you score especially high marks on professional boards? Did you earn honors or other accolades?

Your resume needs to be brief. It should be no more than two pages. You should use action words, and be positive. Remember, you are marketing yourself. However, don't embellish, and if you are still awaiting licensure or certification information, say so. Don't list credentials you don't yet have. Some of the important items your resume should include are:

- **Contact information:** Include your full name (including credentials you have earned) and complete contact information.
- **Education:** List the most recent, and list degrees by date.
- **Objective or current career goal:** Gear the goals you list toward the job you're seeking.
- **Work experience:** Include your job title, major accomplishments, and employment dates.
- **Qualifications and skills:** Try to identify the ones that match the job description. Include your computer and software skills.

- **Other accomplishments:** This can include volunteer positions you have held, and athletics, clubs, and service or religious organizations. (Think back to your college applications.)
- **Honors, awards, or recognitions:** List any you have received through work experiences, school, and extracurricular activities.

Think seriously about your e-mail address. It should be included, but is it something silly? It may be incredibly clever and creative. You may dearly love the cartoon character you've chosen to include in your name, but does it sound professional? Carefully consider signing up for a new e-mail account with a professional-sounding address just for your job search. Free e-mail accounts are available from sources such as Yahoo!, Google, and Hotmail. Your ISP may also allow you to create another identity.

 **Alert**

Neatness counts. Study sample resumes and choose an appropriate format. It should be professional and easy to read. Your word-processing software probably has some templates built in, or you can download others online. Proofread your resume several times, and ask friends to do so. Health care requires attention to detail, so make sure your resume represents you well.

The cover letter is your opportunity to introduce yourself and to try to entice the employer to call or e-mail you for an interview. It should be concise and to the point, but also express your interest in the position and in becoming part of their team. Be aware that if this is a large corporation, your letter may be separated out and never seen, but take the time to compose it carefully. Again, proofread and don't embellish. Integrity and honesty are vital characteristics in the health care field.

Networking Always

You have no doubt heard the phrase "it's not what you know, but who you know." Networking is an important part of finding the career opportunities you want. You actually network every day as you converse with friends, family, coworkers, acquaintances, etc., about your career, goals, ambitions, and dreams. When you need to find a job, you have to call upon everyone you know to think about everyone they know to pass on the information.

In a more formal fashion, you need to attend job fairs and professional organization events. Mingle and pass out business cards with your contact information on them. These cards don't have to be fancy or terribly formal. You can purchase blank business card stock from the stationery or office supply store and print your own. You need your name, credentials, and contact information. Have them handy at all times. This may seem awkward because it's not a business card in the true fashion. However, in the early portion of the 1900s when people made a visit to someone's home, it was customary to hand out a calling card with their name engraved on it. Sometimes they added an address or other contact information. Think of these cards as your calling card. They are essential to making contacts.

E ssential

Keep your resume up to date, and if you hear about an exciting opportunity, send it off as soon as possible to the networking contacts you've met. It is appropriate and expected at job fairs and networking functions to carry copies of your resume. Have them in a neat folder so that they don't become curled or bent.

Use networking opportunities to meet with people who work for the employers and in the positions that interest you. Ask them questions about the standard salary for an entry-level position in their company. (Don't ever ask how much they make.) Ask them about the type of benefits the company offers, such as health insurance, vacation, retirement plans, etc. If shifts and on-call responsibilities play a part in your selected field, ask how they are handled in this company. Ask about orientation and in-services. Don't put the person on the spot, but you should get a feel for whether or not this person and his coworkers are happy and secure in their jobs.

An important lesson you need to learn is that the health care field is a small and mobile community. People you meet will know people you know. You will learn the reputations of the key players in the field, and you will get to know some of them. There is a real sense of six degrees of separation. It may not be from Kevin Bacon, but it will be from someone you know who knows someone who knows someone.

You will encounter a lot of challenges in your career. Health care is constantly emerging and growing and is not now, nor probably will it ever be, perfect. If it gets to a point that you cannot continue to participate or function, move on. But don't burn your bridges. If you have been a very valuable employee, you will be sorely missed, but don't make an issue of it. Resist the temptation at an exit interview to tell off your boss or to bad-mouth the company. It is simply time to part ways and to move in another direction. Don't burn bridges! You may encounter this person in another venture down the road, or you may need a positive reference in the future. Again, you don't know everyone these people know either.

Alert

Take this information to heart and learn that no matter how unhappy you may be in a situation, never burn your bridges. You never know when you might work with someone again, or someone who knows someone, even clear across the country and in the smallest towns.

Health care is a physically and emotionally demanding job. If you haven't been able to keep yourself replenished, you will burn out. That does not mean you need to leave the profession. Look for another niche, or even consider moving into a related field. Much of the education you have may well adapt to, and offer you shortcuts to, a new career path. Get back into the network and find something new and exciting for yourself.

The Interview Process

When an employer contacts you to set up an interview, be prepared to ask a few questions. Some companies may keep you seemingly all day, filling out applications, taking tests, going for a drug test, etc., and others just want to interview you and schedule the rest later. Be sure you know how long they might need you and what you'll be expected to do so you can plan accordingly.

Before the Interview

Arrive early. Be sure to have a copy of your resume and a note-pad. You need to dress in business attire and, of course, be impeccably groomed. Don't wear heavy scents, and use a breath mint before you go in. Be sure you have two working black pens. Have a list of your references with complete contact information. Also have complete contact information for your emergency contact person.

Eat something before you go. Never go to an interview or important meeting with an empty stomach. If you do, be prepared for your stomach to start "growling" at the most inopportune time. Be sure to avoid obnoxious or offensive foods such as garlic and onions.

Be sure you have all licenses, including your driver's license and professional license(s), with you. You should also have your CPR card, if indicated, and your social security card. If you have a green card you must have this as well. Most people don't carry all of these at all times, so be sure you have them with you, as prospective employers will need to make a copy of them for your file. It can be irritating to HR personnel if you neglect to have these items with you. First impressions are important.

During the Interview

Be prepared to explain gaps in your experience or other holes in your resume. Be prepared to explain why you would be a good match for this job. Expect the unexpected. Take a deep breath and think for a moment about anything you aren't sure about or might be uncomfortable discussing. If you have a bad work experience glaring on your resume, just explain that it wasn't the right position for you. Take responsibility and don't bad-mouth others.

Be aware of your posture and body language. Sit up straight and be attentive. Crossing your arms gives an impression that you are closed to communication or input. Smile and always make eye contact.

You should expect to be asked to discuss your strengths and weaknesses in some fashion or another, so be prepared. Many will ask where you see yourself five years from now. Be prepared with an answer, such as one demonstrating a desire to grow and advance in your profession.

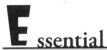

Essential

Follow the lead of the person interviewing you about bodily contact like shaking hands. Some people can be very germ phobic these days. A firm handshake is essential if they offer a hand. Always say thank you and be gracious. If you don't understand a question, say so.

If you have to complete paperwork, read it over first and check carefully what information goes where. Remember, neatness counts! Don't leave blanks. If you don't understand what you need to do, ask. (Having a small pad of sticky notes would be useful so that you can reference areas you need assistance with and complete the rest of the form if you can before asking questions.) If you make errors, ask for a new copy to complete. If possible, take the paperwork home with you so that you can give it more time and attention.

Before you leave the interview, be sure you have had a chance to get all of your questions answered. Know what the job entails, what your responsibilities would be, and what would be expected from you. Have a clear understanding of major policies, what shift you'd be working, how many weekends and holidays you're expected to work, etc. Understand who you'd be working for, who you'd be supervising, how performance is evaluated, how raises are determined, and what opportunities you would have to advance.

The Salary Question

The subject of salary may or may not come up. If they ask you about your requirements, tell them that it will have to depend upon several factors, including such things as your responsibilities, shift, on-call responsibilities, benefits, opportunities for raises (are they merit based? how often and what percentage is the usual amount for this job?), and opportunities for advancement. Usually salary and other benefits can be negotiated when a job offer is made. That may or may not take place at the time of the interview.

Don't enter into a job with false hopes and misunderstandings of expectations. You will only find yourself disenchanted and unhappy. Sometimes this leads to good people leaving the profession; at the very least it affects morale, performance, and productivity. Have a clear understanding of the expectations and responsibilities before you begin a job.

After the Interview

Again, make eye contact and thank interviewers for their time. Shake hands. If they have to make a decision, ask when you'll know what their decision is and if they'll call or contact you either way. Follow up interviews with a written response, again thanking the person who interviewed you and stating that you look forward to working for the company. Send this off right away.

If a networking contact helped you get this interview, touch base with your contact to thank him or her. If you get the job, be sure to thank your contact appropriately.

The Sign-On Bonus

Many employers are now offering sign-on bonuses, especially for hard-to-fill positions. This is a common occurrence for nurses, and it is becoming so for physical and occupational therapists as well as many other health care professionals who are facing shortages in their fields.

Alert

Before jumping at the prospect of a sign-on bonus, be sure you read and understand all of the small print. Not all sign-on bonuses are created equal, and some have specifications that are virtually impossible to meet. There are usually penalty clauses if you don't stay the determined time, so be aware that you may have to repay the bonus if you are unable to fulfill your obligation.

Get it all in writing and have a full understanding of how much you get and what your obligations are. Also have a full understanding of how and when the payments are made and how they are taxed. A large lump sum sounds great, but if it's highly taxed, is it really worth it?

Also be aware that these are hiring incentives. Long-term staff in these facilities may have morale issues and professional jealousies about sign-on bonuses. Salaries and bonuses should always be kept confidential.

The Future of Health Care Jobs

Each chapter has already discussed the future for specific professions. In general, almost all health care professions will continue to grow rapidly over the next decade. There are also many more options that already exist beyond those discussed in this book. Others will continue to evolve as technology improves and new techniques, diagnostics, and treatments are invented and approved.

There will continue to be changes and paradigm shifts in the health care industry due to the current influencing factors, as well as any that may come about from economic changes as well as the political climate of the country.

Cost-containment issues have already forced trends and roles to change, which places more responsibility upon patients for their own health status. This has helped to change some of the litigious climate and eased the focus on malpractice in some areas. It has also changed the focus of the public toward being proactive and demanding preventative education and care. This, in turn, has forced changes in roles for health care professionals and will continue to do so.

Managed care forced many difficult and uncomfortable changes in the 1990s that the health care industry is still reeling from, but many have eased and evolved into changes that have proven to be better in the long run and have brought about positive results. Cost-containment efforts continue to be a necessary evil in the health care industry and will effect changes for many years to come.

Continuing Education

Advances in health care and scientific discoveries are reported every day. Internet access to this information is almost immediate. Drugs are recalled; significant findings are reported regarding diagnostics, treatment options, and other items such as genetics; and lifestyle links are reported on a daily basis.

Keeping up with this information can prove to be quite a challenge for anyone, but it is important to stay abreast of the most important changes and know where to access more information as it impacts your practice or profession.

Continuing education was voluntary for a while, but not everyone took advantage of it, and many felt they didn't need to bother. Now most health care professions require a significant amount of continuing education in order to renew licenses, usually every one to three years. In most cases, choices of education opportunities are still up to the individual. Continuing education should focus on your specific area of practice, assist you in learning new skills and techniques, or broaden your knowledge base.

For some fields, home study and online courses are also available. Professional journals offer continuing-education units (CEUs) for reading articles and taking short quizzes. Continuing education is also given to those working on advanced degrees. Specific information about continuing education can be obtained from your state licensing agency and/or professional organization.

 Fact

Continuing-education units (CEUs) and courses are seminars, workshops, and in-services provided by experts in the field, professional organizations, and sometimes by drug companies and vendors of equipment, software, and treatment modalities. In most instances one CEU is equal to one hour of study. Most professions require the approximate equivalent of thirty to forty-five CEUs every two years.

Health care is a lifelong learning commitment. As trends change and demographics of the consumers change, professionals will have to learn new skills, techniques, and procedures to meet the needs of the public. This is in addition to any technological advances and scientific discoveries. Those entering careers in the health care field need to be willing to make the commitment to seek out the best and most relevant learning opportunities for themselves and their patients.

The pursuit of an advanced degree in your profession can also count toward continuing education and often qualifies for a significant number of continuing-education units. Check with your state licensing board, and time your education with your renewal dates appropriately so that you get the most credit possible.

Chapter 20

Take Care of Yourself

If you work in an environment where you have close contact with patients, you are likely to catch their colds and flu. Over time, you will begin to build up some immunity and not catch virtually everything they have. However, you will always have to take precautions and put your own health and safety first. Standard precautions are a must at all times. Always follow good hand-washing techniques, and wear protective equipment whenever necessary.

Expect to Get Sick Sometimes

Being a health care worker does not give you an automatic immunity to illness of any sort. Sometimes students studying diseases, pathology, and microbiology tend to develop some or all of the signs and symptoms and consequently diagnose themselves with every disease they encounter. This usually fades after a semester or so, but actual exposure to germs is inevitable.

Surrounded by Germs

Hospitals in particular are notorious for harboring germs, and when your patients tell you they could recover more quickly at home, it's often true. Nosocomial (hospital-bred) infections are responsible for far too many deaths each year. One of the most common is pneumonia, which can spread like wildfire if health care workers (and patients) are not careful to utilize proper infection-control measures.

MRSA (methicillin-resistant staphylococcus aureus) and VRE (vancomycin-resistant enterococci) have become huge infection-control issues. MRSA, for instance, can become colonized in nasal passages; it can last for years and cause workman's compensation nightmares. Effective hand washing, using gloves and gowns when indicated, as well as identification of the infection in patients and reporting to infection control staff is essential.

Alert

MRSA and VRE are two virulent, antibiotic-resistant strains of bacteria that reside in hospitals. They are most prevalently found on bed rails and door handles. When an infected patient uses a tissue and then grabs for the bedrail, the germs are left on the bedrail. The nurse or therapist lets the bedrail down and has now transferred the germs to her hands.

Protect Yourself

Health care professionals are usually the worst at seeking care. They think they can treat themselves and often feel infallible. Health care is a physically demanding field and a very stressful one as well. These factors take a toll, help to reduce your natural immunity, and can leave you vulnerable to illness.

If you have any underlying disease processes such as diabetes, asthma, lupus, or other autoimmune diseases, you can find your risks increased because of the stressful demands of the job. You may need to take extra measures to keep your symptoms controlled.

Simple measures such as taking vitamins and minerals as recommended by your physician can help. Consuming a balanced diet and eating at regular intervals is important, as is drinking adequate fluids and emptying your bladder as needed. Getting plenty of sleep and taking breaks will help as well. This is not impossible in a health care setting. It can take a concerted effort and strong teamwork to ensure that it happens. Work with your coworkers to cover each other for breaks and meals, and encourage each other to improve these habits even on the busiest of hospital units.

Blood and other bodily fluids should always be treated as if they were contaminated. When you protect yourself, you also protect your patients and your family and friends.

Infection Control

Hand washing is the most effective form of infection control. It is vital that you wash your hands many times each day if you are in contact with patients. Of course, you will wash each time you visit the bathroom, but you also need to wash your hands before and after any patient contact. If you touch your mouth or your hair, you need to wash your hands again. If you use a tissue, you need to wash your hands afterward. If you handle any trash or patient equipment, you need to wash your hands after contact. When performing any procedures on a patient, you will need to wash your hands in between the dirty and clean aspects in addition to doing so before and after the procedure.

 Fact

Hand washing involves at least twenty to thirty seconds of contact with soap and comfortably warm water. Use friction to scrub the palms, wrists, and backs of the hands as well as the fingers and to clean under fingernails. Rinse from the wrists downward until the water runs clear. Use a clean paper towel to dry your hands and another to turn off the faucet and to open the door after washing your hands.

If you're going to come in contact with any blood products or bodily fluids, you also need to use Personal Protective Equipment (PPE). This equipment includes items such as gloves, goggles, aprons, gowns, masks, shoe booties, and hairnets. You don't need to don the full suit of armor for each event, but you will need to follow protocols and common sense. Blood products and bodily fluids should be considered contaminated for all intents and purposes for your protection and for the protection of the patients and other health care workers.

If any surface is contaminated, you will need to follow protocol for your facility to clean it up. This will usually involve a bleach solution. There may be a need for special spill absorption substances as well.

Keep fingernails trimmed and short. Most facilities frown on or prohibit the use of artificial nails of any sort. Hair should be short if possible or tied back so that it is not flying into your field of vision or contaminating any clean or sterile field. If you touch your hair, you need to rewash your hands.

Manage That Stress Level

Most health care professions are very stressful, especially those that involve direct patient care. Even those of you who may not ever have direct patient contact will most likely have a high degree of stress involved. Health care is a demanding field where precision and accuracy are essential. In most instances success depends on timeliness as well. Most health care workers are overachievers and often perfectionists by nature. These two factor spell stress on their own.

Stress is practically unavoidable in a health care profession due to the physical and emotional demands. When stress is not managed appropriately it can lead to burnout and is a major contributor to health care workers' leaving the field.

Health care often revolves around life-and-death issues. Even when it doesn't, the temptation to become lax or complacent must always be resisted. There is not room for mediocrity in health care. There are many fine skills to be developed by practitioners, and some will naturally be far better at them than others, but everyone must always strive to do the very best job they can. Everyone who works in health care has to put forth their best effort every day, including those in ancillary positions.

All of this adds up to stress, and in order to function at your best, you must be able to manage your stress. It is important to slow down and take stock of things. Your life can get to a point where it is so filled with drama that every little issue can become a crisis. You have to learn to not sweat the small stuff, and to put your efforts into the important matters. To do that, you will have to be able to distinguish between them.

Refer back to Chapter 4 about learning to manage your stress during your education process. Laughter can be one of the most successful tools for breaking the stress barrier. Sometimes just taking a moment to think of something funny, or even just something that makes you smile, will ease the tension and bring a sense of renewal.

Deep breathing, counting to ten (or backwards from ten to one), and closing your eyes and centering yourself for a moment to remember why you chose this profession will all help to release your body's hold on the stress.

E ssential

In a health care setting, something usually needs to be done yesterday. The word *stat* may become part of your everyday vocabulary. This comes from the Latin word *statim*, and means "immediately." In medical terminology it takes on the added implication of "immediately, if not sooner."

For more long-term stress management you need to find ways to get away from all of your stressors. Turn off the cell phone! Regular exercise is one of the best ways to burn off steam and take you away from all that stresses you. Grab your MP3 player. Take a walk or a jog. Ride a bike.

You might prefer to find a quiet place and turn down the lights, listen to some soothing music, and reduce the stimuli. Have a massage. Practice yoga or self-hypnosis. Read a book for pleasure. Listen to books on CD or a podcast while traveling to and from work. Go to the movies and lose yourself in the story. Watch some television that is purely silly and noneducational. Devote at least twenty to thirty minutes each day to uninterrupted relaxation and stress management.

Be Proactive about Your Own Health

Exposure to illness is not the only issue for health care workers. On-the-job injury is also a potential for harm. For instance, nurses have the highest risk for back injuries of any profession. Health care workers who have direct patient contact all risk injury while assisting patients and need to protect their backs and other joints. An injury can be a career-ending event.

Proper Body Mechanics Prevent Injury

Proper body mechanics are essential to everyone, but are especially so for health care workers involved in direct patient care. One wrong move can cost you your job and your health.

Lifting is one of the most dangerous things anyone can do. Whether lifting a box or piece of equipment, or assisting in moving a patient, there are a few rules that must always be followed. These include:

- Never try to lift or move a patient by yourself. Always summon help, and wait until they arrive.
- Move as close to the object or patient as possible.
- Never twist; always sidestep or pivot.
- Always keep your lower back in its naturally curved or arched state.
- When lifting, place your feet firmly, set apart about the width of your shoulders, to provide a solid, wide base of support.
- Keep your head up and your shoulders back. Your upper back should be perfectly straight.
- Tighten your stomach muscles and keep them tight. Bow slightly at the hips and then squat. Use your legs, not your back! Push up from your knees, using your momentum to assist you.

In Case of Injury

If you do get hurt, report the injury immediately and have it checked out. If you need treatment or therapy, be sure to get it without delay. Early intervention and treatment are essential to a positive outcome. Understand your rights and don't be intimidated. Be pro-active and protect yourself. It is also important to understand that damage can be cumulative, especially in back injuries. One small wrong movement can trigger a serious situation.

 **Alert**

Always be sure you know how to use something before attempting to use it. If in doubt, always ask for help. Don't take shortcuts. If the equipment has a safety mechanism, use it. For example, many needles now come with a shield to protect from needle-stick injuries, but if you don't use them, they cannot protect you.

If You Get Sick

If you are sick, stay home. Don't share your germs with others. Your patients and coworkers don't need any more exposure. Rest, drink fluids, and eat what you can. If you need to, see your physician. If you need antibiotics, take them until they are gone.

You can do your part to help avoid illness by being proactive. Take your annual flu shot. During cold and flu season, be sure to get plenty of rest and avoid crowds as much as possible. And, of course, always adhere to proper hygiene and hand washing.

If you need a mental health day to renew yourself and reduce stress, take it. Be kind to your coworkers and try to plan ahead, but if you can't, take the time. You must take care of you, so that you can take care of others.

Avoid Burnout, Reward Yourself

Most health care professions are physically and emotionally demanding. You probably chose this profession because you want to do something meaningful and help people. Giving is a wonderful quality, but if you don't take care to renew and recharge your resources, you will soon find you have nothing left to give.

In health care you don't produce a product or other tangible goods. You don't always see the final fruits of your efforts, and you don't often receive accolades and applause for them either. In many instances you will only participate in a short segment of the health care process for a patient. You might be the x-ray technician taking the film to determine if the patient has pneumonia. Or you might be the prosthetist who fits the new leg for the patient but never sees them learn to walk again. Even nurses and doctors often don't see how their care makes a difference in someone's life except in short time frames.

Learning to find your own rewards in your professional life can be as challenging as the job itself. It is easy to see how you could become disillusioned or frustrated. It is not always easy to understand how to deal with these feelings and how to avoid them.

E ssential

Burnout is a very real challenge for many health care workers. The desire to help people is usually a deeply rooted passion and it's hard to understand how that passion can die. It doesn't have to, but you do need to recognize that it is perfectly natural for all human beings to need to feel that they have a purpose and to be thanked and recognized for their efforts and help once in a while.

You also have to learn that it is okay to say no sometimes. If you need time to recharge yourself, you have nothing more to give at that moment. Don't agree to work an extra shift or to take on an extra assignment. Take care of you. If you don't, you'll allow resentments to build.

Learn to center yourself and remind yourself how and why you came to this profession. It is important to you to give and to help people. If someone doesn't seem appreciative of your help, understand that it is likely because they aren't feeling their best. That should not deter you from doing the best job you can. It's important to you. You chose to do this job and worked hard and struggled to get here. Thank yourself. Applaud your own efforts and pat yourself on the back.

If you're in management, take time to thank your employees often. They need your praise, your recognition, and your appreciation. Even if you have problem employees, you can put forth the effort to show them that they matter. This may even go a long way in improving the problems. You'll earn the respect of your employees, and your efforts will go further than you might imagine toward retention of staff. Your appreciation of others will be returned to you in many ways.

Explore Other Options

If you haven't heeded the above advice and find yourself burned out, stop and consider the options. Before you decide to give up your career entirely, explore the pros and cons of your situation. Perhaps the particular niche you're in is no longer well suited to you. Explore other options within your field. A different aspect of health care with different levels of physical and/or emotional challenges could be just what you need.

Perhaps you just need to find a new department or another employer. Be honest with yourself about why you are unhappy. Do you need to improve a set of skills? Is there a communication problem? Do you need an arbitrator or someone to intervene and resolve some issues?

Perhaps you have other skills and talents that you'd like to explore and utilize in your job. Is there another approach or opportunity where this could happen?

Sometimes a leave of absence or long vacation is in order. Sometimes simple things such as redecorating your office can help as well. Having something new to look forward to can be important in helping to cheer up your attitude.

Create Your Rewards

When something goes right, something is especially exciting, or someone actually says thank you, those are the moments you need to remember. When you recognize that your efforts helped someone achieve a goal, take credit for it. It may not be at all appropriate to run through the halls exclaiming your success, but you can reward yourself.

Start a journal and find a special box to keep it in. Write yourself a thank-you note or certificate of appreciation. Record the event on a slip of paper. If you don't have time to write in your journal, or aren't inclined to do so at all, write yourself little notes and keep them all in your special box. Take it out and review them from time to time, and especially when you are doubting yourself or feel like giving it all up. Of course, you need to be careful of confidentiality, so don't include information that would identify patients to others. Over a period of time, you'll see that you have made a difference and that your choice was a good one.

You can also set goals for yourself. Try learning new skills or conquering a fear, such as confronting a coworker who bullies you. When you achieve the goal, reward yourself with trinkets, or take yourself somewhere special. Enjoy your career and personal growth experiences.

Learn to Leave the Job at Work

There will be occasions when you need to prepare for something, such as a presentation, or do some research outside of work in order to catch up or expand your knowledge base. This may be especially true when you are new to your profession, but you need to learn to not mix your work with your home environment. You need a place to retreat and get away. Perhaps spending an hour at the library on your way home can accomplish this.

Consider whether your habit of bringing work home stems from something that you can resolve by purchasing an item such as a PDA (personal digital assistant), which can house databases and offers access to the Internet. If you've been spending time at home researching medical information, you might consider having one of these in your pocket for quick reference while working instead.

Alert

Consider why you bring work home. Are you doing this because you are too slow at your job? Or do you spend too much time goofing off? Are you short staffed? How long will you be expected to continue this? If there are issues that you need to deal with, don't put them off. You need your time away from work.

Can you accomplish the same thing by staying a little later or going in a little early? This may not be ideal either, but at least you're not allowing your work to enter your home. Keeping the two separate is important. Sometimes you cannot help but mix the two if, for example, you have to be on call for the night. Even then, try not to mix in any more than is necessary. Take and make necessary calls in another room if possible.

You may live and work in the same area, which gives rise to the possibility that you'll encounter patients in the community, such as at the grocery store. You can be warm and friendly, but you also may need to set limits with them and tell them to call you at work and not discuss business when you run in to them. Never give out your home or other private phone numbers to patients, no matter how much they beg for it. Remember to keep your relationships professional. Just as you respect their right to privacy, expect patients to respect your privacy as well.

Chapter 21

You as a Professional

Embarking on your career as a health care professional will be an exciting and rewarding challenge for your professional lifetime. Choosing to help people, especially those who will be at their most needy and vulnerable, is a fine and noble gesture. Some may never thank you, but know in your heart that your efforts are necessary and are appreciated by those who need you and by your coworkers. Take pride in your work, and always care for your patients as if they were your most cherished loved ones.

Keep Up to Date with Your Field

Almost every field in the health care industry has its own professional organization or is associated with a combined group of similar professionals. Most of the organizations produce their own trade journals. From these stem multiple journals, newsletters, and other publications for professionals in your field. Specialties within the profession may also have their own associations and sponsored publications.

There are also vast numbers of trade journals, newsletters, and online publications that are not published by professional organizations but are written by professionals and often published by medical publishing houses. Specialty areas such as oncology, pediatrics, neurology, home health, and public health are usually focuses of publications specific to physicians, nurses, and therapists.

They may offer articles that can be read, and then offer a short test that can be taken for continuing-education purposes. They also highlight and honor those practitioners who have made a difference in the profession or to patients.

Professional journals also help you to keep up to date with the latest technology and trends to provide state-of-the-art care to your patients and to make your practice successful and profitable. Again, they may be geared to your particular specialty. For instance, if you are a podiatrist, you may seek publications that are devoted to the specialty of podiatric medicine instead of subscribing to a general medicine publication. Administrators would find a publication for the hospital administrator more beneficial than a general health care publication.

 Fact

Professional journals disseminate information about your professional organization and its efforts, such as political lobbying to enact changes in the scope of practice, education, or licensing procedures. And they provide notification of legislation that adversely affects the profession or consumers and encourage professionals to contact their own legislators.

Subscriptions to trade journals can be expensive, but the cost is usually tax-deductible (check with your tax advisor). Many times a facility will subscribe and make the journals available to staff members or keep them in the facility's library.

Your local community library may have copies of some journals. Hospital and medical school libraries will have copies of many more. The *Magazine Industry Market Place* is a large reference book that lists all trade journals and is updated yearly. Most public libraries have a copy in their reference section.

Some trade journals are available online for smaller fees and varying levels of access to materials. They may offer fee-based access to articles, some of which may be of particular interest to you or your coworkers. If you can't subscribe, consider reading what you can online.

Other alternatives include sharing a subscription with a few colleagues. Designate someone as the primary subscriber and the one to scan the journals for relevant articles and information, and then circulate the journal with a routing slip and tabs highlighting the important articles. You might also find it beneficial to meet periodically either on a specific or an informal basis to discuss articles you have read and share your knowledge with your peers.

Setting Career Goals

Setting career goals is important for everyone, not just health care professionals. Goals keep you focused and working toward something that is important to you and gives you a feeling of accomplishment. Goals provide impetus for change, give you momentum, and don't let you burn out or become stagnant. Goals help you to continue to strive to be the best at what you do.

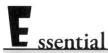

E ssential

People (especially interviewers) will often ask, "Where do you see yourself in five years?" The answer is not so much about whether you aspire to become the world's greatest brain surgeon or rival da Vinci in medical illustration. It is more important to understand whether you have aspirations and goals or if you aspire to be doing the same thing for the next thirty years.

It's important to understand that the health care industry is changing and growing. It isn't staying the same. You might find the perfect job and love the people you work with. It's close to home and the management is about as perfect as it can get. You could be very happy there for the rest of your professional life. And then one day you start to hear the rumors. A new company has bought out your perfect facility. You'll have a new boss in a few weeks and procedures will change. Right out from under you, the perfect job is gone. The changes might work out to be great, but it's still not the same. Or your boss moves on for personal or professional reasons and you suddenly have the boss from hell.

It is important to re-examine your professional life periodically and to make changes to keep yourself fresh and interested and happy in your work. You should always keep abreast of the options. This will help ensure that you are prepared to make a move should life dictate the necessity. It's always good to be aware of your worth, including the kind of salaries, benefits, and working conditions that others in your field are earning.

Employers often eliminate positions to encourage new blood, and unfortunately sometimes to find new workers at lower salaries. This has been commonplace in other industries and is becoming more popular in the health care industry as well.

 Fact

Employees generally don't stay and earn "the gold watch" for twenty-five years of service any longer, and employers don't expect employees to stick around that long. The trend for workers in other industries has been to make a move every three to five years in order to attain significant salary increases and improve benefits.

Sign-on bonuses and other tools for recruitment have sparked morale issues and caused long-term employees to become disenchanted at not being rewarded for their loyalty. With severe shortages in so many fields, facilities are re-examining some of the recruitment tactics and spending more time on retention issues in an effort to decrease some of the turnover that has been caused by their creative hiring techniques.

Thinking outside the box is necessary to solving shortages, but management has to take into consideration retention issues as well. Many more trials and errors will ensue in this area as shortages continue toward crisis levels, especially for nurses and some therapists.

Grow with Your Profession

As the demands of the aging population increase and technology continues to improve and change, so will your profession. You will need to be willing to continue to grow and change, and you will need to see the changes as opportunities to improve your skills and to make a bigger and better contribution, as well as to find greater satisfaction in your career.

Some people are terrified of change and experience physical symptoms and illness if they have to change. Health care is probably not a good choice for those individuals. Learning to recognize new diagnoses and to find new and innovative treatments and cures cannot take place in a stagnant situation.

Learn from your peers and explore opportunities to find mentors who can enlighten and educate you and ease your fears of the unknown. Concentrate your continuing-education efforts on learning new skills and developing your talents through workshops and seminars, or by returning to school for an advanced degree. Avoid taking the easy route with continuing-education units (CEUs) just so you can quickly take and pass a test to be done with it. Use the continuing education as an opportunity to expand your horizons, not just to prove that you know what you already learned.

E ssential

As the need for more professionals continues to grow, so will the need for those who can educate students in the field. If you enjoy teaching others, consider the possibility of becoming a mentor or a teacher in your field at least part-time.

Share your knowledge. If you have learned a new technique or skill, consider holding a workshop or in-service for your coworkers. Time is limited, and knowledge and information are crucial. By sharing information and techniques with your coworkers, you help to increase the overall knowledge base.

If your profession develops new specialties and opportunities, consider moving into the new realms. This helps to keep you from becoming burned out and affords you opportunities to maximize your skills and abilities.

You may also look for entrepreneurial opportunities. Opportunities for consultants and independent contractors are becoming quite popular. With the many changes in health care reimbursement, such as the new Medicare Part D drug coverage, other issues surface. This program got off to a very rocky start due to the wide variations in formulary and payment schedules. Consultants who can understand the program and how to access information on plans and formularies have become much needed.

Health care literacy affects over fifty percent of the population. Helping patients to understand their responsibilities and how to access care—including how to obtain transportation, how to maneuver the maze of a managed-care environment, and how to decipher prescription instructions—are just two examples of areas in which patients fail due to an inability to comprehend the health care process. Consultants who can assist patients in these areas are always needed. Someone will eventually figure out how to turn this into a lucrative endeavor.

Wellness and promoting health is a big issue. Presenting workshops and seminars for the general public to inform and educate them on ways to prevent illness and promote a healthy lifestyle is also very popular.

Podcasts are gaining in popularity, as they can be downloaded to MP3 players and taken with you. Multiple programs can be designed, and a subscription process can easily be set up to promote your information through this media and constantly update your subscribers. Web casts are another media option for sharing information and holding workshops and seminars to reach a broad audience.

The Pros and Cons of Joining Your Professional Organization

Professional organizations are made up of members of the profession who are working toward a common goal of promoting and improving the profession. They advocate for the members of the profession as well as for the consumers to improve the delivery and quality of health care. They bond together to offer members information, perks, and opportunities they might not otherwise have.

The cost of joining a professional organization can be steep, and many times this is the deterrent. However, the dues are tax deductible (consult your tax advisor). Some people, however, just don't find a need to join organizations. Perhaps the most important consideration for joining your professional organization is the statement it makes about your personal commitment to your profession and your professionalism. It adds credibility to your resume and to your business. Some of the other benefits include the lobbyists and advocates who work to improve the profession as well as the health care in this country. Another is the personal and professional growth opportunities that becoming an active member offer to you.

Organizations are always in need of new blood to help organize such things as their annual conventions, workshops and seminars, and continuing-education opportunities, as well as to work on legislative committees and other organizational building teams. Helping your organization work to improve your profession as well as to help improve the overall health care in this country can be a rewarding opportunity.

 Fact

For those who prefer not to be so actively involved, membership serves other purposes. Insurance benefits, including health and life insurance, are often available through professional organizations. And getting malpractice insurance through a large group can result in much more affordable rates and even better coverage.

Professional organizations also offer tremendous networking opportunities for members to share ideas and brainstorm, to vent and commiserate, and to give members a sense that they are not alone in the challenges presented by their particular profession and health care in general. Opportunities to learn about new techniques, career options, etc., are invaluable benefits to group members.

Educational opportunities through seminars and workshops at annual conventions and throughout the year are sponsored and conducted by the organization as well as by members. These are usually open to nonmembers as well, but cost savings is the perk to members.

Group discounts for professional as well as personal services are often a perk to members of any organization. Members usually get substantial discounts for events and educational opportunities offered through their professional organizations.

Many members who lead very busy professional as well as personal lives depend on their professional organization to brief them on important industry changes, legislation that impacts their practices, advances in technology, and scientific discoveries. Most organizations publish a trade journal as well.

Through your professional organization you will also find access to mentors and have an opportunity to participate in mentoring others should you so desire.

The Growing Need for Information Technology

A vast amount of medical research data and information is disseminated every day. Health professionals cannot possibly keep up with the explosion of information, and consequently not everyone has access to the very latest in techniques and procedures. This is due in large part to the fact that less than 20 percent of hospitals and only about 5 percent of physicians' offices are equipped to handle electronic medical records.

This is all a good indication of the fact that there is a long way to go in getting practitioners as well as facilities to go online to receive and stay abreast of this information or to participate in research opportunities.

Computer technology took a long time to become an everyday part of practitioners' lives and offices in the first place. Hospitals and other health care facilities were some of the last holdouts in introducing computerized components to their everyday functions as well. Computer literacy has not been emphasized, and the expense and learning curves have been allowed to be good excuses to delay the computerization process.

Alert

The consequence of insufficient computer literacy is that it still takes about fourteen to seventeen years for medical breakthroughs to become standard practice. This is not the case in other industries where effective use of information and data is regularly used to measure quality and plan for improvement.

The opportunity is here. Health care software is a multimillion-dollar-plus industry and growing. The use of PDAs, MP3 players, and electronic notebooks and tablets is becoming much more commonplace with practitioners. Billing codes have become much more definitive so that data can be better collected and studied. Politicians have set goals for creating an infrastructure not only to promote electronic health records, but also to utilize the information contained in those records to promote higher quality standards and to better study diseases, treatments, and outcomes.

Access to health information and utilizing that access to promote improved health care are essential to the health care industry. In combination with that, computer literacy is a must for all health care workers.

Continuing education is an opportunity to learn about advances in your field. Almost all licensed health care workers are required to take some form of continuing education on a regular basis. Stay informed and subscribe to updates and e-mail alerts to keep abreast of research and advances in the medical field in general. Take in-services, seminars, and workshops to help improve and broaden your knowledge base.

Making a Commitment to Excellence

Health care involves life-and-death issues affecting fellow human beings. As a health care worker you need to dedicate yourself to the patients who will be served by the work that you do. Make a commitment to excellence. There is no room for mediocrity. Whether you are a practitioner or medical photographer, your input can make a difference in someone's life every day. Always strive to do the best job you can possibly do.

A study in the *New England Journal of Medicine* (March 16, 2006) shows that most Americans receive mediocre medical care. This is unacceptable. The only good point in the report was that factors such as race and socioeconomic status didn't matter. Rich or poor, male or female, you got basically the same level of mediocre care, specifically, patients received the care that was recommended only 54.9 percent of the time.

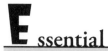
Essential

Whatever your role in the health care industry, make a commitment every day to do your best. Think of the people you impact as if they were all your most cherished loved ones and provide nothing less than you would expect for them.

As a member of the health care team, some of the things you can do to help improve the quality of care include advocating for your patients within your community and facilities as well as with your legislators, learning how health care is reimbursed and what factors influence the rules and decisions that govern this process, understanding health care literacy problems, and working with your patients to ensure that they understand their responsibilities.

Appendix A

Additional Resources

Career and Education Web Sites

The following is a sample of the multitude of health care education and career-related Web sites that provide resources and information. Many also have active forums to post questions and comments.

About.com

About.com has many health guides who are nurses, physicians, dentists, N.D.s, therapists, and other health care professionals. This site provides information about the field, in addition to resources for professionals and laypeople. It also has active forums. The Nursing Site guide is Kathy Quan, the author of *The Everything® New Nurse Book* and *The Everything® Guide to Careers in Health Care.*
✍*www.nursing.about.com*
✍*www.about.com*

U.S. Department of Labor

The Bureau of Labor Statistics, U.S. Department of Labor, *Occupational Outlook Handbook*, 2006–07 edition, offers statistics and information about many health care careers, including education, salary information, and future outlook. ✍*www.bls.gov/oco*

Healthcare Career Resource Center

This site offers a comprehensive list of health care careers from ORACLE ThinkQuest Education Foundation Library. It has many links to summaries of information about duties, education, salary, and outlook. ✍*http://library.thinkquest.org/15569*

WorldWideLearn

This site's Guide to College Majors in Alternative Medicine is an informative discussion of alternative medicine options and the educational preparation needed.

✐*www.worldwidelearn.com/online-education-guide/*
health-medical/alternative-medicine-major.htm

CollegeBoard.org

Information on SAT and ACT college entrance exams as well as links to financial aid and other college entrance information are available on the CollegeBoard.org Web site.

✐*www.collegeboard.org*

FAFSA

Access and submit the Free Application for Federal Student Aid (FAFSA) application online for financial aid consideration.

✐*www.fafsa.ed.gov*

Financial Aid

FinAid is one of many sites with information about financial aid.

✐*www.finaid.org*

The GRE

Information on how to prepare for and register to take the Graduate Record Exam can be found at this site. ✐*www.gre.org*

Fast Company.com—"The Brand Called You"

"The Brand Called You" is an article on Fast Company.com's Web site by business management guru Tom Peters about considering yourself the CEO of a business called "you."

✐*www.fastcompany.com/online/10/brandyou.html*

CareerDesignsOnline—Your Career as a Business

This self-help workbook is available from this site on how to find your next career.

✐*http://careerdesignsonline.com*

HealthLiteracy Consulting
Helen Osborne, a health literacy expert, discusses the issues involving literacy in health care today. There are links to many articles and resources on this site. ✍*www.healthliteracy.com*

Home Health 101
This site offers practical information for home health professionals. ✍*http://homehealth101.com*

House-Calls Online
This is a site for home health professionals with links to resources and other home health sites.
✍*http://housecalls-online.com*

Suite101.com
This site has recently undergone a makeover and has a whole section devoted to health. Most of the writers for this section are medical professionals. Kathy Quan writes for the HealthFieldMedicare section, which includes up-to-date career information for health care professionals.
✍*http://healthfieldmedicare.suite101.com/*

Books

Farr, J. Michael, *America's Top Jobs for People Without a Four-Year Degree* (Indianapolis, IN: JIST Works, an imprint of JIST Publishing, Inc., 2001).

Field, Shelly, *100 Best Careers for the 21st Century* (Foster City, CA: IDG Books Worldwide, Inc., 1994).

Swanson, Barbara M., *Careers in Health Care, 5th ed.* (New York, NY: McGraw-Hill Companies, Inc. 2005).

Wischnitzer, Dr. Saul, and Edith Wischnitzer, *Top 100 Health Care Careers, 2nd ed.* (Indianapolis, IN: JIST Works, an imprint of JIST Publishing, Inc., 2005).

Professional Journals and Publications

There are over 8,000 trade journals in the health care industry. Many have online editions or Web sites where you can request sample issues and purchase subscriptions. Below is just a sampling. You can find a complete listing of health care trade journals at your local library in the reference book *Magazine Industry Market Place.* Ask your librarian for assistance.

Journal of the American
Medical Association
✍*http://jama.ama-assn.org*

The American Chiropractor
✍*www.theamerican*
chiropractor.com

American Journal of Nursing
✍*www.ajnonline.com*

The Journal of the American
Dental Association
✍*http://jada.ada.org*

Journal of the American
Dietetic Association
✍*www.adajournal.org*

Male Nurse magazine
✍*www.malenurse*
magazine.com

R.N. magazine
✍*www.rnweb.com*

Journal of the American
Physical Therapy Association
✍*www.ptjournal.org*

Health Care Informatics
✍*www.healthcare-informatics*
.com/index.php

Managed Healthcare Executive
✍*www.managedhealthcare*
executive.com/mhe

Entrance Exams

In earlier chapters you may have encountered a reference to admissions exams required by certain schools or programs such as medical school, dental school, nursing school, pharmacy school, or optometry school. Most master's degree programs will require such tests as the GRE, GMAT, or MAT. You will have to check with the individual school's admissions requirements to determine which of these may be required.

The MCAT

The Medical College Admissions Test is required by all podiatry schools, some veterinary programs, and most medical schools to help them determine which applicants to accept. In addition to the MCAT scores, the admissions officer or admissions team will consider your grades, extracurricular activities, and references, as well as your personal interview and any other requested information in making a decision about your application. The MCAT is given twice a year, in April and August, and there are application deadlines.

There are four separate sections to the exam and it is timed.

- **Writing Sample:** consists of 1 question (time: 60 minutes)
- **Verbal Reasoning:** consists of 65 questions (time: 85 minutes)
- **Physical Sciences:** consists of 77 questions (time: 100 minutes)
- **Biological Sciences:** consists of 77 questions (time: 100 minutes)

For further information see the MCAT Web site: *www/aamc.org /students/mcat/start.htm*

The DAT

The Dental Admissions Test is administered twice a year, in April and October, and is required by most dental schools. In addition to the DAT scores, dental schools also look at grades, extracurricular activities, references, and your personal interview to make a decision concerning your application.

There are four parts to this test.

- Reading comprehension
- Perceptual ability
- Quantitative reasoning
- A survey of natural sciences: Biology, inorganic chemistry, and organic chemistry

For more information see the Web site: *www.ada.org/prof/ed/ testing/dat/index.asp*

NET

Most nursing schools for both R.N. and L.P.N./L.V.N. students are now requiring an admission test. Check with the institution for testing dates and other information. At this time there is no standardized exam; however, the National League for Nurses, which accredits nursing programs, has developed a pre-exam, and it is expected to become a standardized test in the future.

Nursing admission tests typically include reading comprehension (which should be at a minimum at the tenth-grade level), math skills (from basics through algebra), a reading rate exam, an evaluation of test-taking skills, a stress level profile, a social interaction profile, and a learning style evaluation.

For further information, contact the admissions office at the nursing school of your choice.

PCAT

The Pharmacy College Admissions Test is developed by PsychCorp (a brand of Harcourt Assessment) to test candidates' academic ability and grasp of the scientific knowledge necessary for a successful pharmaceutical education and career. The PCAT is given three times each year, in January, June, and October. Most pharmacy schools require this test, which consists of 280 multiple-choice questions in five content areas:

- Verbal Skills
- Reading comprehension
- Biology
- Chemistry
- Quantitative ability (math)

For more information, contact Harcourt Assessment and search for the PCAT at their Web site: *http://harcourtassessment.com*.

The OAT

Optometry schools may require the Optometry Admission Test, which tests applicants' comprehension of scientific information as well as their academic ability. There are 100 multiple-choice questions in three content areas:

- Biology
- General chemistry
- Organic chemistry

You can get further information about this test and apply online for testing at their Web site: *http://opted.org*.

The GRE

The Graduate Record Examination is required by many postbaccalaureate degree programs such as master's programs. It can be taken via computer or as a written exam. There are specific specialty tests available, but most programs in health care just require the general exam. Be sure to check with your admissions department for specific information. There are seven sections to the test, which measures verbal, analytical, quantitative (math) skills, and comprehension.

For further information see the Educational Testing Services Web site for GRE information at *www.gre.org*.

The GMAT

The Graduate Management Admission Test is required by most schools of management for their master's degree candidates. These schools usually offer an M.B.A., but for health care purposes, the GMAT is usually required for such programs as hospital administration and may be required for other health care administrators as well.

There are three sections, which cover verbal, quantitative (math), and analytical writing, and may include items such as problem-solving questions, reading comprehension, critical reasoning, and grammar.

For further information check the Graduate Management Admission Council's Web site: *www.mba.com*.

The MAT

The Miller Analogies Test is given to graduate school candidates who are seeking advanced degrees in analytical programs. It tests the candidate's ability to analyze information rather than merely memorize it. The MAT is available in both written and computer-based formats. It tests your fluency in English, your ability to recognize relationships between ideas, and your general knowledge in such fields as math, literature, fine arts, science, philosophy, and history.

Many businesses and corporations utilize this exam in the hiring process for executives. It is licensed for use by Harcourt Assessment.

For more information search for the MAT at the Harcourt Web site: *http://harcourtassessment.com/*.

Index

The Everything® Career Guide Series

THE

EVERYTHING
GUIDE TO BEING A
PARALEGAL

Secrets to a successful career!

Steven W. Schneider
Attorney-at-Law

Trade Paperback
ISBN: 1-59337-583-2
$14.95

THE

EVERYTHING
GUIDE TO BEING A
REAL ESTATE AGENT

Secrets to a successful career!

Shahri Masters
Author of The Everything® Homeselling Book, 2nd Edition

Trade Paperback
ISBN: 1-59337-432-1
$14.95

THE

EVERYTHING
GUIDE TO BEING A
SALES REP

Winning secrets to a successful–
and profitable–career!

Ruth Klein

Trade Paperback
ISBN: 1-59337-657-X
$14.95

THE

EVERYTHING
GUIDE TO STARTING AND RUNNING A
RESTAURANT

Secrets to a successful business!

Ronald Lee, Restaurateur

Trade Paperback
ISBN: 1-59337-433-X
$14.95 ($19.95 CAN)

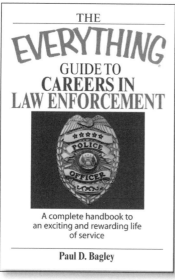

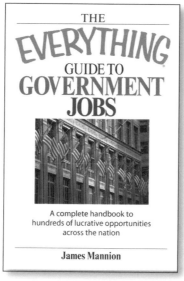